OFFICIALLY WITHDRAWN FROM
NORTH CENTRAL
REGIONAL LIBRARY

Studies in Supernatural Literature
Series Editor: S. T. Joshi

Lovecraft and Influence: His Predecessors and Successors, edited by Robert H. Waugh, 2013.
Lord Dunsany, H. P. Lovecraft, and Ray Bradbury: Spectral Journeys, by William F. Touponce, 2013.
Critical Essays on Lord Dunsany, edited by S. T. Joshi, 2013.

Lord Dunsany, H. P. Lovecraft, and Ray Bradbury

Spectral Journeys

William F. Touponce

Studies in Supernatural Literature

THE SCARECROW PRESS, INC.
Lanham • Toronto • Plymouth, UK
2013

Published by Scarecrow Press, Inc.
A wholly owned subsidiary of The Rowman & Littlefield Publishing Group, Inc.
4501 Forbes Boulevard, Suite 200, Lanham, Maryland 20706
www.rowman.com

10 Thornbury Road, Plymouth PL6 7PP, United Kingdom

Copyright © 2013 by Scarecrow Press, Inc.

All rights reserved. No part of this book may be reproduced in any form or by any electronic or mechanical means, including information storage and retrieval systems, without written permission from the publisher, except by a reviewer who may quote passages in a review.

British Library Cataloguing in Publication Information Available

Library of Congress Cataloging-in-Publication Data

Touponce, William F.
Lord Dunsany, H. P. Lovecraft, and Ray Bradbury : spectral journeys / William F. Touponce.
pages cm. — (Studies in Supernatural Literature)
Includes bibliographical references and index.
ISBN 978-0-8108-9219-4 (cloth : alk. paper) — ISBN 978-0-8108-9220-0 (ebook) 1. Fantasy fiction—History and criticism. 2. Civilization, Modern, in literature. 3. Dunsany, Edward John Moreton Drax Plunkett, Baron, 1878–1957—Criticism and interpretation. 4. Lovecraft, H. P. (Howard Phillips), 1890–1937—Criticism and interpretation. 5. Bradbury, Ray, 1920–2012—Criticism and interpretation. 6. Modernism (Literature)—History and criticism. 7. Science fiction—History and criticism. I. Title.
PN3435.T66 2013
809.3'8766—dc23
2013015582

♾ ™ The paper used in this publication meets the minimum requirements of American National Standard for Information Sciences Permanence of Paper for Printed Library Materials, ANSI/NISO Z39.48-1992.

Printed in the United States of America

Contents

Introduction	vii
Lord Dunsany, or Beauty	1
H. P. Lovecraft, or Shock	57
Ray Bradbury, or Nostalgia	109
Index	139
About the Author	143

Introduction

Literature is full of secrets, but perhaps it offers no stranger matter for our consideration than melodies unheard by those who made them, than Siren songs that never came to the Sirens' ears. —Arthur Machen

As a story, the experience of modernity has yet to be told completely in all of its rich narrative complexity. Perhaps it never entirely will be, the very act of narration in genre implying a certain limited point of view, and the repression or casting into shadow of other points of view. Ideological struggles over the meaning of modernity continue, but one thing seems clear to the writers considered in this study: the resources of realism for enriching our inner lives are limited if not exhausted.[1] Each of the writers investigated here—Lord Dunsany, H. P. Lovecraft, and Ray Bradbury, whose works together span the twentieth century—defined himself as primarily a storyteller or fabulist, with occasional longer narrative adventures into the fantastic (Dunsany and Bradbury were also active in creating a fantastic drama, but their stories have had the widest influence). Considering collectively their careers and the extent of their creative output, which is expressed in hundreds of stories of the fantastic, it is as if they were saying to us that we should never tire of telling realists Nietzsche's story of how the real world became a fable.[2]

To these writers the real was becoming ever more and more fantastic, a point that Ray Bradbury was fond of making. Although they were in some cases (Dunsany and Lovecraft especially) drawn toward the overwhelming ideological prestige of realism later in their careers, mixing realistic technique with the themes of the supernatural or science fiction, I have been constantly amazed at how these gifted storytellers use the tropes of fantastic fiction to get at the heart of the matter: the condition of being modern. At their imaginative best, in hundreds of stories, these authors have created magical fables and allegories of experience that, while using certain techniques of realism, lie beyond its reach. Bradbury could, for instance, compress all the horror and wonder of modernity into a single supernatural story, such as "The Scythe" (*Weird Tales*, 1943), in which a man displaced by the Dust Bowl becomes the figure of the grim reaper.

In connection with Bradbury, the master figure of the specter or ghost has come to be seen as provocatively indicating what the world of modernity feels like, a figure for the lack of fullness in the world, and hence in experience.[3] To those theorists of modernity I turn to in this study, notably Walter Benjamin for his account of the storyteller, the early Georg Lukács for his theory of the novel, Mikhail Bakhtin for his account of laughter and the carnival tradition, and Theodor Adorno and Max Horkheimer for their critique of the excesses of modern positive science, modernity is still haunted by what it repressed. Bakhtin investigates the degradation of laughter in rationalism from the seventeenth century onward. Adorno and Horkheimer see in Odysseus's denial and repression of himself in the episode of the Sirens the very model of bourgeois identity (expressed in their remarkable collaboration, *Dialectic of Enlightenment*, first published in 1947) and the fate of literature in class society. For Benjamin, what was being lost in modernity was the traditional experience of community conveyed by the storyteller.

For these thinkers the narrative of modernity goes something like this: as the supernatural support for human values disappeared, it became increasingly clear that we no longer perceived the world as having an immanent meaning given by God. The world itself had become "godforsaken" and problematic, even demonic, the first literary instance being *Don Quixote*.[4] New forms of official culture and authority, however, took the place of the church in the rationalist states created in the seventeenth and eighteenth centuries. And even though belief in the supernatural has plainly been on the wane since the nineteenth century and the rise of scientific modernity, in literature, and perhaps in some forms of philosophy as well, the sense of being haunted, both by the past and in the future, has increased in intensity at least since the 1808 publication of Goethe's *Faust*. The emergence of the haunted heroes of Gothic romance has since been established as a further connection with allegorical modes of meaning in which fear and dread became part of the very destiny of mankind. This was first underlined by Lovecraft in a discussion of spectral literature—a term that he seems to have coined.[5] The study of Gothic modernism continues to uncover spectral moments within the discourse of modernity, which now seems inseparable from the "conjuration and abjuration" of ghosts and spirits.[6]

If modern experience is now somehow spectral, part of the reason has to do with the growth of rationalism and science. A passage from Joseph Wood Krutch's 1929 study *The Modern Temper*, which was influential on both

Lovecraft and Bradbury, nicely sums up the de-centering effect of scientific modernity from the point of view of liberal humanism:

> Three centuries lay between the promulgation of the Copernican theory and the publication of *The Origin of Species*, but in sixty-odd years which have elapsed since the latter event the blows have fallen with a rapidity which left no interval for recovery. The structures which are known variously as mythology, religion, and philosophy, and which are alike in that each has as its function the interpretation of experience in terms which have human values, have collapsed under the force of successive attacks and shown themselves utterly incapable of assimilating the new stores of experience which have been dumped upon the world. With increasing completeness science maps out the pattern of nature, but the latter has no relation to the pattern of human needs and feelings.[7]

Krutch's sense of modern experience was tied to scientific experiment, and to what science reveals about nature. For Krutch, human beings had themselves become despairing fantastical creatures, living in an illusory world that no longer existed. But Krutch also realized that human nature, as understood by science in the laboratory, had also proved problematic: "human nature is too phantasmagorical, too insubstantial, to 'unreal' to submit to such treatment."[8] In looking at the drama of the past and in considering the possibility of modern tragedy he argued, contra Nietzsche, that modern man was so diminished by science and "enlightenment" that the sense of tragedy was no longer possible or even relevant. Human beings were problematic creatures, living now in sufferance to science in a universe not made for them, denied the dignity that tragedy would have afforded them. The mood of modernity was melancholy. Walter Benjamin confronted the same problem of tragic experience in his study of the mood of melancholy in German baroque drama, which I will come to in a moment.

To be fair, not all American views of modern experience were as stern as Krutch's, especially those more immersed in the context of pragmatism. Roughly contemporaneous with Krutch's *The Modern Temper* was John Dewey's *Art as Experience* (1934). Dewey argued that the experience of art could be integrative and was a good deal more optimistic about science providing a guide to human values, to what we should want and need. Nonetheless, he too talks about the difficulty of having a coherent experience in the modern world: "No one experience has a chance to complete itself because something else is entered upon so speedily. What is called experience becomes so dispersed and miscellaneous as hardly to deserve the name."[9] The modern average person in Dewey's analysis no longer seems capable of putting together doing and undergoing into a coherent whole.

Art remained for Dewey one of the ways in which authentic experience—my main concern in this study—could still be posited and felt, but he points out how much artworks have lost their "indigenous status" in being largely confined to museums and galleries by the rich as evidence of their good standing in the realm of culture. Dewey in the opening pages of his study explicitly acknowledged that the growth of capitalism (changes in industrial conditions) had been a powerful factor contributing to the separation of art from everyday life, art collectors being mainly capitalists, though he does not pursue an economic analysis.

As liberal democrats bent on reform, Krutch and Dewey do not call for a radical critique or removal of the social conditions underlying the "crisis of experience." But other thinkers of the same period, roughly the 1920s and 1930s, were more concerned with the ways in which capitalism as a mode of production was actually destroying cultural memory (though all sort of ersatz experiences could be bought and sold). In particular, Walter Benjamin's essays about the impact of technology on the aura of traditional art objects and on the concomitant emergence of "exhibition value" in institutions such as museums have been very influential in recent cultural debates about modernity.

It is my view that the writers of the fantastic considered in this volume, whose works span the twentieth century—Dunsany began publishing during the Edwardian period and Bradbury was still publishing collections in the first decade of the twenty-first century—have devised stories in which the experience of the supernatural is linked in complex ways to the experience of society under capitalism, to the ways in which industrial (and later consumer capitalism) was undermining the very possibility of extended and integrated experience (*Erfahrung* in Benjamin). As a matter of fact we can pretty much identify modernity with industrial capitalism in Dunsany and Lovecraft, considering their frequent diatribes against The Age of the Machine.

And if it is true, as Northrop Frye asserted, that romance and fantasy are inevitable for writers who don't believe in the permanence of their own society, then there ought to be a way of reading these authors and their chosen genres as inherently critical of modern society, to uncover the social in their texts. Though certainly not revolutionaries bent on transforming society in any programmatic sense, and even while denying that history or human life in itself has any transcendent purpose or meaning, I find that Dunsany, Lovecraft, and Bradbury each conducts a critique of capitalism as destructive of history and coherent experience.

However different in conscious politics and personality, each of these writers is fundamentally opposed to a society based on commercialism and universal exchange. Though they might be imaginatively attracted to other, earlier forms of trade, such as merchant's capital in the eighteenth century, they all share a strong opposition to commercialism. While struggling to assert the qualitative interests of the artist and the finely crafted tale, they find in supernatural fiction's inassimilable monstrous figures, cursed and banned books that are dangerous to read, and pantheons of strange and grotesquely malevolent gods a store of ironic tropes, since none of them really believes in the existence of the supernatural, that reveal the *spectral* nature of capitalism.[10]

Dunsany and Lovecraft utterly rejected machine civilization. It may at first seem idiosyncratic and even quaint when we discover the many pages in Lovecraft's correspondence that mention his hating to type his handwritten manuscripts, but he gives such a vivid description of how composing and transcribing on the machine robbed him of creativity that obviously his repugnance involves more than just a personal affectation.[11] The handwritten manuscript for Lovecraft bore the traces of individuality, of the storyteller's personal aura. Dunsany as well wrote out his stories with a quill pen, or dictated them. In my view each of these authors revives certain features and traces of traditional storytelling, making the supernatural tale into a comment on the destruction of the aura—that sense of uniqueness we attribute to a work of art from the past—in modern society.

However insightful, Krutch and Dewey are not today considered important theorists of modernity. Krutch claimed only to be describing the mood of modernity as it appeared to him, and Dewey's discussion of art is largely confined to the art of past ages. But since Krutch's time the "crisis of experience" brought about by technological modernity seems to have worsened. If not for the average person, then certainly among intellectuals or thinking persons the mood has darkened considerably. Like other Marxist thinkers, Benjamin and Adorno stressed that modernity was bringing about fundamental changes in the very structure of perception and everyday experience, substituting for the traditional experience of life in an integrated community (*Erfahrung*) that of the impoverished passing moment (*Erlebnis*). For all those who lived in cities and who worked in factories, workers and ordinary middle-class consumers alike, *Erfahrung*, experience organized and articulated through collectively shared, traditionally fixed meanings, was being divided under conditions of modernity into the shock-like instantaneity of *Erlebnis*, privatized subjective experience, and information, consisting of facts that remained completely unrelated to personal life, expressed in newspapers and the like, which were not being related to the public by true storytellers. Dunsany, as we will see in the first chapter, had asserted these very same problems of modernity in the Edwardian period, nearly two decades before Benjamin came to articulate them.

From the outset of his career, Benjamin was searching for a much broader framework for understanding experience than what was provided by the intellectual culture he knew. Part of his expanded context of discussion was an attempt to tie modes of perception to definite historical stages of communication and to literary forms, starting with an early stage of enlivened, naive storytelling such as we find in the epic (in the tales of Odysseus, for example) as precursor of the novel. He writes:

> Historically, the various modes of communication have competed with one another. The replacement of the older narration by information, of information by sensation, reflects the increasing atrophy of experience (*Erfahrung*). In turn, there is a contrast between all these forms and the story, which is one of the oldest forms of communication. It is not the object of a story to convey a happening *per se*, which is the purpose of information; rather, it embeds it in the life of the storyteller in order to pass it on as experience to those listening. It thus bears the marks (*Spuren*, traces) of the storyteller much as the marks of the potter's hand.[12]

At the end of this passage Benjamin thanks Proust for restoring the figure of the storyteller in modernity, through his aesthetic use of involuntary memory, which in turn plays a central role in Benjamin's definition of aura. In the full account, Benjamin alludes to a degenerating sequence of modes of perception and narrative modes of consciousness, from story to novel, to fragmented news item to mere sensation. But from the opening paragraph of this essay he makes it clear that an economic base is at fault. People were being robbed by the capitalist system of what seemed their most inalienable possession: the ability to exchange (*auszutauschen*, in the sense of barter) stories. Experience (*Erfahrung*) had fallen in value (*im Kurse gefallen*; implying the circulation of commodities).

Actually for Benjamin the storyteller was already a figure who, while not quite ghostly, was already receding into the distance. Indeed, it was the advent of modernization itself that brought about our sensitivity to the aura. Modern shock and fragmentation constituted the aura as a problem precisely through making us realize that it is what the present lacks. At the center of Benjamin's readings of such key modernist authors as Baudelaire, Kafka, Proust, and Brecht (of whom he was a personal friend) is the notion of modern experience being conditioned by the decay of the aura. Authentic aura, represented by the masterpieces of the past constituting high culture, was threatened by modern techniques of mechanical reproduction, which could reproduce the art object in multiple copies, making it a commodity like any other in mass culture. But, Benjamin also reasoned, there might be revolutionary potential waiting to be unlocked in new forms of communication such as film.

In a poetic definition, Benjamin characterized the aura in connection with photography in almost supernatural terms, as a strange weave of space and time, as the unique apparition of a distance no matter how close the object may appear to be.[13] For Benjamin, traditional art objects possessed aura in returning our gaze from a distance, their atmosphere of beauty being more like a medium in which the human subject breathes and expands, like the experience of a natural landscape. But there is also considerable evidence suggesting that in addition to its visible qualities, tactile experience is also at the basis of what Benjamin meant by the aura (as in the artisanal trace left by the storyteller in the passage quoted above).[14]

As for the emotions involved in auratic experience, I know of no more poignant expression of the distance of the aura in Benjamin's sense of the term than the Proustian opening paragraphs of H. P. Lovecraft's *The Dream-Quest of Unknown Kadath*, which create a mood of almost-vanished memory combined with the pain of lost things. But the hero of this story, Randolph Carter, discovers in the end that his dream city is actually contained in the memories of his real historical childhood in Boston. Randolph Carter in other stories becomes a spectral figure, unable to assume again his human form because he cannot read or translate a certain parchment that belongs to a (inhuman) tradition of cursed books. Carter in his inhuman form may be an ironically distanced image of Lovecraft's own spectral authorship of such stories as "Out of the Aeons" (1933), since he made his living as a ghostwriter.

At any rate, Benjamin understood that in order to become a part of Marxist materialist aesthetics, the notion of aura, just as it is in Lovecraft's wonderful allegory, had to be modified so as to accommodate history understood as a collective reality. That is, aura had to be understood not just as belonging to cult art objects, or to the occult experiences of the dream, but as appearing in all things that are the product of human labor, however veiled in form or ideology they may be, as "the key to the possibility of experience in/of the modern everyday."[15] Yet he resisted his friend Adorno's attempt to see in aura an extension of the effect of reification, or alienated human labor, as another version of commodity fetishism and held to his own image of "dialectics at a standstill" (like the photograph).[16]

The term in Benjamin's critical discourse thus moves between two opposed meanings, one arcane or even demonic and the other profane.[17] In his more revolutionary moods, he was wont to speak of aura as in need of demolition. To have any revolutionary potential to address current conditions, art must dispense with past notions of eternal beauty and embrace the fleeting experience (*Erlebnis*) of shock, an artistic practice he found in Baudelaire's use of allegory.

Though he prepared himself unsuccessfully for an academic life by writing on Goethe and then the allegory of German baroque drama (which made him something of a specialist on seventeenth-century melancholy), Benjamin was particularly interested in mass culture and the new arts of photography and film. He wrote several influential essays in the late 1920s and 1930s about the revolutionary potential of these technologically based media to transform our lives. These essays define the aura in ways that have become central to the discipline of film studies. The gaze that the object seems to return to us became central to his thinking during this period. He was among the first theorists of film (and of photography) to embrace the work of Freud and to argue that the cinema presents us with the uncanny experience of an "optical unconscious" that lies outside the normal spectrum of sense impressions. The camera sees what ordinary human vision cannot register.

Perhaps a few brief examples can make some of this abstract discussion of the experience of the aura more concrete. The shocking effect of one of Lovecraft's most well-known stories of the modern supernatural, "Pickman's Model" (1926), actually hinges on the distinction between photography and the traditional aura of painting. In the story Pickman's paintings shock the conventional art community, which perceives them as too horrible and too demonic even to exhibit. Pickman's forte is in depicting faces. But there is something disturbing in them that goes beyond the limits of decent representation, creating a quality of uneasiness, for the paintings allude to the exchange of humans with demonic creatures in the myths of changelings. At the end of the story the narrator discovers that the painter was working from photographs of actual demonic creatures. Here Lovecraft uses photography (which had an early preoccupation with the aura of the human face in the unique daguerreotype) to demystify the auratic and the hierarchical social structures a ritualized aura of the exhibition—"exhibition value" in Benjamin's terms—preserves. Modern photography, in which the snapshot generates no aura itself, shocks and stupefies us (or at least the twist ending would have it so). Yet the story itself has acquired a certain aura as embodying Lovecraft's aesthetics, and was anthologized twice during his lifetime. Bradbury is perhaps more ambivalent about finding new aesthetic possibilities for horror and unease in the ruin of consumer culture and the fetishistic experiences of the commodity world. Sometimes, he seems to revel in the destruction and decay of the aura and the creation of junk. In Bradbury's post-apocalyptic story "The Smile," entertainment consists in lining up to spit at what is left of the *Mona Lisa*, a fragment containing her smile.

Benjamin was always pointing out that modern art had a way of shocking us out of familiar and habituated ways of thinking. He described Dada in its ruthless annihilation of the aura as anticipating film in some of its effects. (Kurt Schwitters, one of the founders of Dada, was famous for saying that anything the artist spits is art.) Modern art movements such as surrealism motivated Benjamin to undertake his Arcades Project, which is among other things an intricate and visionary Freudo-Marxist decoding of the phantasmagoria of fetish-like objects produced by capitalism in the nineteenth century.[18] He wanted to introduce the modern discovery of desire and the unconscious into his readings of modernity. Interestingly, Lovecraft often spoke of supernatural horror in architectural terms, as the fearful passage through an endless Gothic maze, "the black arcade." As we will see, Lovecraft transformed the shock of modernity into a spectral aesthetic by introducing the experience of the labyrinthine city into his stories, giving them a sense of duration actually based on the continuous experience of shock.

But at the same time that Benjamin was searching for revolutionary potential in these new media, he also uncovered the ways in which the traditional forms of the past survived and were transformed by storytellers such as Franz Kafka, and especially in the prose writings of Baudelaire's *Paris Spleen* (a modern version of melancholy). Indeed the figure of the storyteller embodied for Benjamin all of the auratic powers of memory and tradition that were on the wane in the modern world. As I mentioned, Benjamin saw the figure of the storyteller as receding from our culture, a situation leading to loss of traditional wisdom and a condition of homelessness pervading modern culture. Our age had become the age of information and newspapers.

But in his 1936 essay on the Russian author Nikolai Leskov, whose translation into German Benjamin was introducing, he suggests two main types of experience still to be found in the folktale/fairy tale tradition and in the modern short story generally: "the lore of faraway places, such as a much traveled man brings home, and the lore of the past, such as is manifested most clearly to the inhabitants of a place."[19] Benjamin left no doubt in his introduction that he preferred the more communally based short story to the novel, which he thought a form appealing to and increasing solitude and alienation.

I cannot do adequate justice to the analogical subtlety of Benjamin's thought, which is often abrupt and startling, in this brief introduction, but this essay has been a suggestive inspiration, if not the exact model, for what I have attempted to do in this study, that is, to link the experience of reading fantastic fiction to social experience. Benjamin was first received and discussed as a Marxist materialist critic of both official and mass culture (he left an intriguing note on the disavowal of experience in Mickey Mouse cartoons), but his legacy is still being explored. Pioneering many of the now familiar textual strategies of deconstruction, including the current revival of allegorical modes of reading cultural texts, his essays enacted and resembled the contrary potentialities of allegory he was so adept at finding in those writers he studied.

Ever since his 1928 study of baroque drama (*Trauerspiel*, mourning play), allegory for Benjamin was not so much a literary mode as an intuitive way of perceiving reality, an outlook. It is preeminently the kind of experience that arises when the world is apprehended as no longer permanent or a living totality; as the gods withdraw, the world becomes fragmentary and enigmatic, it ceases to be purely physical and becomes at the same time a collection of dead yet spiritual signs. In Benjamin's exposition, allegory's post-romantic reputation for conventionality and inauthenticity, in contrast with the living symbol, stems from a historical attempt to deny the role of the trace or writing in experience.[20] Symbols only provided a momentary glimpse of totality, whereas the allegorical could provide a more comprehensive view of man's place in nature. When he began to think about Marx, he saw in the latter's analysis of commodities an allegorical (or spectral) approach to meaning, since commodities mysteriously contain invisible social relations. The allegorical emblems of the baroque returned as commodities. Allegory became for him "the armature of modernity."[21]

His method of reading the traces of the past (the trace being another notion he pioneered) was redemptive, yet melancholy, and his writings on history's "weak messianic force" influential on such thinkers as Jacques Derrida. He had the ability, much prized among Marxist thinkers, to read the traces of social relations in objects fetishized by commodity production.[22] In his own generation he was a decisive influence on eminent Marxist theorists such as Theodor Adorno. Adorno in his *Aesthetics* made aura the subject of several complex discussions of the relation of the artwork to natural beauty, mood, and atmosphere.[23]

In the current generation of Marxist thinkers one thinks inevitably of Fredric Jameson, whose *The Political Unconscious* (1981) explores narrative as a socially symbolic act and launches Marxist interpretation as essentially allegorical: "It is in detecting the traces of that uninterrupted narrative [history as class struggle], in restoring to the surface of the text the repressed and buried reality of this fundamental history, that the doctrine of a political unconscious finds its function and necessity."[24] Unfortunately Jameson, after a favorable reading of romance in the theoretical first past of his study, goes on to study Honoré de Balzac, George Gissing, and Joseph Conrad, writers strongly placed in the tradition of realism. He offers us no extended reading of modern fantastic narrative as a socially symbolic act in *The Political Unconscious*, though he did go on to examine science fiction and utopian literature in later critical studies. This study is written in the belief that our experience of supernatural horror and the weird, of the "black arcade" contained in a story such as Lovecraft's "The Horror at Red Hook," can be understood as an architectural layer of the political unconscious conceived along Jamesonian lines.

For his part, despite the equivocations on the notion in his writings, it seems clear that Benjamin himself felt the irreparable loss of aura personally as something to be regretted. Despite the posture of his more avant-garde or Marxist-inspired "revolutionary" essays that art under mechanical conditions of reproduction might open up new possibilities of perception, he was filled with nostalgia for his lost childhood in Berlin. So too, in various ways, all of the writers considered in this study evoke nostalgia as perhaps *the* painful experience of modernity. Benjamin gave unequivocal prestige to the storyteller as the bearer of authentic experience (*Erfahrung*). And so too I hope to show that my three authors responded to the condition of modernity by creating stories in which the figure of the storyteller in Benjamin's sense is restored and reinvented.

The German word *Erfahrung* is related to the verb for journeying, *fahren* (the prefix *Er* means "completed"); so there is a strong sense of the completed journey already at work in Benjamin's use of the word, which unfortunately does not exist in English. Another word for experience used by Benjamin in opposition to *Erfahrung* is *Erlebnis*, derived from the verb *leben*, "to live." *Erlebnis* is experience as lived through, but not necessarily integrated into, conscious life. Another reason then why I call on Dunsany, Lovecraft, and Bradbury as storytellers is because their stories render the fragmented nature of modern experience endurable by giving it the quality of having been fully experienced, even when that experience may turn out to be spectral.

Benjamin himself was no stranger to supernatural fiction and even wrote an essay on E. T. A. Hoffmann as a storyteller possessed and driven by a kind of grotesque and demonic perception of the world that was critical of bourgeois Berlin in the early nineteenth century.[25] So as far as Benjamin was concerned, some of the more salient features of auratic experience in the wider cultural definition Benjamin gave to it—the mourning for beautiful semblance, the longed-for return of the gaze, the temporal disjunction and shock-like confrontation with the demonic and the grotesque—could perhaps be better appreciated in supernatural fiction than in realism. Benjamin's writings are therefore of great relevance to understanding a writer like H. P. Lovecraft, who in a pioneering essay on supernatural fiction defined aura and atmosphere as the key element in understanding the historical persistence of the weird tale.[26]

As a matter of fact, Benjamin's 1939 essay "On Some Motifs in Baudelaire," which gives us his most elaborate discussion of the aura, provided me with the overall plan for this study. In this essay Benjamin distinguishes four distinct aspects of the mood of modernity: beauty, shock, nostalgia, and melancholy. These three moods of modernity identified by Benjamin allow me to examine my four writers according to what mood seems to predominate in their aesthetic. Thus each chapter begins with a discussion of that writer's dominant aesthetic and, after a brief biographical survey of life and writings, goes on to examine the stories as a working out of that aesthetic. It is obvious that all three writers share elements of beauty, the shock of the grotesque, nostalgia, and melancholy, the latter two not being entirely separable, but nonetheless one of the moods tends to predominate in each writer. For Benjamin, moods were also revelatory of historical and political experience. But by placing my three writers in diachronic order, I aim also to examine them in the broadest possible horizon of meaning, the historical and dialectical relationship each author has to the development of capitalism, from industrial capitalism of the early twentieth century to today's global late capitalist economic formations.[27]

For Dunsany, newspapers, as products of modernity and the age of information, were ephemera and anathema to real storytelling. Dunsany's oral-based tales accordingly have many of the qualities of the much-traveled man. But Lovecraft expanded the traditional supernatural tale by contrasting sources of information such as newspapers, the *public* and *uninquiring* face of a story, with the horrific and actual hidden truth uncovered by the narrator. Lovecraft, while increasingly rooted in the antiquarianism of New England and especially of Providence, wrote of strange cosmic journeys. Bradbury too had a strong sense of nostalgia for small town America, but wrote in the tradition of carnival and grotesque realism.[28]

I should say at the outset that the experience of beauty, shock, nostalgia, and melancholy are of course present in varying degrees in each of the writers considered in this study. Dunsany was no stranger to shock, as his stories about his experiences in World War I will attest. Lovecraft, who described himself as a scientific indifferentist, but who thought that his dissatisfaction with objective reality and his interest in fantasy brought him very close to melancholy, professed a fascination with Albrecht Dürer's allegorical engraving of that figure.[29] Bradbury's *Fahrenheit 451* is a deeply melancholic book, but Bradbury found a medicine for melancholy in his nostalgia for carnival and the idyllic past of his childhood. And so on. Each of these writers could be read as in some sense nostalgic or melancholic with regard to modernity, and they would hardly be modern writers if they did not respond to the many shocks of the twentieth century with new versions of the beautiful and the grotesque.

To Lovecraft the modern weird tale was a product of a long tradition of atmosphere and aura that in turn needed to be received by the critic and reader in a mood of awed listening created by the storyteller. I think we need to understand more about that tradition of storytelling and how it is related to modern society. Accordingly, I have tried to write a criticism of the fantastic exploring comparatively the implications of what the Marxist-sociological tradition of dialectical thought might have to offer the study of the fantastic in culture. I am indebted to that tradition for whatever insights the reader may find herein, but especially to Benjamin, who so strikingly illuminated and located the (largely unconscious) need for fantastic storytelling in the transformations of perception brought about by modern society.

I find that Dunsany best reminds us of what we have lost in terms of beautiful semblance, and that Lovecraft invites us to take pleasure in the deforming shock or disintegration of the beautiful aura into grotesque and demonic shapes. Both of these writers invented new gods in strange pantheons to express their allegories of modern experience. But Bradbury, feeling that the world was filling up with a bitter melancholy at the waning of experience (*Erfahrung*), calls on popular nostalgia and the carnival tradition, degraded by modernity, in order to resist the authority of the modern technological state with its world of information and facts. As I wrote this study of Dunsany, Lovecraft, and Bradbury, thinkers in the Western Marxist tradition, especially Benjamin, together with Bakhtin, formed a small group—a spectral company, if you like—that helped me make a difficult journey into the meaning of modernity. I hope they will do the same for you. In addition, I would like to thank the very real presence of S. T. Joshi for his encouragement and guidance.

NOTES

1. M. M. Bakhtin and P. M. Medvedev, *The Formal Method in Literary Scholarship* (Cambridge, MA: Harvard University Press, 1985), 134. "One might say that human consciousness possesses a series of inner genres for seeing and conceptualizing reality. A given consciousness is richer or poorer in genres, depending on its ideological environment. Literature occupies an important place in this ideological environment. As the plastic arts give width and depth to the visual realm and teach our eye to see, the genres of literature enrich our inner speech with new devices for the awareness and conceptualization of reality."
2. Friedrich Nietzsche, *The Portable Nietzsche*, edited and translated by Walter Kaufmann (New York: Penguin, 1976), 585–86.
3. See the review of five recent studies of modernism by Daniel T. O'Hara, "Modernism's Ghosts," *Journal of Modern Literature* 26, Nos. 3/4 (Summer 2003): 154–58. One of the books reviewed, Amy Hungerford's *The Holocaust of Texts*, offers a reading of Ray Bradbury's *Fahrenheit 451* as personifying texts as if they were the spirits of the dead.
4. Georg Lukács, *The Theory of the Novel*, translated by Anna Bostock (Cambridge, MA: MIT Press, 1971), 103–4. Lukács published his famous study in the same year, 1920, as Lovecraft wrote "Ex Oblivione," a prose poem proclaiming the modern world demonic. In general, I have been guided in my understanding of experience as a cultural theme by the magisterial work of intellectual historian of modernity Martin Jay, and in my understanding of the deepening crisis of experience in storytelling by the writings of Walter Benjamin and Theodor Adorno. Jay's chapter on Benjamin and Adorno and the crisis of experience has been particularly invaluable to me. Martin Jay, *Songs of Experience, Modern American and European Variations on a Universal Theme* (Berkeley: University of California Press, 2005).
5. H. P. Lovecraft, *The Annotated Supernatural Horror in Literature*, edited by S. T. Joshi (New York: Hippocampus Press, 2000), 31. Lovecraft is discussing Maturin and refers to Balzac's praise of *Melmoth the Wanderer* (1820) as an allegorical figure. In more recent allegory I have in mind Mr. Dark of Ray Bradbury's *Something Wicked This Way Comes*.
6. David Glover, "The 'Spectrality Effect' in Early Modernism," in Andrew Smith and Jeff Wallace, editors, *Gothic Modernisms* (London: Palgrave, 2001), 29–43. Glover's title refers to Derrida, 31.
7. Joseph Wood Krutch, *The Modern Temper* (New York: Harcourt, Brace & Co., 1929), 9.
8. Krutch, *The Modern Temper*, 57.
9. John Dewey, *Art as Experience* (New York: Capricorn, 1958), 45.
10. For the spectral in Marx, see Jacques Derrida, *Specters of Marx*, translated by Peggy Kamuf (London: Routledge, 1994). Derrida's textual analyses of Marx are persuasive, but instead of finding Marx and communism spectral, I have asserted capitalism's spectrality in the writers I have chosen. In this I follow Marx's own analysis of the ghostly, supernatural character of money in *Capital* and elsewhere, which Derrida himself pointed out. Marx constantly used figures of the supernatural (especially werewolves and vampires) to describe the workings

of capital. See Stanley Edgar Hyman, *The Tangled Bank: Darwin, Marx and Freud as Imaginative Writers* (New York: Atheneum, 1962), 133–35.

11. See the pages listed under "Typewriters" in S. T. Joshi, *An Index to the Selected Letters of H. P. Lovecraft* (West Warwick, RI: Necronomicon Press, 1991), 38.

12. Walter Benjamin, "On Some Motifs in Baudelaire," in *Illuminations*, translated by Harry Zohn (New York: Schocken, 1969), 159.

13. Walter Benjamin, "Little History of Photography," in *Selected Writings*, Volume 2, Part 2, edited by Michael W. Jennings et al. (Cambridge, MA: Harvard University Press, 2005), 518.

14. For an account of the tactile in Benjamin, see Richard Shiff, "Handling Shocks: On the Representation of Experience in Walter Benjamin's Analogies," *Oxford Journal of Art* 15, No. 2 (1992): 88–103.

15. Miriam Bratu Hansen, "Benjamin's Aura," *Critical Inquiry* 34 (Winter 2008): 351. According to Hansen, by the time of his highly influential 1936 essay called "The Work of Art in the Age of Its Mechanical Reproduction," Benjamin had largely dropped the occult and demonic associations of the term and come to speak of it as irremediably in decay. Aura was not to be understood as an eternal value bearing the unchanging meaning of an object but rather as the *manner* in which it can mean something for a contemporary public, inseparable from the historically changing ways of its reception.

16. For a discussion of Benjamin's notion of the aura in relation to Marx's notion of commodity fetishism, see Gyorgy Markus, "Walter Benjamin or The Commodity as Phantasmagoria," *New German Critique* No. 83 (Spring–Summer 2001): 3–42.

17. For Benjamin's reflections on occultist discourse, see "Light from Obscurantists," in Walter Benjamin, *Selected Writings*, Volume 2, Part 2, 653–57.

18. Benjamin was also interested in architecture, and worked on a massive project concerning the Paris arcades and their role in creating a modern consumer culture. The nineteenth-century Paris Arcades housed the first consumer dream worlds, which in the twentieth century appeared as commodity graveyards. These imaginative glassy locales inspired the surrealists who in turn influenced Benjamin, and the collective history of modernity. See Walter Benjamin, *The Arcades Project*, edited by Rolf Tiedemann (Cambridge, MA: Harvard University Press, 1999).

19. Walter Benjamin, "The Storyteller: Reflections on the Work of Nikolai Leskov," in *Walter Benjamin, Selected Writings*, Volume 3, edited by Howard Eiland and Michael W. Jennings (Cambridge, MA: Harvard University Press, 2002), 144.

20. For a useful account, see Bainard Cowan, "Walter Benjamin's Theory of Allegory," *New German Critique* No. 22 (Winter 1981): 109–22. Cowan points out the similarities between Benjamin's theory of allegory as experience and deconstruction.

21. Walter Benjamin, *Selected Writings*, Volume 4, edited by Howard Eiland and Michael W. Jennings (Cambridge, MA: Harvard University Press, 2003), 183.

22. Karl Marx, *Capital*, Volume One, translated by Ben Fowkes (New York: Vintage, 1977), 138–39.

23. Theodor Adorno, *Aesthetic Theory*, translated by Robert Hullot-Kentor (Minneapolis: University of Minnesota Press, 1997), 274–75. I explore Benjamin and Adorno's ideas about aura as modeled on beautiful semblance in nature in my chapter on Dunsany.

24. Fredric Jameson, *The Political Unconscious: Narrative as a Socially Symbolic Act* (Ithaca, NY: Cornell University Press, 1981), 20.

25. Walter Benjamin, "Demonic Berlin," in *Selected Writings*, Volume 2, Part 1, edited by Michael W. Jennings (Cambridge, MA: Harvard University Press, 1999), 322–26.

26. H. P. Lovecraft, *The Annotated Supernatural Horror in Literature*, 23. Lovecraft emphasizes the attitude of awed listening that the weird tale requires, just as Benjamin does in his essay on Hoffmann.

27. For a discussion of the different periods of capitalism, see Lucien Goldmann, *Cultural Creation*, translated by Bart Grahl (Oxford: Basil Blackwell, 1977), 52–55. Goldmann distinguishes three distinct periods in the history of Western capitalism: a lengthy period of liberal capitalism (also called laissez-faire) stretching from the Enlightenment to the end of World War I, the imperialist period, or capitalism in crisis, lasting from 1918 to 1945, and consumer

society or mass society, in which we live today, each correlated with the imaginary universes of writers. I have loosely followed Goldmann's periods, although my authors obviously overlap in them to a certain extent.

28. Mikhail Bakhtin, *Rabelais and His World*, translated by Helene Iswolsky (Bloomington: Indiana University Press, 1984), 52–53. Bakhtin explains that modern realism broke with the carnival tradition and limited itself to naturalist empiricism.

29. H. P. Lovecraft, *Selected Letters*, Volume 5, edited by August Derleth and James Turner (Sauk City, WI: Arkham House, 1976), 343.

Lord Dunsany, or Beauty

Romance, the literary mode in which Lord Dunsany (Edward John Moreton Drax Plunkett, 18th Baron Dunsany, 1878–1957) wrote most successfully and influentially, projects a world that is closer to our innermost desires, the world as we would like it to be in contrast to the often frustrating world of experience (in Dunsany's felicitous phrase, romance lies beyond the fields we know). According to Northrop Frye, romance shows better than any other mode the archetypal function of literature in visualizing the world of desire, not as an escape from reality, but "as a genuine form of the world that human life tries to imitate."[1] Most readers of romance today understand that it is mainly about adventure, and that its primary literary form is the quest, but on closer historical examination it seems that romance also had a social function, of articulating whatever remained unfulfilled or repressed in society. For Dunsany romance projected a powerful spell of idealized beauty that he thought absolutely necessary to modern culture, in which he saw beauty as an autonomous realm being destroyed at every turn.

As we shall see, quests for beauty abound in Dunsany. The city, that archetype of civilization, is one of the primary imaginary embodiments of beauty in Dunsany. At the same time, idealized cities express a cultural ideal in Dunsany, and his heroes thirst for them. What is more, he reinvented and revisited the sociology of all of the traditional forms of storytelling related to romance—heroic legend, fable, myth, and the supernatural tale. Storytelling as a source of wisdom remained of paramount value to him throughout his prolific career. Even when he no longer wrote romance stories *per se*, and turned to the realistic novel, he was still firmly opposed to realism as a mode depicting things simply as they are (i.e., naturalism). In *The Story of Mona Sheehy* (1939), for instance, Mona's expansive fantasies about herself as the daughter of the queen of the Shee make her critical of the debased forms of romance she sees around her.[2] The Jorkens tales too, ostensibly written to make use of Dunsany's extensive travel experiences in Africa, are actually tall tales that play a game of the impossible with an incredulous reader, and thereby create a modern Baron Munchausen.

That being so, he would perhaps be pleased to find that romance as a higher literary mode has of late undergone a reexamination by critics interested in the social function of art, such as Fredric Jameson and Northrop Frye. Far from being considered naive, escapist and trivial, and tied to the machinery of commodity production, it now appears that true romance preserves the archetypal experience of a non-alienated society, bearing within it a revolutionary potential. Frye in particular saw romance as the one genre that was never satisfied with the status quo, no matter what the society.[3] Of course Dunsany never consciously saw beyond romance to a socialist future (as did William Morris), and his view of the ultimate horizon of human history was in the last decade of his life quite grim.[4] Nonetheless, moments of utopian longing and a desire for collective activity can easily be detected in his early writings. As we shall see, these longings tend to focus on the storyteller as a figure who transmits values from the past. In this chapter I try to understand his felt ideological need for images of beauty that call us to a life beyond the isolated individual in light of these recent theories of romance.

Dunsany's emphasis on the need for idealized beauty may today seem quaint, and, romance being an aristocratic form in origin, may be considered a mere reflex of his conservative politics. But actually his artistic concerns were always broader than his class origins would seem to indicate. Indeed, for him the inescapable purpose of serious art, by which he meant all kinds of creative activity in society, lay in bringing more beauty into the world at every level of society. It is well to remember that the human desire to capture beauty was *the* central preoccupation of Western artists, poets, and philosophers for many centuries and in fact constituted a rich tradition that embraced many different ideological positions and artistic styles.[5] For his part, Dunsany felt that his greatest achievement lay in the tradition of romantic beauty and, like many writers before him whom he admired, the artisanal in culture (Keats and Shelley among the romantic poets and Tennyson).

As will become clear, the whole of Dunsany's aesthetic rests on a complex dialectical relationship between natural beauty and art beauty. In the Marxist view of this relationship, art is conditioned by epochal shifts in the social mode of production. As Raymond Williams observes, "We have mixed our labour with the earth, our forces with its forces too deeply to be able to draw back and separate either out."[6] For this reason alone, it is never enough simply to understand the conscious politics of a writer. Rather, a careful analysis of the dialectical images of man's "metabolism" with nature expressed in literary works has also to be considered. This is all the more necessary in the case of Dunsany, whose intense bodily love of the natural landscape is evident in nearly everything he wrote. His habit of personifying natural forces as sometimes indifferent, cruel, and Darwinian is perhaps unconscious but in the last analysis not accidental. It was determined by both the cultural milieu—when at school at Eton the young Dunsany memorized whole sections of Tennyson's *Idylls of the King*—and by the shape of alienated nature in the late Victorian period.[7]

It is not my intention to review here the debates about the origin of art in collective humanity or to lament its fate in class society. It seems obvious to me that in a class society such as we have constructed, various classes try to recruit art into serving their particular purposes. Dunsany's work is no exception, and reflects all of the contradictions of art and beauty under capitalism in the modern period, which I will be concerned with exploring throughout this chapter. But here I would say that, despite his conservative politics, Dunsany's romance writings are saturated with a longing for the more collective and less exploitative relationship to nature that existed before the advent of industrial capitalism. A glance at the lengthy and elaborate Robin Hood–like building of his dream castle in Spain at the end of his fantasy historical novel *The Chronicles of Rodriguez* (1922)—his version of *Don Quixote*—is enough to convince even the casual reader of that.[8]

Marxist critics have long speculated that among so-called primitive peoples, beauty was a deeply felt cultic and magical experience belonging to the collective.[9] Art, in the form of ritual and myth, was from the beginning a necessity for human survival in nature (this is also the view of Ray Bradbury, discussed in the third chapter). If anything, reading Dunsany's stories of the Pegāna mythos has made me aware of the fact that the pantheons of many historical religions included gods representing beauty (Freya for the Norsemen, for example). In the Marxist view, this cultic experience of the uniqueness of beauty based on the appearance of a god probably represented an attempt to gain some magical control over the natural environment. Magic has never really left the purposes of art, despite the advent of science and the Enlightenment. In Benjamin's terms art, even under the problematic conditions of capitalism, still possesses an identifiable aura.[10]

However that may be, it is this cultic experience of beauty based ultimately on the natural world that represents the epicenter of Dunsany's fantasy. He conceived of beauty in the traditional manner as having a unique "aura" or atmosphere that remained inviolable and at a distance.[11] However, as we will see, Dunsany felt that beautiful semblance, as the very ground of the experience of beauty, was being destroyed by modern industrial capitalism. Thus beauty was increasingly represented as threatened in his writings. Another threat was posed by the modern masses with their urge to grasp and possess things at close range, itself one of the chief effects created by commodity fetishism. Thus on the level of the political unconscious his best writings generate a remarkable and authentic dialectical tension between the fantasy worlds he created—as absolutely far away in space and time as he wished them to be—and the modern world with its idols of the marketplace. Increasingly, these two worlds, enchanted nature and debased society, were more and more starkly contrasted as Dunsany's experience of the modern world deepened. By the time of the publication of his book of aesthetic parables, *Fifty-One Tales* (1915), after the outset of the Great War, we find stories of bourgeois women buying idols of pagan gods in shops and even a live sphinx, thereby meeting their doom. But the possibility of liberation lies under the very paving stones of London's streets ("The Sphinx in Thebes," "The Trouble in Leafy Green Street," "Taking Up Piccadilly").

In what follows I will argue that Dunsany's Pegāna mythos, despite its dated period novelty, retains for us today considerable power to represent what Marxist critics call the decay of aura in modern society. These stories also have the power to question the centrality of a realism that has been dominant in Western literature for well over a century and a half. Following recent reevaluations of romance that reexamine its potential for cultural subversion, and using Northrop Frye's sequence of historical modes, I will argue that however conservative in politics Dunsany consciously may have been, there is always a political unconscious to consider in his writings.[12]

For these reasons I find Dunsany to be a fascinating if contradictory figure, his cultural sensibilities largely shaped by the restlessness and rapid change of the Edwardian period. Today this period is viewed not merely as a transitional time between the Victorian period and the upsurge in modernist writers of the 1920s, who created a definitive break with Victorianism. The most recent research places Dunsany among those artists responding to the rapid urbanization and dehumanization of the urban middle class and of the poor during the first decade of the twentieth century. Dunsany is now seen as typical of fantasy writers, openly displaying anxieties about the "cracks in Edwardian confidence."[13]

I therefore open my discussion of Dunsany's aesthetics with his attack on realism published in 1911, which is solidly in the Edwardian period.[14] This article was in fact published at the same cultural moment that H. G. Wells was suggesting in a survey of the novel that the assurance of Victorian fiction had shifted toward a more doubtful, skeptical attitude.[15] Dunsany's doubts were clearly about the hegemony of realism as the dominant mode in theatre. In his view a narrow realism had taken hold of theatrical representation, reflecting society back to itself as nothing more than a series of trivial and often sordid problems to be solved. Realism, while true to life, did not question the stated goal of middle-class life—the accumulation of money; it merely reflected it. Yet decadence, Dunsany observed, was being produced in factories, with beauty banished, frightened away by advertising. What is more, Dunsany was deeply troubled by the flood of information being spread by modern technologies of communication. The old forms of romance, which once offered a coherent understanding of the world, were rapidly disappearing, with nothing of value to replace them.

Dunsany was writing at the beginnings of modern consumer society and specifically about London theatre. London was at that time the very economic center of capitalism in the modern world. As such, the system of exchange value, what he called the age of trade, was most in evidence there, filling everyday life with a heap of commodities and a value system organized by advertising. In his view, putting representations of this world on stage could only rob the theatre of its unique beauty and importance. His response was to insist that the dramatist should look for his stories somewhere far away from the fads and fashions of empty bourgeois lives. This brings up the central problem of Dunsany's orientalism, which I will take up in a moment. Extending his argument to encompass what source materials he considered appropriate to the modern stage, Dunsany argued that traditional stories expressed the collective wisdom of the people and could still give a meaningful shape to human lives. Without them meaningful experience was impossible. Therefore, he felt called upon to restore the figure of the storyteller to the stage.

The tone of this article places poets and dramatists of a traditional sort on the high moral ground of educators. Civilization must be led by drama to the task of discovering higher goals than commerce. In Dunsany's account of then current literary modes, romance figures as an earlier mode were deemed better at representing real, as opposed to artificially stimulated, goals and desires. In arguing that it can be viewed as a higher form of realism, Dunsany seems to have anticipated Frye's observation that the terms "romantic" and "realistic" are not to be understood absolutely, but are relative and comparative.[16] Most interesting in my view is the fact that Dunsany's diagnosis of the problem of realism links it to industrial capitalism and the rise of bourgeois society, quite in the manner of Marxist critics like Fredric Jameson, albeit on a much less sophisticated level.

At the time of this article articulating and defending his dramatic practice, Dunsany's talent for the evocation of a distant and oriental beauty was already well known. In a series of story collections beginning with *The Gods of Pegāna* (1905), Dunsany had found his unique voice and style, with stories that mimicked the pose of a traveler remembering an intense beauty experienced long ago and far away. But Dunsany, for all his advocacy of traditional storytelling, was in fact an innovator, and is seen today as a progenitor of *fabulation*, the creation of a narrative in which the characters, including the storyteller, feel themselves as knowingly belonging to the inviolable world of story and not to the real world. In modern fantasy the characters may even become aware of themselves as owing their mode of existence to the story, which is constantly being retold.[17] For instance, the reader of *The Gods of*

Pegāna is aware at the outset, even if the gods are not, that Dunsany's gods and their world are the dreams of another god, MĀNA-YOOD-SUSHĀĪ. One of those dreamt gods, Trogool, who is neither man nor beast, is himself the reader of a book, *The Scheme of Things*, and knows that his readings will one day end, bringing an end to the gods and to men.

By 1912 the Anglo-Irish poet W. B. Yeats was already retrospectively celebrating Dunsany's oriental novelties in his Cuala Press series, while lamenting if only Dunsany would write stories for the Irish Renaissance based on Celtic mythology instead of the East. Yeats included selections from two of Dunsany's plays and summed up his early glory by saying that he had unleashed more fabulous beauty into the world than the travel writings of Sir John Mandeville, and more color and ceremony than either Edgar Allan Poe or Thomas De Quincey. With this extravagant praise Yeats also precisely identified the essential novelty to be had in Dunsany's writings: a traveler's quest for an absolute and fabulous beauty that was haunted by the destructive power of Time.[18] Beauty for Dunsany could arrive only from afar, most often from the East, in fabulous travelers' tales tinged with accounts of marvelous cities.

Dunsany's writings are indeed saturated with reinvented figures and tropes from the orient, the reason for this being, in my opinion, twofold: the orient had long represented otherness in Western culture, and for Dunsany, who strongly felt the ugliness of modern urban life, had not beauty become *the other*? This is a question I will pursue further in my reading of the stories, but allow me to state here that I think Dunsany uses the rich repertoire of these figures (the Sphinx, Egypt, Eden, Troy, Babylon, the Arabian Nights, etc.) in a way that does not primarily represent them as ideologically subaltern to the West. Dunsany's imagination romanticizes but does not *colonize* the East. Beauty, to remain beautiful, must remain untouched in order to preserve its aura of distance.[19]

Natural beauty, on which is based the experience of artistic beauty, posed certain limits to the human imagination. Nature was a productive force far surpassing anything man could achieve. Like the romantics Dunsany saw nature as enigmatic and silent about man, but in its meanings saying more than could be put in human language.[20] But he came to feel that we are aided in our search for unity with nature by our minds, which, having evolved within nature, respond deeply to beautiful appearance as revealing the depths of our own consciousness. In his autobiography, which is largely a tracing of natural images in his writings, Dunsany mentions, for instance, the multicolored movement of kelp in sea currents in the Mediterranean, as seen from the top of Gibraltar, as expressing his own youthful consciousness of the East and of his own wandering spirit.[21] The gloaming, the twilight of day, a time when a mysterious beauty seems to opalesce, and another world seems about to appear, was also a magical experience for him, and he recreated it many times in his fantasies. Words too—especially poetry—seemed to him magically attuned to an ancient harmony of mind and environment.[22] So, while the difficulty of creating new beauty remained for all artists, natural appearance might suggest an enchanted landscape to the poet's imagination, even if in the end one could not add much to the store of the world's beauty.[23]

Not wishing to go beyond natural landscape, in Dunsany's reveries imaginary cities, like Babbulkund (i.e., Babylon), arise as constructed by man seemingly out of the natural landscape. Remote and fabulous destinations for the seeker of beauty, these cities carved out of nature retain a magical relationship with it, but nonetheless point up an ideological limit in Dunsany's conception of beauty in art. Dunsany obviously understood that mankind must create itself out of the domination of nature, no matter the society or mode of production involved. "Realistic" political economies, like that depicted in *Robinson Crusoe* (which Marx mocked as the illusion of liberal economists), hardly make a difference in this respect. If Dunsany's fantasy worlds must create new beauty, then they must also seek, as far as possible, modes of production not based on the dominantion of nature.

To my mind, there is little question that Dunsany identified modernity with industrial capitalism, which was destroying the English countryside. In fact, by the time Marx wrote *Capital* (1867; English translation 1886) it was widely understood by writers and intellectuals that industrial capitalism, which first came to prominence in England, was now bringing about a global transformation of man's relationship to nature. This capitalist transformation of time and space destroying the memory of the past was bringing about a crisis of experience that culminated in the Great War. This is the reason why the traveler's tale in Dunsany, as the bearer of traditional wisdom, seems always to tell of the imperilment of beauty, attesting to the root meanings of the peril and risk (the Latin *experiri*, to test, try, prove) involved in far-off quests for beauty.[24]

As it happens, Dunsany was himself a primary witness during his life, not only to the destruction of natural beauty in England, but also to its disappearance as the subject of art. Concerned about his legacy during a lecture tour of the United States in 1953, Dunsany mused about how the American newspapers had conspired to make him seem like an eccentric British peer for his interest in beauty. He wanted to be remembered and honored as a poet, but had to concede privately that the main part of his life could perhaps better be found in fox hunting.[25] In conversation with people he met on the tour Dunsany expressed his distrust of modernism for abandoning the quest for beauty. In particular he expressed his disgust with T. S. Eliot's drama and poetry.[26] He tried to be charming in public, but knew that he was being advertised and consumed as a relic of a forgotten age by the media.

For Dunsany, beauty still had a strong connection with truth and justice.[27] Beauty in his view was not just a mask hiding power relations. As it happens,

I agree with Theodor Adorno, who was always trying to understand the nature of the social in art, that the best response that critics can make to the alienation of art in modern times is to try to understand the social in artworks as having a relative autonomy resistant to their very conditions of existence:

> Art, however, is social not only because of its mode of production, in which the dialectic of the forces and relations of production is concentrated, nor simply because of the social derivation of its thematic material. Much more importantly, art becomes social by its opposition to society, and it occupies this position only as autonomous art. By crystallizing in itself something unique to itself, rather than complying with existing social norms and qualifying as "socially useful," it criticizes society by merely existing, for which puritans of all stripes condemn it.[28]

Adorno is one critic who still believed that art had an intimate connection with the truth, which was expressed through a dialectical interplay between form and content. Adorno devoted a large section of his *Aesthetics* to understanding the relationship between natural beauty and art beauty, which anyone seriously interested in understanding Dunsany's aesthetics should read. In these sections, Adorno eloquently argues that true (i.e., authentic) aesthetic experience is deeply involved with what is still not reconciled in experience. In particular, the thrill or shudder we feel in experiencing certain overwhelming works of art points us toward our underlying relationship to nature, which has been repressed or forgotten.[29] Dunsany found that intense thrill of aesthetic beauty in the hunt, and no amount of ideological analysis can explain away the sheer promise of freedom and joy he felt in such experiences. Hunts are described or alluded to in all of his major works as the source of human happiness.[30]

As the reader of this chapter will discover, I find Dunsany to be most authentic as a writer when he exposes us to a longing to be reconciled with nature, a longing that is stronger, perhaps, than that to be found in any other fantasy writer, Tolkien and Lewis included. But his writings are not especially consoling as regards the capacity of human beings to achieve reconciliation. They are imbued with the pain of real history. These moments of dialectical negativity in his works remove him, in my opinion, from the charge of being an "escapist" writer or of being merely an affirmative author supportive of bourgeois culture.

In any sociological account of Dunsany's writing, Marxist or otherwise, his class origins and education would be important to understanding his aesthetic, so let us begin with them before going on to discuss the literary modes in which he chose to write. To start with some very general observations, Dunsany belonged to a socially declining class, the landed Anglo-Irish aristocracy.[31] Historically in Britain, the aristocratic landowning classes were in conflict with the rising power of the capitalist bourgeoisie.[32] This social background of class conflict helps us understand why Dunsany possessed throughout his life an almost instinctive dislike for all things commercial, remarking in a letter to an American producer of his plays, Stuart Walker, in 1916 that as soon as art took on a value it threatened to became a commodity, like cheese.[33] Given his remarks to Walker, I doubt that anyone could seriously question that Dunsany's views about art being valueless are in the last analysis political, needing to be taken in the context of the increasing commodity fetishism of everyday life in industrialized Britain.

As far as his biographical life is concerned, Dunsany's education prepared him ideologically to be a part of the ruling elite of the British Empire. He attended Eton, where he was immersed in classics, especially the Greek dramatists, and trained for a military career at Sandhurst. But in becoming a writer he did not live out his father's wishes for his son's career. On his father's death in 1899, he became the eighteenth Baron Dunsany, and soon left the military after fighting in the Second Boer War (1899–1900). Thereafter, while continuing to support the British military presence in Ireland and the British Empire abroad, Dunsany left the management of his Irish estates to an uncle and pursued the traditional occupations of the landed aristocracy—cricket, hunting, and travel—after briefly and unsuccessfully running for Parliament on the conservative platform of tariff reform.[34]

His first volume of stories, *The Gods of Pegāna* (1905), was self-published during the Edwardian period and reflects, as previously indicated, the aesthetics of the times. It seems to have been prompted by a need to create a conscious piece of oriental fantasy.[35] It brought him the admiring attention of important figures in the emerging modernism of Anglo-Irish literature, such as A. E. (George William Russell) and W. B. Yeats, who soon invited him to write plays for the Abbey Theatre. Dunsany resisted the urging of Yeats to be become involved in Irish mythology and culture. Perhaps because of his decision to construct his own mythology, he suffered throughout his career from the accusation of dilettantism, of not being a serious writer. The argument that all true art lies in the pursuit of beauty and is therefore perfectly useless—an opinion that he seems to have gotten from Oscar Wilde's aestheticism—did little to change the public (and really bourgeois) perception of him as one of the idle rich.

In Irish politics he was a Unionist, and was wounded and hospitalized during the Easter Rebellion of 1916. Too old to serve directly in the Great War, he nonetheless spent a total of four months at the front and three weeks in the trenches in 1917–1918 in support of the British Expeditionary Force in northern France. One of his tasks was laying barbed wire in the Nomansland of the Somme.[36] He came under bombardment by German artillery fire, which he vividly described in his writings. As we will see later on, this crisis of experience—he found he could no longer coherently narrate what was happening around him using the old literary forms he knew—had a profound effect on Dunsany's later writings, and influenced the shaping of what many consider his greatest achievement, *The King of Elfland's Daughter* (1924). Later in life he witnessed the birth pangs of the Irish republic, the collapse of democracy in Europe during World War II, and the end of the British Empire, which he had long staunchly supported. He wrote much patriotic material during his lifetime, some of which is plainly propaganda for the ruling elite.

Whatever his conscious political convictions in support of British imperialism,[37] and of the sporting life of an aristocrat, and however fervent his rejection of modernism as sordid, he chose to write in a form of literature that is recognized today as largely subversive of established power and authority, and even as being proletarian in its deepest desires. He may not ever have consciously considered supporting socialism (as did William Morris) or understood history in terms of class struggle, but the experience of capitalism, with its dominance of nature through technology, is something Dunsany deeply felt as *wrong*; therefore, capitalism is, I think, the ultimate interpretive horizon of nearly everything he wrote that is of lasting significance today. In my readings I will trace the adventures of Dunsany's cultural dialectic between natural beauty and art beauty, and between the beautiful and the sublime, and place it in relationship to the capitalist mode of production. In what follows, Dunsany's works will be read as mediating social content to the reader; the social will never disappear entirely, and I hope that the reader of this chapter will be surprised to find, as I was, how often "revolutionary" ideas about political economy and social justice emerge alongside aesthetic ideas about romance.[38]

To comment on all of Dunsany's works would be beyond the scope of this study, and besides, a very thorough and engaging critical survey of his entire output already exists.[39] Instead I will focus primarily on his stories of the Pegāna mythos, with attention given to certain of his other collected stories and a brief glance at his novels, but setting aside his drama and poetry. The sociology of the novel is rather different than that of the traditional fantastic story, in which Dunsany excelled, because it developed with the rise of the bourgeoisie and individualism. I will comment on this important difference and what it meant to Dunsany's aesthetic at the end of the chapter. But as we will see, the thematic development of Dunsany's narrative worlds follows roughly the same sequence of five historical modes—a mode is based on the powers of action available to the hero—distinguished by Northrop Frye in *Anatomy of Criticism*, beginning with myth.

In Frye's account a myth is a story about a god who is superior in kind to the natural environment and the rest of mankind. In this mode the storyteller is an oracle of the god or a prophet. Myths are *believed*, and have a central cultural authority. In romance (medieval times) the hero is still quasi-divine, but superior in degree to other human beings and slightly superior to the natural environment. The laws of nature are also slightly suspended. Magic can happen, and reality approaches desire as wishes are fulfilled (King Arthur). In this mode the gods have withdrawn, and the function of the storyteller, who may be a wandering minstrel, is to remember. The marvelous journey and the crossing of the boundaries of consciousness become major themes. Here Frye locates legends, folktales, fairy tales, and their literary affiliates, such as Chaucer. The primary interest is in telling the story, as in the Celtic romances and the Icelandic sagas.

In the high mimetic mode (the Renaissance), the hero is superior in degree to other humans and is often a leader with an important social position, an aristocrat or part of the nobility, but not superior to the laws of nature, which have become absolute. The distant goals of the romance quest, the Holy Grail or the City of God, modulate into "symbols of convergence" attracting a centripetal gaze. Desire is conditioned by the social reality of the court and the capital city. The typical story is one of the fall of a leader or prince through *hamartia* (this category contains most epic and tragedy in the Aristotelian sense). Here Frye locates such national epics as *The Faerie Queene* and *Paradise Lost*.

The low mimetic mode (eighteenth and nineteenth centuries) finds its early heroes in the romantic poets themselves, who seem to live on a higher plane of existence than mere nature. Eventually the intensely individualized hero gives way to an ordinary person who labors under natural law. Comedy, realism, and naturalism dominate this mode. Desire is once again conditioned by social reality, this time the reality of bourgeois society. Many stories tell of a virtuous figure succumbing to the forces of society (Hedda Gabler, Tess). One could fit Dunsany's two "realistic" novels, *The Curse of the Wise Woman* (1933) and *The Story of Mona Sheehy* (1939), in this category, because the heroine has to give up her illusions (in this sense they are examples of "critical realism"), though arguably in the first novel it is the narrator himself who abandons his belief in the supernatural.

Finally, in the twentieth century irony begins to dominate storytelling, with the hero inferior in power and intelligence to other humans and to the environment; the laws of nature seem arbitrary and meaningless, and reality destroys desire. The hero is an ordinary person who may fulfill the role of the *pharmakos* or scapegoat, who takes the blame for society's sins and who is cast out so that others may live (the hero as victim in the detective story). Here we could place Dunsany's novel of the return of the supernatural and its effect on an English rural village, *The Blessing of Pan* (1927).

Frye's literary modes, with romance acting as a kind of center, are considerably more nuanced than I have room to present them. To begin with, each mode had its own naive and sophisticated version, depending on the audience. Furthermore, tragic and comic outcomes, in which the hero is either destroyed by society or integrated into it, operate in each successive mode.

Frye also believed that he could detect a return to myth in the ironic mode (Kafka and Joyce), the whole cycle repeating itself in modern literature. Important for this study is the fact that Frye, like Benjamin, conceives of the modern storyteller as a craftsman, as someone less than a prophet or legislator, as in previous ages. This was also Dunsany's view.[40] The modern storyteller made the maximum claim, not for his personality, but for his art. Indeed, Frye's comments on the traditional storyteller, either as a wanderer contrasting the worlds of memory and experience or as rooted in the lore of a specific place (in which case the story travels), are very reminiscent of Benjamin's discussion.[41]

For my purposes Frye's notion of modal counterpoint in the writings of a single author helps me understand a writer like Dunsany, who used elements of the supernatural in a contrapuntal way throughout his career.[42] I also find it intriguing to consider that Dunsany's literary universe appears to unfold in roughly the same sequence of modes—myth, romance, high mimetic, low mimetic, and irony—that Frye distinguishes in Western literature. Most critics who have examined Dunsany's career over its entire length have held the view, first enunciated by H. P. Lovecraft, that sees him as starting out naively and powerfully (insofar as tone is concerned) and then gradually becoming more sophisticated and shallow, eventually parodying his earlier self. I have no doubt that this is true *generally* about the increasingly comic aspects of his writing, but I think that comic and tragic outcomes, as well as an ironic tendency in Frye's sense, were present from the beginning.[43]

This sense of ironic displacement can be strongly felt in *The Gods of Pegāna*, in which Dunsany presents us with an array of gods aware of their own belatedness, and threatened with their own disappearance.[44] This self-knowledge is kept a secret to their own prophets, who must then give voice to the paradoxes of not knowing. Furthermore, the gods are aware that they are dreams of the main god, MĀNA-YOOD-SUSHĀĪ (only this god's name is capitalized), who will one day forget to rest and destroy them. Here the novelty of Dunsany's orientalism makes its first (and perhaps most humorous) appearance, for MĀNA-YOOD-SUSHĀĪ is not a deity who rests from labor after creating, as Jehovah did on the seventh day, or to whom one can even pray, nor is his creation uniquely done one time only. Indeed, MĀNA-YOOD-SUSHĀĪ sleeps and wakes in endless cycles lasting millions of years. He is an idle god (*deus otiosus*), who rests all the time and who forbids his own worship.[45] In orientalism, generally, the East was seen as passive, mysterious, and unformed. Dunsany repeats this notion to a certain extent in his master god, but clearly MĀNA-YOOD-SUSHĀĪ is not a god who lends ideological support to the Protestant work ethic! Indeed, the other gods fear what will happen when this reposeful god ceases resting. Probably out of boredom, the smaller or lesser gods create man and beasts for their own amusement, and play with them cruelly.

In the narrative world Dunsany creates, the laughter of the gods at human life is cruel. Human existence can only be grasped as a game played by these amoral gods. No doubt there is some Nietzschean influence here, and I will have more to say about this later, but from the beginning we are unsure whether or not the destinies of gods and men are controlled by Fate or by Chance. These two mysterious figures cast lots in the cosmogonic mists before the beginning of time to decide whose game it would be, but we are never told who won! Other gods in this motley pantheon include Skarl the Drummer (who keeps MĀNA-YOOD-SUSHĀĪ at rest); Kib, the sender of life; Mung, lord of all deaths; Sish, god of time; Dorozhand, god of destiny; Slid, lord of all waters; Limpang-Tung, god of mirth and melodious minstrels; Roon, god of going; and Sirāmi, lord of all forgetting. Some of these gods, like Slid, are only known poetically through compilations of their oracular Sayings. But eventually a cycle of myths emerges as told by a storyteller celebrating their spheres of action and revealing their conflicts with each other. If I had to pick a god to preside over the political unconscious of this text, it would be Yoharneth-Lahai, god of dreams and fancies, but more about this later. In addition, there is a host of household gods who live close to man and who sometimes rebel against the lesser gods in order to play their own games of life and death with man.

The subtlety of Dunsany's approach to storytelling is difficult to convey in a summary fashion, for it depends on a close reading of the changing modalities of his narrative. However, the basic technique involves Dunsany the narrator letting the reader know, in various ways, that the provenance of the story lies in its endless retelling. Characters in his narrative world relate to each other primarily through the act of storytelling. We often see and interpret things through embedded layers of storytelling, each subtly changing the experience of the story. Dunsany makes frequent use of the anonymous phrases "it is told" or "men tell" and their stylistic variants to introduce or embed his stories, so that we are always already aware that we inhabit a story-shaped world. Let us briefly examine one story about a god, "The Eye in the Waste," for what it can reveal to us about the nature of Dunsany as a storyteller at this early moment in his career.

The story is set in the remote city of Bodrahan, where all caravans end. Beyond the city stretches a waste of seven increasingly depleted deserts from which no traveler returns. Yet the story tells of something no man has presumably ever seen (except in a tale): in the center of the last desert stands a monumental statue, Rānorāda (meaning "the eye in the waste"), carved out of a living mountain by the other gods in the likeness of the god Hoodrazai. The giant statue is illustrated with somber intensity by S. H. Sime, Dunsany's favorite illustrator and collaborator, and evokes the sublime. On the base of the statue an inscription the size of a riverbed reads, "To the god who knows." Hoodrazai was apparently a god of mirth and joy until he overheard the murmurings of MĀNA-YOOD-SUSHĀĪ, and learned the making of the gods. So far, in Frye's terms, we are located in a mythical mode of meaning with a tragic outcome. However, Dunsany soon indicates how Hoodrazai's myth is changed in being told to the resting camel drivers by the old men who are merchants of the marketplace of Bodrahan.

In being retold in the marketplace, Hoodrazai's myth loses some of its cultural authority. In fact, since Hoodrazai was saddened, indeed devastated (perhaps this is why his statue is located in the ontological seventh desert, the Desert of Deserts), by the wisdom he gained from listening, the camel drivers all agree that wisdom should be banished into the desert while they enjoy themselves drinking wine. Thus they both accept the traditional wisdom of the story and deny it at the same time. Dunsany himself, as narrator, appears to agree at the end with this demotion of myth's authority, sensibly observing that who, indeed, could credit this tale told by camel drivers who heard it from the old merchants in the marketplace of remote Bodrahan.

Dunsany creates more novelty by reversing his own narrative ground rules in the following story, "Of the Thing That Is Neither God Nor Beast." Initially set in Bodrahan, it is the story of the god Tragool and his book and the prophet Yadin, who has a vision of him. It being accepted from the previous story that wisdom has been banished from cities into the desert, prophets must seek it there. Sure enough, like any true prophet, Yadin has a desert vision, which engages him in a beautiful cosmic reverie of flying with migrating flamingoes. Yadin's vision of these birds and of the god Tragool— figured as an erupting volcano in Sime's illustration—was based at least in part on Dunsany's own personal experience.[46] Yet it is thought to be a hallucination by some of the people. Still others, however—the old storytellers of Bodrahan—give it credence.

In this manner *The Gods of Pegāna* creates a rich medley of interwoven sketches and oracular sayings and modulated myths. Another, larger narrative category of the social comprises the stories told about the prophets who must mediate between the people, who want to know how to improve their lot in life, and the gods. These are often ironic in tone. Some tell of negative prophets, like Yonath, who preaches that it is best not to know; others, like Kabok and Yūn-Ilāra, are in the end destroyed by Mung, who is against prophets. Often these figures are blasted by the knowledge they receive from the gods, and are forced to make up comforting illusions about the afterlife (aided by Yoharneth-Lahai, god of dreams and fancies) in order to survive in human communities. Let us examine the career of Imbaun, who has five stories told about him, and who gives us the comforting vision of Pegāna as an afterlife.

As High Prophet in Aradec, Imbaun is first given a vision of man's future by Dorozhand and becomes his prophet. The vision of mankind killing each other in future wars is not a hopeful one (in one war men slay other men with mists, which seems eerily prescient of World War I). Another battle goes on with nature, as man overthrows the deserts. Human cities rise and fall out of the deserts, but Imbaun is kept from seeing the end of the gods and The Secret of Things, written in an unknown tongue. In the following story Imbaun meets Zodrak, a simple shepherd who became one of the gods. Again, the knowledge that Zodrak has to impart is largely made up of ironic reversals. Calling himself a fool, Zodrak finds that his wisdom should lie in not knowing what he has done, for in wanting to give mankind both love and riches, he sent gold into the world and thereby mixed love and gold together, creating grief and spoiling the beautiful scheme of the gods (who do not know of riches). This story announces the theme of gold as a corrupting agent of universal exchange for the first time in Dunsany.

Imbaun is also visited by Yoharneth-Lahai, who apparently provides him with a vision of Pegāna as an afterlife for humans. As luxuriously beautiful as it is (illustrated in decadent and languorous splendor by Sime for the frontispiece of the volume), this vision of a rose-scented garden of pleasure without toil clearly serves the purpose of keeping Imbaun in business with the people. In fact, Imbaun's rhetoric refers flatteringly to the wisdom of the people in believing that their afterlife will be with the gods in Pegāna. Although we are led to suspect that Imbaun has cynically given his people a fabrication to save his job, still the vision is quite captivating, and we ourselves are easily drawn into the aesthetic experience of Pegāna. Sime's drawing depicts naked figures, both male and female, reclining on the lush grass of an orchard lawn, while behind them the central waterspout discharges mists. Definitely *not* a desert landscape, this is clearly influenced by the oriental view of Paradise (also represented in the text by Wornath-Mavai, Dunsany's version of Eden).

In Dunsany's prose there is also a great blue pool, alone in the mountains, in whose waters one may behold the entire shape of one's life. Interestingly, none in Pegāna choose to seek out this pool or to know about the suffering and sin that lie reflected in it. As appealing as the landscape is in sensual pleasures, Pegāna is ultimately seductive because going there involves forgiving one's enemies, in the Nietzschean sense of giving up the reactive spirit of vengeance that can take over the human will. Indeed, the next story, "The Sayings of Imbaun," speculates that man may live again on some other world (the theme of eternal return).[47] Ironically, in the last story about him, Imbaun is executed because he directly tells the king, who is afraid of death, that he will die. Thereafter, Dunsany says laconically in the concluding line, there arose prophets in Aradec who did not speak of death to the kings.

With the entry of kings and prophets into the world of Pegāna, we begin to slide into the next historical mode Frye identifies, romance, with its heroes who may be semi-divine. The next collection, *Time and the Gods* (1906), does indeed contain many stories about kings and their prophets, as well as more etiological and origin myths about gods like Slid (who apparently comes from outer space). These origin stories continue and complete the cosmogonic myth of MĀNA-YOOD-SUSHĀĪ as *deus otiosus*, telling how the world has changed, been made richer or poorer, since its creation. But the stories of kings and prophets still seem to be set broadly within the economic and social horizons of the ancient world. In *The Sword of Welleran* (1908) we begin to find heroes like those of medieval legend, and the relationship between lord and village, as well as the building of a holy abbey, is the social background evoked in such stories as "The Fortress Unvanquishable, Save for Sacnoth." Fairy tales and fables about ordinary people encountering the fabulous begin to appear more often in the later collections, like *A Dreamer's Tales* (1910) and *The Book of Wonder* (1912).

I will come to each collection individually, but before leaving Dunsany's debut collection, I want to discuss a story that is recognizably a literary myth, "The River." As such, the story is a symbolic act unfolding on three interpretive horizons, personal, social, and historical.[48] On the first level, this story creates and amplifies beauty through cosmic reverie. It is told by an unidentified first-person narrator (Dunsany) lying in the desert, which is described as being beyond all cities and sounds. We know from this statement that the dreamer's reverie—and ours as readers—is not going to be interrupted. In the night sky above him spreads the majestic starry flow of the River of Silence, Imrana. Soon the dream-built ship of the god Yoharneth-Lahai appears, taking on human passengers who are weary of the clamor of cities and who lay down on the deck among their own forgotten fancies and songs. As they sail toward Pegāna, Sirāmi, lord of all forgetting, removes any too-painful memories. This ship of story, whose very timbers and rigging are made of human dreams and hopes, is, among other things, a vision of the journey to the afterlife. The story ends with an account of how the gods themselves, when MĀNA-YOOD-SUSHĀĪ awakens, will board their golden galleons and sail into the Silent Sea and be gods of nothing.

This story's beautiful images can be read on one level as evoking in the reader a reverie of the starlit cosmos (aided by Sime's illustration that depicts a sky crowded with astonishingly large stars), but also, on another level, as constellating a kind of aesthetic response to the social dehumanization of the Edwardian period. The reader may recall that the Edwardian period was one that witnessed increasing urbanization due to industrialization, and that Edwardian fiction considers the city as a significant social and political fact.[49] In Dunsany's finely crafted art, all those who are weary of the noise of cities board the silent ship, where the silence allows them to remember old fancies and songs that were never sung and forget painful memories. They are rowed to their destination not by real rowers but by the inhabitants of old stories (princes are among those mentioned).

Unfortunately, space does not permit me to comment at length on the complex onomastic field Dunsany sets up with oriental names in this and in other stories,[50] or the dreamlike atmosphere of its images (neither a river of water nor a river of fire, Imrana the River of Silence arises from the drumming of Skarl and flows into the Sea of Silence), yet clearly this silence is semi-allegorical and represents a paradoxical return to nature outside of language. Those who board the ship do so willingly under the (nonlinguistic) sign of Mung. They are dead, and death gives them a completed shape and authority, restoring dignity to their lives. Clearly too "The River" evokes some of the aura of the storyteller, for silence is a necessary part of that aura.[51] We must be silent in order to hear/read the story. Furthermore, by dreaming in reverie, Dunsany the storyteller participates creatively in the sacred time of his own cosmogonic myth, which states that the world was created by a dreaming god, MĀNA-YOOD-SUSHĀĪ. Because the boat also recycles old dreams back to living humans, Dunsany overcomes the irreversibility and linearity of modern time, transforming a natural landscape into a cultural milieu.[52]

On the historical level, Dunsany's story of a reposeful dream-ship journeying on the River of Silence creates an experience of the beautiful in images that do not entirely ignore the pain of real history—the phrase "galleons of gold" suggests Britain as a maritime nation and colonial power shaped by war and sea trade. Instead, the story sublimates and redeems that history on a higher level. On closer inspection of its details we realize that the rigging of the ship is made from people's hopes, and that some of those boarding the ship have no home in the world. This dream-ship is clearly saturated with utopian longings.[53] In the end, class society is ameliorated by its journey. Now, we might think at first glance that this collection of stories is as absolutely far from the real world as possible, but here we find ordinary people being rowed to Pegāna by the princes imagined in their stories, and the gold of empire seems destined for exclusively aesthetic purposes. The story effects, then, a fantasy transformation of the real conditions of society.

Dunsany's next collection, *Time and the Gods* (1906), tells more stories of gods, kings, and prophets, but with an unexpected emphasis on the passage of time for each category of existent.[54] The gods, who are generally amoral and unconcerned about human suffering in Dunsany, begin to experience the same losses as humans do. The opening story, "Time and the Gods," tells of the dream creation of the beautiful city of the gods, Sardathrion, made of onyx and gleaming marble, surrounded by a great desert that keeps the ordinary person from ever visiting it (except in stories and visions like those of the narrator, who doubts his own vision). In addition to the aesthetic pleasure it provides, Sardathrion is a powerful sign that the gods are gods, and they presume it will last forever. It is replete with musical fountains and poets, who sing of its beauty to the gods who walk among them disguised as humans. Inzana (the Dawn), child of all the gods and the subject of another story, plays there with her golden ball, the sun. But neglected by the gods, who are busy sacking human cities, Sardathrion too falls prey to Time, who is depicted as more primordial than the gods, with a bloody red sword at his side. The rest of the story takes the form of a lament for the lost city and a search for its fragments of remembrance. In their lament and search for souvenirs and fragments of the past, the gods become more human (and more modern).

This opening story signals Dunsany's innovative use of different temporal modes by having his gods undergo "human" experiences. The experience is one of intense nostalgia for lost beauty and pleasure, but one that will last for longer than human time allows. One feels that Sardathrion will always henceforth be a ruin for the gods. As it happens, two separate and contrasting stories also tell of parallel human attempts to overcome the depredations of irreversible and linear time. In the first story, "The Cave of Kai," King Khanazar overcomes time—at least in his later years—by means of a singer of tales (a harper) who can preserve through his art the epic deeds of the king against the oblivion represented by the cave of Kai, where his yesterdays are stored by a strange creature, part god and part beast, with the face of a warrior, who does not negotiate or give up the past in exchange for riches. The singer, who can also call up memories of the king's (paradisal) childhood, is himself described as a shadow in the cave of Kai who stands between Kai and the world. All this invites a kind of allegorical reading of the power of storytelling to free us by recollection from the destructive work of time.

The pain of existence in time is ironically emphasized by the second story of a king and his quest. "In the Land of Time" tells of a king and his armies who campaign forlornly against time. The story retells some of the legend of the Buddha, for Karnith Zo is motivated to go on his quest because he is appalled by the ravages of time on his people. Karnith Zo eventually returns home defeated, with an army of aged men who are easily overcome by enemies. However, in later years these same conquerors sometimes listen to the strange stories that are still told about the king and his army. In a sense, then, and despite the defeat he endures, Karnith Zo survives in the fabulous stories people tell about him. Because these two kings are not superior to the natural environment, they could be read as modulations into the high mimetic mode, with comic (in Frye's sense of integration into society) and tragic outcomes, respectively. The narrator of Karnith Zo's story, in fact, makes clear that he is relying for parts of his chronicle on the tales of deserters from the king's armies, thus subtly shifting from a mythological narrative world to one based on historical "fact."

With regard to temporality, both of the stories about kings take place in an epically distanced and completed past (though men of these days still know the tale). But in the second part of the volume we encounter a longer narrative, "The Journey of the King," which seems to strain at the limits of traditional storytelling. Gathering together different prophetic narratives, it tells the story of King Ebalon, who wants to know what lies beyond death in the form of a journey. No less than twelve separate prophets give him different versions of that journey, none of them conclusive or finalizing for him. Consequently, "The Journey of the King" introduces the beginnings of social "novelness," not at all typical of traditional narratives, into Dunsany's storytelling. Indeed the text seems structured by a series of unsatisfactory ideological positions, but it would be difficult to identify them as representing different classes in Dunsany's society at the time.[55]

In general, by now it should be fairly clear that journey and the social experience of storytelling are identified in Dunsany. If one goes on a journey, then at the end there is a coherent story, no matter how disastrous, to tell; journeys are not simply a collection of anecdotes lived through.[56] But in this case, not knowing his end, and therefore the completed shape of his life, is the problem for the king, and for the reader of this story. We cannot read the story as having a complete transmissible form given at the moment of death. Furthermore, the embedded stories themselves raise individual interpretive questions as well, since the king has to decide which of the accounts of the afterlife to credit, if any.

Let us examine the internal sequence of these spectral stories and the responses of the king to try and understand how the aesthetic whole should be interpreted. The story opens with King Ebalon making a break with pleasure and women by sending away his dancers, cupbearers, and singers from his presence. The first mention of female storytelling in Dunsany, they will return at the end, bringing back the pleasures of storytelling. The king now desires wisdom concerning the afterlife, and twelve prophets appear in a series before him, each with a different vision. The first to speak is Samahn, a prophet of the old gods who are becoming enfeebled because no one prays to them anymore (a new god of light, lurking in the afterworld, threatens to make an appearance). His vision describes a journey to a Sea of Souls, where great thoughts are communicated without the use of language. Unfortunately, reincarnation of the soul into the prison house of the senses follows this blissful state, and complete forgetfulness ensues. The king commands Samahn to return to his temple and to continue worshiping the old gods, who were easy and pleasant.

Following Samahn, Ynath's tale of a primal sea outside of time also evokes anamnesis, though the details of a central garden of the gods facing eastward are considerably more orientalized. In this account, the king is said to have once held a most beautiful dream that he discarded when he entered time to become the king. The king acknowledges that he once held a dream, but time swept it away. Monith, the next prophet, tells the king a story that is hard for him to accept: he will exchange souls with a beggar that he once rode over in a royal procession.

By evening people in the city begin to mock the king and his prophets. The king believes the next prophet, Ynar, to be mad, for he believes that in the afterlife the king will take no journey but, instead, will find his dreams to be more real than the fading world he now takes to be real. Remorse will be a dream, too, but very real. The prophet admits to his madness, but claims he is aware of his soul and master of it, whereas the king is merely possessed and manipulated by strange gods he does not know. Since it cannot be decided who is wrong, the prophet claims victory and departs, with a threat to call upon the unnamed gods he knows but does not serve. He returns to his temple on a crystal peak in the mountains.

By contrast, the next prophet, Thun, lives by the sea but has no temple. He is the sad prophet, and for his melancholy story he sings the dirge of Shimono Kani, the youngest of the gods, who made a harp of the heartstrings of the dead old gods. The story is similar in theme to "The Cave of Kai," but here the singer of the tale has a cosmic or eschatological function added to his social one: when the king hears the voice of the singer after feasting, he remembers only fragments of the beyond and a feeling of sadness for the death of the old gods. However, each soul being a note and therefore a possibility, the dirge of Shimono Kani has the cosmic function of remembering souls trapped in the prison house of earth and recalling them to the life of the spirit, which plays another variation on the theme of anamnesis that runs through these stories. Someday the dirge will be played in full, perhaps at the king's funeral procession. Then he too will become part of a universal song, overwhelming the silence that sits at the end of things.

The sixth prophet is simply called the Prophet of Journeys, and he tells once again of a dream journey, this time by caravan, which after crossing the immense Waste of Nought full of mirages eventually reaches a real city, the City of Ceasing. The seventh prophet, Zornadhu, who inhabits a garden valley full of poppy fields, has to be found and persuaded to leave his blissful home. Not understanding the function of bartering for gold that exists in cities, he has to be forcibly taken away, leaving no one to lament the death of his beloved poppies, which are his metaphor for dead souls. He gives the king a lament for his lost poppy fields, and a vision of human life passing through the dreams of whatever gods also dream there.

In an important passage summing up what I take to be Dunsany's own views, King Ebalon gives a very Nietzschean response, claiming that he is weary of the otherworldly, shadowy, and metaphysical dreams of all these prophets.[57] He reveals that he believes that the gods made him to love the green fields of earth. King Ebalon, wanting to remain among the gardens of earth as long as possible, asks for a prophet who can sing to him the glories of the gods who inhabit the orient sky, but would leave to other men what glories these gods who move beyond the twilight shall in the end give to the dead. When he looks at the sky (at divinity), his perceptions remain rooted in the earth. He has become weary with the metaphysical desire to go beyond the barrier of the sky, finding sufficient meaning in the sky's shimmering of possibilities.

To create a sense of the beautiful in the king's language here, Dunsany uses the words "opal" (King Ebalon rules Zarkandhu, a kingdom to the south of the opal mountains) and "orient" and "twilight" in a dense cluster of images bearing both archaic and modern connotations.[58] "Orient" has a range of meanings traditionally associated with exotic beauty: it can signify the East, and includes here Dunsany's feeling for the orient; and it can describe a pearl of exceptional luster. An opal as well manifests this quality of shimmering iridescence, as does the twilight (Dunsany's favorite time of day). Indeed, these word images appear often in his writings, especially in *The King of Elfland's Daughter*, which I will discuss later. But here let me remark that all these images of natural beauty work together to create the feeling of distant shimmering unlimited possibility, and indeed this symbolic sense of twilight is strong in the remaining prophetic stories. The stories that the king has heard so far about the afterlife all are lacking in this sense of open possibility. The dirge of Shimono Kani is after all for the dead gods, and his song will one day be completed. Let us examine how the other prophets respond to the king's request for a prophet who knows the gods but who can tell of the earth.

The next series of prophets tell stories that are hardly more consoling, but in telling of the meaning of the gods they touch more on the meaning of life in this world. Indeed the prophet Yamen, the next to speak, does not mention the gods at all, but instead gives the king an account of what life would be like if he were to get his wish and never age naturally. The problem is one of increasing experience leading to an inescapable crisis. For as others of his generation die, the king will have a surfeit of experiences that he cannot share: he will be a hunter (i.e., the aristocratic classes) yearning for the chase but finding that there is nothing left to overcome. Increased wisdom will not bring solace; even knowledge itself will become entirely negative. Lastly, in future years the king will find himself among men who have changed in a way he does not understand, not having learned how to barter with gold (the beginnings of capitalism). These new men of a kingless, jesting age who inhabit cities (i.e., modern states) will hold dominion over the earth, but man shall remain alienated from nature. Even this situation shall end when nature dies, in the entropic heat death of the earth. The shadows of the gods will dissipate, but the king, always young, will live on. Yamen tries to show the king that the blessings of the gods given out of due time always conceal a curse, but the king tells the prophet to urge the gods who loved the earth to continue to care for it even when it grows cold.

The prophet Paharn tells the king a lengthy embedded story of Kithneb, a fellow shepherd who rejects the gods of the earth (fashioned out of red clay by his mother) and who goes in search of the gods beyond the twilight sky. Kithneb, though clearly not an aristocratic figure like the king, like him does not want to engage with the marketplace. He hears the voices of the gods but does not understand the meaning of their utterances. Driven to find out what they mean, Kithneb consults another prophet, Arnin-yo, who tells him how to sail around the whirlpool—called Brimdono—that guards the passage to the land of the gods. At the end of his journey Kithneb does hear and understand the meaning of the gods directly, without the distorting lies of prophets, but Brimdono takes him. The king continues to hear in his imagination the exulting roar of the destructive whirlpool, a force of nature.

Mohantis, a hermit prophet, tells the king of his vision of a dream river, Munra-O (personified as feminine), to which many types of vessels journey. This is pretty clearly an allegory of England as a capitalist and maritime nation, for there are golden ships of Pride of Power and of Pomp of Cities floating along its waters, taking souls to earth. Mohantis and his journey earthward, however, are enabled by a different ship, a smaller boat of birch bark made by Tharn, god of the hunt. Tharn bestows upon him the glamour of the hunt, which allows him to participate in the lives of wild animals and nature at large in the dark woods. Tharn also imbues him with a mistrust of cities. Because of his opposition to civilized life—his boat is not a grand galleon of gold but is craftily self-made from the bark of a tree, with little transformation of materials—I think this god is meant to represent a non-exploitative relationship to nature, for nature is not being transformed into a mere resource to be exploited for profit and personal gain.

Myths of Actaeon notwithstanding, Mohantis could be described as happy in his hunter's vision of Tharn. Though still based on violence, nature reciprocally glances back at him through the eyes of hunted animals. With the next prophet, Ulf, we return to a world that holds little consolation. Indeed, Ulf's vision of the afterlife tells of a sea and a river that make up the Tears of Men. In Ulf's vision the king will journey on this river until he finds the hall of the gods, where Time with bloody hands sits on the throne. The gods themselves, who sought to make Time their slave and servant, have been overcome by him.

With this penultimate vision the king bursts into a lament that he shall never find the gods and know whether they are really kindly. The other prophets try to convince the king that this vision is false and that theirs is the only true one. The king sits long in silence, saying nothing, but eventually calls back his dancers, singers, and cupbearers to entertain the prophets at a farewell banquet. Because they have each prophesied against the other, the king rejects them all but announces that the power of his wine is greater than their spells, and his dancers more wondrous than prophecy. Dancing—a Dionysian art without an artifact—will prove more powerful than truth.

The exiled dancers proceed to perform their response, creating the maze of the dance, the labyrinth being the only aesthetic structure that Nietzsche held would be consistent with our modern perplexities of soul that the king has encountered in listening to these stories.[59] One of the dancers, Dream of the Sea, resolves the many metaphysical (and political) and temporal contradictions of the prophetic narratives by telling/dancing her own magical version of the afterlife: a romantic tale of an enchanted island bathed in the red glow of sunset, where night never fully comes on and where the sorrows of the world never reach the king because they break up on the reefs. Dunsany does not directly report, but rather gives us an impressionistic summary of her story, which evokes a self-enclosed aesthetic world outside of time and experience, without prophetic wisdom, but where the beautiful lure of song never ceases. During the festivities the king notices a hooded prophet who does not partake of the food and wine and who has not yet spoken. Later in his apartments the king meets *The End*, who knows the king's journey but will not tell it, for he is literally death and the end of Dunsany's fragmentary story.[60] Following him out of the castle, the king embarks on his last journey.

A study of Nietzsche's influence on Dunsany's aesthetic ideas would no doubt yield much that would advance our understanding and interpretation of this labyrinthine text, with its welter of metaphysical images. However, my concern is primarily with the social in the collection generally, so I must conclude my discussion of *Time and the Gods* with a story that is obviously a parable of capitalism and the crisis of experience. In "Usury," natural beauty is shown to have links with domination and exploitation under capitalism. As Marx pointed out, "Nature does not produce on the one hand owners of money or commodities, and on the other hand men possessing nothing but their own labour-power. This relation has no basis in natural history, nor does it have a social basis common to all periods of history."[61] In Marx's analysis, capitalism is the historical result of a whole series of modes of production, beginning with barter, which we have already seen mentioned in Dunsany.

In *Capital* Marx distinguishes, both formally and historically, usurer's capital and merchant's capital as earlier forms of industrial capital.[62] As it happens, Dunsany wrote at least one story about each phase of capital ("Idle Days on the Yann" is about merchant's capital, "The Kith of the Elf-Folk" concerns industrial capital), which we will examine in the course of this chapter. Usury, the lending of money at a rate of interest, is an older form of capital, outlawed by the Christian culture of the Middle Ages and condemned by the Protestant Reformation and certain modernists as *contra naturam*.[63] Jews were allowed by their religion to lend money to non-Jews, but not amongst themselves. The objection to usury by traditionalists of all stripes was that the usurer did no productive work in society; he owned wealth but did not use it for the good of society.

"Usury" is the first story in which God is given in the singular and capitalized (no pun intended). Dunsany tells us that the men of Zonu hold that Yahn is God. He is depicted as grasping and greedy and an expert in the law, both unfortunate stereotypes of Jews as moneylenders during the Middle Ages. (Sime's illustration, significantly, is used as the frontispiece to the entire collection, as if to point up economic realities. I can detect, however, no elements of anti-Semitic caricature in his depiction of Yahn.) At any rate, the men of Zonu were once shadows who lived beyond the rim of Pegāna, knowing little of joy and nothing of sorrow. But Yahn possesses a heap of jewels, each jewel being a life. He lures and brings the shadows under his control by offering them a bargain in which each one of them will be given a life—described as full of natural beauty, a landscape residing within the jewel—in exchange for their experiences. The experiences of the shadows—which they do not own—will enrich the value of the jewels by cutting (with their grief) and polishing them (what Marx would call labor-power). In summary, Yahn retains control of the jewels, but the shadows get a life on loan. In Marxist interpretation these images allegorize the real history of class struggle, making it clear who is the exploiter and who is the exploited, while at the same time creating a fantasy mode of production in which the experience of nature becomes a commodity.[64]

Yahn also controls what the nature of experience should be: the shadows are to produce only scenes for the jewels that are pleasing to him. Soon it becomes part of the law that each shadow have a gleaming life on loan and other shadows as servants as well. However, when men begin to argue that they should possess the jewels themselves because they have labored on them (a reference to Locke's view of the origin of the right of property), they find that the law—of the liberal free market on which they made the bargain and sold themselves—supports Yahn. Being the epitome of greed, and over-skilled in the law, Yahn continues to exploit new shadows. I think he represents all forms of what Marx called interest-bearing capital. The only relief humans have from this oppression seems to be the hope that someday Yahn will be satisfied and leave them, or the hope that the older, more powerful gods will return and make a hard bargain with Yahn, banishing him. And the Lives of Yahn? No one knows for certain what will happen to them when the gods of old return.

With the publication of *The Sword of Welleran* (1908), Dunsany moved into more contemporary time, though he continued to offer a medley of modes. Taken together, the title story and "The Fortress Unvanquishable, Save for Sacnoth" are viewed today as having founded the genre of heroic fantasy, but in Frye's terms they are clearly romance, for the hero is superior to nature and magic is operative (in less serious terms, they were an influence on the sword and sorcery genre).[65] Dunsany rejected soldiering as a career for himself, but nonetheless there is a strong martial spirit to be found in some of his stories. In both these stories beauty and power reside in a legendary sword, and the narrator portrays himself as a traditional romantic storyteller/dreamer presenting his experience of the story.

As a romantic quest for exotic beauty, "The Fall of Babbulkund" is a small masterpiece of oriental fantasy, which, despite the suggestions of extreme decadent pleasures—King Nehemoth has four harems, Princess Linderith wears the brilliant jewel Ong Zwarba while others go in simple garments, and in the middle of the desert a crystal-bottomed artificial lake is illuminated by hundreds of slaves at night to ease the king's musings—nonetheless manages to envisage a relationship to nature different than that known in the West, for Babbulkund has been carved out of a white holy mountain by artisans who loved their work. Like all of Dunsany's oriental fantasies, its aesthetic effect of otherness is created with archaic words and invented phrasings, an experience that is difficult to summarize or paraphrase. But the connotations are in the main Egyptian and partly Babylonian, and therefore pre-capitalist.[66]

Babbulkund, which in the end is never seen by the narrator except in stories, is a crossroads for caravans from Arabia, India, and China, all of whom sing songs of the fabulous wares in its marketplace. Typical of romance, an undertow of allegory is suggested when we are told in the first traveler's tale that the city is located near the River of Myth (Oonrāna) and Waters of Fable (Plegáthanees), which flow together. Part myth and part fable, Babbulkund is destroyed because of a religious abomination committed by its king, the last in a long dynasty of pharaohs who have ruled the city. Nehemoth worships Annolith, a god forbidden to all others. There are echoes of the Babylonian exile of the Jews in the story told by the people fleeing the city's destruction, but the prophet sent by an Old Testament–like God to prophesy against Babbulkund is himself seemingly devastated by the prospect of its destruction. Although the prophet cannot disobey God, he too loves and mourns the passing of Babbulkund's beauty.

"The Whirlpool" and "The Hurricane" are personifications of nature in the earlier mode of myth found in *The Gods of Pegāna*. Love and Death are also personified in "On the Dry Land." Though each of these stories could be shown to have a political unconscious in the images of nature we find in them, a conscious critique of industrial capitalism is operative in two stories, "The Kith of the Elf-Folk" and "The Lord of Cities." The former story is a modern fairy tale that some might find a bit tendentious—as always when we read a story with an overt political target—but to my mind it contains sufficient beauty of poetic language to stand on its own as a fine, emotionally moving story. It's certainly comparable in craft and style to any of the art fairy tales invented by Hans Christian Andersen, though it is a good deal less sentimental and seems directed at adults. In its observation of local wildlife, this story is rooted in the lore of place, unlike the travelers' tales we have so far encountered.

Indeed, the beauty that we find in the story is not orientalized, though the marshland preserves its aura of distance in the glamour of its perilous pools. The narrator, who claims to have been born in the hour dusk, and whose imagination can participate in the drama of the natural environment at that time of day, tells an affectionate tale of the Wild Things, little brown creatures who live in the marshlands of East Anglia and who are related to elves. As such, they do not have souls and cannot die. However, one of the Wild Things is drawn to the light, song, and ceremony of a church built near the marshes and desires to have a soul and to worship God and seek Paradise. Feeling sorry for her longings, her kith make her a soul out of natural substances found in the marshland, mist and birdsong and the gossamer of a dewy spider web, combining these things together with treasured memories of the old marshes and reflections of the stars in the water (in other words, her soul is a landscape).

Her kith tell her that once she places the soul in her breast she cannot give it back, but must find another human to take it before she can return to her former state. This condition sets up the second chapter of the story, which unfolds through an increasingly ironic series of reversals of perspective and values. Almost at once she had become a beautiful young woman who could now see the inner beauty of the marsh, ironically because she was now distanced from it. The Wild Things cannot see the beauty of the marshland because they are immersed in it. Here Dunsany gives us a very clear indication that beauty is something constructed historically by human beings. But be that as it may, and despite the inwardness given to her by it, her natural soul makes it hard for her to adjust to human society, for she frequently sees spectral things, ghosts for instance, that normal humans do not perceive. Although she tries to worship in church in the staid manner required, she falls in love with the young curate, Mr. Millings, because of the beauty of the biblical names of far-off rivers and cities he uses in a sermon (this is meant to satirize Dunsany's own use of the prose cadences of the King James Bible in his Pegāna stories).

Now called Mary Jane Rush, she is sent away to work in a factory in the Midlands (possibly Birmingham, its largest manufacturing city and a center of the industrial revolution) because she had publicly announced her love for the curate. In the factory Mary Jane finds only soulless work. I cannot be certain that Dunsany ever read Marx's description of how machinery was deskilling workers in the modern factory, but Dunsany's alienated description of the experience of this special class of worker—the machine worker (often a woman or a child), whose only job it was to tend the giant machines and looms of the textile industry—matches Marx's account point by point.[67]

Mary Jane's only job is to pick up the ends of broken threads and feed them to the spinning machine. Marx saw the factory as one place in which the unified intellectual faculties and the aesthetic qualities associated with traditional labor were being stripped away as humans became slaves to machines.

Soon Mary Jane's beautiful soul finds only ugliness in the industrial landscape around her, and she wants to get rid of it, but, in the story's deepest class irony, she finds that she cannot find anyone among the poor because they all have souls, but that's *all* they have. Again, this is close to Marx's own view that the urban proletariat was created by capitalism to have only one commodity, their labor-power, to sell on the free market. As it happens, Mary Jane is able finally to get rid of her soul by moving up in the social classes. One day outside the factory gates she begins to lament in song her loss of the marshes. Her voice is so natural and beautiful and moving that it deeply impresses a certain Signor Thompsoni, who takes her to London to train for the Covent Garden Opera. Now known as Signorina Russiano, she becomes a kind of celebrity, but still does not feel free.[68] One evening after a ravishing performance, she meets Cecilia, Countess of Birmingham (undoubtedly a peerage bought with money), and discovers that she does not have a soul! Mary Jane offers her the soul, but the countess is not persuaded, it seems, by the beauties it has to offer. But, thinking herself lucky, she finally accepts the offer, and the little Wild Thing escapes the city and returns to great rejoicing among her kith in the marshes.

This is the first story in a Dunsany collection set in a recognizably real world. But as such it is mainly significant for its fantasy critique of industrial capitalism and class society. That critique is continued in "The Lord of Cities," a Rousseau-like reverie of a solitary walker in the English countryside who, following a road and river, comes upon a mysterious town called Wrellisford that the industrial revolution (that fever of the West) has somehow bypassed. The wanderer comes upon an old abandoned mill draped inside with spider webs. He spends some time admiring and touching the black tapestry of the spider webs, a work of natural art described as too delicate and beautiful to be handed on by merchants. Later that night, at home and in his bed, stimulated by the touching of this marvelously complex material woven of infinite threads, his mind constructs an artistic form of dialogue in which the road and the river speak of man's purposes with cities, with the road affirming that beauty is historically constructed out of nature by man's imagination and labor—indeed nothing is beautiful without man's presence to see it—but with the stream remaining hopeful that the sea will give back some of the beauty the river has carried down to it in the end. Then the spider speaks the concluding paragraphs about inheriting man's world after man has disappeared. The point of this semi-allegory is that natural beauty will always be superior to man's creations in the long run.

Dunsany is reminding us too that while class conflict undoubtedly exists, labor is first and foremost a process between man and nature. The river and the road are in Marxist terms part of the means of production, and just as Marx often gives voice to commodities in *Capital* to make a polemical point about our ignorance concerning the social relations they mask, here Dunsany gives voices to the necessary parts of the economic base of the mode of production to make us aware of our ultimate dependence on nature. Interestingly, Marx himself discusses labor in nature, such as the spider, but concludes that humans have a prior mental conception or conscious purpose with nature, which separates us from it.[69]

Marx's discussion here is uncharacteristically shaped by abstract concepts. By contrast, Dunsany offers us a graduated series of concrete dialectical images of the political unconscious, from the human-dominated (the road) to the more natural (the river), and finally invites us to consider the labor of nature itself. The images and voices of this story are designed not to help us conceptualize our difficulties with nature but to dream with feeling about how natural beauty and art beauty are distorted under capitalism, and to imagine how the artwork might negate the heteronomy of domination:

> The transition from natural beauty to art beauty is dialectical as a transition in the form of domination. Art beauty is what is objectively mastered in an image and which by virtue of its objectivity transcends domination. Artworks wrest themselves from domination by transforming the aesthetic attitude, shaped by the experience of natural beauty, into a type of productive labor modeled on material labor. As a human language that is organizing as well as reconciled, art wants once again to attain what has become opaque to humans in the language of nature.[70]

Now, in wresting itself from domination, Dunsany's story begins with the wandering figure of the narrator discovering the unity of art and labor in the spider's tapestry hanging in a disused old mill (image of human production negated). It is a visual experience, but also a tactile one, and as the narrator's hand reaches into the web, it creates a textual metaphor for unlimited possibilities of beauty. Later in the evening this deeply subjective experience of non-dominated nature is transformed by reverie into an objective work of art, an autonomous form that expresses all the contradictions of art under capitalism in the speeches of the road and the river. Dunsany then gives the non-human artisan, the spider, the last word, negating man's ugliness but also affirming that man's cities will one day become beautiful under nature's sovereignty. The tone is perhaps not one of reconciliation, but nonetheless the spider's images unite beauty and labor with natural history, which is what modern man seems unable to do. Because of the mastery of the spider's images, we have no trouble imagining the silence of nature and the nights jeweled with stars the spider sees as coming to man's cities. By means of the work Dunsany himself becomes silent. Art has converged with natural beauty.

The reader will perhaps have grasped by now that one of the primary ways in which ugliness—whether natural or human—is transformed into the beautiful in Dunsany is through allegory.[71] The spider's narrative of his increasing sovereignty over man is semi-allegorical and plays off of a thematic opposition between ugliness and beauty (as does the story of the Wild Thing's soul). It speaks in beautiful images about the futility of humans trying to dominate and control nature, which in the end produces only more ugliness. Similarly, throughout Dunsany's writings, which are heavily imbued with the classicism that personified such things as the Furies, we find negative experiences such as the devastations of war, famine, disease, time and fate, etc., represented in images that allow them to be presented as having or containing a certain beauty or sublimity.

The sublime has not been discussed much in this study so far, but we have seen it before, in the statue of Hoodrazai in the Desert of Deserts and in Trogool, the volcano, who reads our fate. In this collection we can point, if not to the spider, then to both of the romantic swords that are at the heart of the opening two stories. One, Sacnoth, is made from the metallic armor of a slain (ugly) dragon and is used to overcome an evil sorcerer, and the other is used to repel an enemy army besieging a beloved city. Both weapons are strongly felt to have magical and primordial powers associated with nature, and to be characters in the narratives themselves, not only because they have names and stories, but also because they are either created out of nature or handed down by ghost-like supernatural hero figures. The Sword of Welleran in particular sublimates the horribleness of warfare to the martial spirit. We will encounter martial allegory again in the painful images of Nomansland Dunsany records in his writings about World War I.

Dunsany in his discussion of romance himself explicitly linked the beautiful with the sublime.[72] Later, he cautioned his readers not to search for allegories in his work (especially his plays). By this caution he did not mean that he never employed allegory, but only that if you had to search hard for meanings in his work then allegory had already failed its function, and you were trapped in a maze of interpretation.[73] Most critics of romance have, however, pointed out the necessity of giving interpretations of its images. What is more, most critics of romance as a literary mode have observed its deep affinity for allegorical images.[74] Given Dunsany's historical distance from us, his images of natural beauty, such as the spider web, may seem clear enough in their immediate meaning, but for reasons I have explained, they do need to be understood in the broader context of a Marxist interpretation of art under industrial capitalism.

Thus I come to discuss one of Dunsany's most complexly layered allegories of the beautiful and the sublime in relation to history, "Poltarnees, Beholder of Ocean," the opening story of *A Dreamer's Tales* (1910). Poltarnees is actually a mountain that forms the western border of the Inner Lands, comprised of three small utopian cities living in harmony with nature where everyone knows everyone else. Here Dunsany seems to be evoking traditional *Gemeinschaft* communities based on shared mores and religious values and having a common fate, rather than modern civil societies based on the pursuit of rational self-interest (*Gesellschaft*). The former is the type of society that H. P. Lovecraft yearned for and which formed the basis of Dunsany's influence on him (see discussion in the next chapter). So harmonious are these cities that the old and holy figure of Romance appears among them, though completely veiled (Sime depicts the masked figure astride a unicorn and accompanied by a large, leopard-like creature). The people worship religious legends of the sea, beyond Poltarnees, which no one has ever seen. The only problem seems to be that the young men of these communities feel called upon to cross the mountain and bring back the experience of the sea, however perilous it may be. However, no one has ever returned with an account of the experience. And the sea in their view remains unappeased and hungry.

Figuring that a far-surpassing natural beauty must be at the heart of the problem, two of the ruling kings call upon a third to submit his beautiful daughter, Hilnaric, to a series of tests, for she may prove more beautiful than the sea and be able to call a young man back to explain the mystery. Despite his fears about blasphemy, her father eventually agrees to the tests, and in a series of beautiful descriptive passages she is judged more beautiful than the moonrise, the morning, and the sunset. Dunsany tells us that her face became a resting place for mysteries and dreams, but still no one can be certain whether or not she is more beautiful than the sea. No one, that is, until the hero appears. As we might expect, Dunsany's hero Athelvok is a hunter, and he becomes legendary to the princess through his story of how he killed a large beast with horns known as a gariach. The King of Arizim promises him that if he can reach the summit of Poltarnees, gaze at the sea, and come back, telling what magic or lure lies in the sea, he can have his daughter in marriage.

So far events have followed the pattern of desire laid down by the story-shaped world of romance. The hero next swears an oath to his beloved that he will return, and we fully expect that he will (for he embodies in his youth the glory of heroes of old), but our expectations are thwarted by the ending. Even the princess seems to know, by some strange lore, that her hero will not return. For Athelvok's experience of the sea is something deeper and more powerful than the beauty he has known thus far, something that would make him want to live on in the consciousness of a broken promise. In aesthetic terms, Athelvok's experience is that of the sublime, of the pain and suffering endured by people (the English nation) who have a real history of maritime shipwreck and death. And as always when Dunsany represents the negative, the frightening and tyrannous sea is personified as a gigantic figure mourning the destruction he has caused to humanity, and making reparations. The figuration also gives voice in this manner to the pain of dominated nature, for nature weeps tears for itself as well.

The enclave that Athelvok eventually enters is full of previously unimagined and marvelous merchandise from alien lands. The sea himself offers new colors to experience. These riches, while on one level representing the literal wealth of a trade society, also paradoxically represent the theme of otherness and difference, which the beauty of the Inner Lands, always seemingly close at hand and the same, did not offer. Nature there seemed under the spell of the identical.[75] In order to break this spell Dunsany's hero had to go on a perilous journey from which he could not return. In terms of experience, the story represents an encounter with the new and the other, moving its hero beyond where he was at the outset. Athelvok realizes that he cannot bring back this death-haunted experience to those who live in the Inner Lands, for they would not understand him. He, and others like him (in this new economic mode of mercantile wealth), will not make the return journey. The story ends on an ironically bitter note: Hilnaric uses her dowry money to build a temple where men may curse the ocean. There is perhaps no finer story in Dunsany's oeuvre illustrating the theme that art, to be authentic, must remain unreconciled, a broken promise.[76]

Another, even more downbeat, version of the perilous journey that is experience is "Carcassonne," which takes place in an atmosphere of medieval knights and quests. The story opens with a festival and a description of the hall of King Camorak: its walls are crowded with heroic weapons; the harp of Arleon, who figures prominently in the story, is actually a weapon used by him in war to urge on the king's armies engaged in battle, and to amaze enemies. Above the weapons the ceiling is painted with the stories of fabulous heroes. In such a charged atmosphere it is easy for the knights of King Camorak to dream of ever more glorious quests. At the festival banquet, however, a diviner tells the king that he is destined by Fate never to come to Carcassonne, a city inhabited by elves and fairies who have retreated from man's presence, created by the blowing of elfin horns (a Tennysonian motif that appears later in *The King of Elfland's Daughter*). Typical of Dunsany, what we learn of this fabulous city comes from songs chanted by the singer of tales, Arleon. Men have dreamt that a witch now lives there, guarded by dragons. She sings old songs that have a direct connection with nature, taught to her by the sea. Fearfully beautiful and lonely, she seems an allegorical figure of the unattainability of our reconciliation with nature.

Arleon leads the subsequent quest of King Camorak and his knights, who believe that they may turn aside one of the dooms of Fate and thereby possess the future as their own. Instead of reaching Carcassonne, however, the king and his men themselves become a proverb for wandering and a disconsolate legend. They turn to idleness, are worn down by local battles (sometimes with natural agencies, such as mountains, thwarting them), until only the king and Arleon are left alive. These two, now old gray wanderers, reflect on their experience. Arleon admits that he no longer knows the way to Carcassonne, and the king allows that his quest has failed. Nonetheless the two go off, still seeking Carcassonne. The Beckett-like narrator/storyteller concludes by coldly saying that they probably did not get far into the deadly marshes that lay before them, and that no story of anyone reaching Carcassonne is known.

As Northrop Frye has observed, the age of romantic heroes is largely a nomadic age, and its poets are frequently wanderers. But although the marvelous journey is one plot structure that seems inexhaustible, there are negative versions of the quest designed to contrast the world of memory and desire with that of experience.[77] One would have to say that in the case of these two stories, which both start out in the world of romance but end in irony or even tragedy, Dunsany has transformed romance to reflect on implied conditions in society that no longer allow romance a central cultural importance. We are made to feel its loss.

Although he was clearly opposed to the industrial and money-lending forms of capital, Dunsany was a lot less hostile to its mercantile forms. As we have seen, caravans and sea trade routes are the implied background of many of Dunsany's stories. No doubt this is based on the real historical transmission of traditional travelers' tales. But Dunsany tended to idealize and to orientalize merchants, especially in such stories as "A Tale of London" (collected in *The Last Book of Wonder*, 1916). This is understandable given Dunsany's interest in exoticism and given the tendency of romance generally to idealize both good and evil. Indeed, Dunsany imagines that fantasy stories themselves might be traded to gain entry to a fabulous city in "The Idle City," a story anthologized by Jorge Luis Borges.[78] It's important to note, however, that it is their use value (the stories can be used to entertain a king who suffers from insomnia) that is important, not their exchange value. Money in these stories, when it is seen at all, is purely a medium for exchange of values, and not an end in itself.

In this collection we have one of the most beautiful expressions of Dunsany's aesthetic of the traveler or wanderer: "Idle Days on the Yann," an explicit dream-fantasy that was followed by two sequels rounding off the Pegāna mythology. The narrative opens a general realm of dreams to which all dreamers may have access (prefigured by "The River," analyzed above), an aesthetic ideal that influenced Lovecraft.[79] There is no trouble getting to the Land of Dreams; the narrator emerges from a wood to board the ship *Bird of the River* (as was prophesized), and the captain, armed with a scimitar, seems to be expecting him. The purpose of the narrator's journey is purely aesthetic: to catch a glimpse of the fabled marble cliffs of Bar-Wul-Yann, the Gate of Yann. But right from the outset we feel in this aesthetic experience the presence of the holy gods and of the social. Diverse prayers and songs heard on board the ship and in the various cities visited help elevate the tone and keep us immersed in the story-shaped world. The narrator himself chooses to pray to Sheol Nugganoth, a god of the jungle no longer worshiped.

Indeed, for the first part of the journey lush jungle imagery predominates in descriptions of vegetation, wildlife, and cities. Dunsany's poetic style is graced by a number of epic similes lending an archaic grandeur to nature. At one point Dunsany compares the lazy butterflies lighting on the large, waxy flower blossoms on the shore to merchants spreading their gleaming silks out on the snow when the caravans go to the northern regions. This simile launches a complex chain of imagistic associations. But after setting up the captain's pavilion on the deck, the men exchange stories, each of his own city or of the miracles of his god. We learn that the captain's journey involves taking merchandise (thick warm rugs called toomarund carpets) to Perdóndaris to exchange for nautical items of use in his home, Belzoond. In this manner a system of equivalences is set up between the butterflies (natural beauty), the products of man (the silk of the merchants), the captain's pavilion (a beautiful restful space with golden tassels), and the exchange of stories. This marvelously interwoven dream-like passage ends with the narrator watching the butterflies float by through the open flaps of the pavilion, and falling asleep.[80]

On a more abstract level a system of exchanges based on use value is set up in the reader's imagination. Money as a social equivalent will of course figure in the trading at Perdóndaris (Dunsany even invents a fantasy coinage, the piffek), and commodities will be exchanged based on sharp bargaining, but although there is clearly some profit to be made, Dunsany's imagination does not venture beyond the fair exchange of human use values. We get no indication that the production of these items was merely for profit, or that they are in any way shoddy. Indeed Dunsany creates a warm comic scene out of the exaggerations of value between the captain and the merchants. What is more, after the bargaining, the captain treats the narrator to a rare, heavy yellow wine, set apart among his sacred things, that has its own origin story in a hunting expedition. The narrator in turn thinks of the noble things he has yet to accomplish. The story is by no means overtly political, but it's hard to imagine this social and dialectical process as part of modern capitalism!

As we know from classical times, ancient cities were always the abode of a god whose presence blessed them and whose festivals were celebrated therein. Each city visited on Dunsany's journey has its own peculiar, dream-like relationship to the gods, but we don't get the sense of any systematic religious allegory. In Mandaroon the people are all asleep because they believe that when they wake the gods will die. In Astahan the people claim to have manacled Time and worship all the gods he has not yet slain. In Perdóndaris, where there is much singing and dancing in the streets over a recent escape from a thunderstorm, they worship a god they do not know. Among the wonders of this city is an ivory gate recently carved from the discarded tusk of some giant animal, heralding its imminent return. Fleeing the city in fear, the narrator later reports that he has since heard of the destruction of Perdóndaris by some unknown creature. Lastly, in Nen, Dunsany encounters the Wanderers, a wild dark tribe of storytellers and strange performers (magicians really) who invade the city every seven years. With these people Dunsany alludes to the supernatural tale of horror in which invasions of the normal world are common. Even though he does not understand the language, he would love to hear their hymn to the night, to which the wolves howl, but the captain must move on.

There is a sense at the end, after the twilight sighting of the marvelous barrier Bar-Wul-Yann, of being hallowed by the journey. Indeed, one thing that the story seems to offer a modern reader is a return to the sense of the sacred, which is always tied in Dunsany to the experience of the beautiful. The imagination works in this story to transfigure the ordinary world, to give us a sense of the aesthetic *value* of the beautiful, as Dunsany has told us romance should do, but never was there a romantic vision that did not suffer the weakening brought about by time. The narrator ends by saying sadly to the captain that he can travel no more in the Land of Dreams. For Northrop Frye, the central form of romance is dialectical, taking place between the transcendent upper world and the demonic lower one. Furthermore, romance internalizes the cycles of the natural world and makes them into images of human desire, a necessary starting point for imagining a better world.[81] We can see this dialectical process, in which the very way we currently understand the category of world is at stake, operating in each facet of Dunsany's story I have distinguished. The transcendent upper world is what we can glimpse of the gods in mysterious and beautiful cities; we encounter the demonic lower world in the Wanderers. In the middle flows the beautiful and proliferating river Yann, offering a non-alienated experience of nature based on humanized use value, which really concerns the problems of *our* modern world. As for the idleness evoked in the title as necessary for aesthetic experience, it is well to remember that no less an aesthete than Oscar Wilde thought that socialism would bring about an expansion of the individual's senses, severely limited under industrial capitalism. But the social solidarity that the narrator finds with the captain and his crew goes far beyond this narrow individualism envisaged by Wilde. It is important to understand, though, that it is nature itself that sets limits to the human imagination. We never go beyond Bar-Wul-Yann to the sea, though we catch glimpses of it. For Dunsany nature is never entirely assimilated to the human body, to civilization, creating a social totality.[82] It always retains something of its sublime qualities that surpass man, hence the beast that destroys Perdóndaris, who is never directly represented. What the experience of the non-human is in Dunsany can perhaps better be understood in the context of Lovecraft in the next chapter. Here I want to remain focused on the fate of beauty.

As a wanderer's tale and a dream quest "Idle Days on the Yann" accomplishes so much in a short space that it is indeed astonishing (Yeats anthologized it with lavish praise, the reader may recall). I doubt that there is any other story in Dunsany's oeuvre that so concentrates his concerns about the fate of beauty in the modern world, though he would go on to develop many, more "realistic" variations on this theme. Although he remained concerned about beauty, Dunsany turned more and more to parody and satire (as in the two sequels to this story) of the obstacles in the real world preventing access to the Land of Dreams.[83] The stories collected in *The Book of Wonder* (1912) and *The Last Book of Wonder* (1916) are in the main humorous variations on traditional forms of storytelling, while *Fifty-One Tales* (1915) is, as I have mentioned, a collection of short aesthetic parables.

The real break in the social nature of Dunsany's storytelling comes with his experiences in World War I. In his autobiography Dunsany relates that when he saw the aftermath of death and devastation produced by machine civilization in the Battle of the Somme, where the British army in particular suffered so many losses, he was left with an impression of ruin that had no parallel in history. Dunsany kept trying to express the devastation, and the sense of loss, but traditional models of storytelling were no longer adequate equivalents to this traumatic experience.

One story in particular, "The Prayer of the Men of Daleswood," which opens the collection *Tales of War* (1918), provides an ironic portrait of storytelling in such circumstances. It tells of the collective efforts of a platoon of men, all from one very small traditional English village, to preserve the memory of what Daleswood meant to them. Realizing that they may all very well be killed in the next offensive, they think about writing down their experiences on a large chalk boulder (the German thermite bombs will destroy mere paper). But they can find no adequate form in which to express their memories. The language of magazine fiction, with which they are familiar, seems inadequate to express their beautiful memories of the English countryside. Frustrated, and in the face of annihilation, they decide to inscribe only a short line asking God to remember them and their village, God being the ultimate omniscient storyteller and ideal reader.[84] Dunsany's ironic stance is to give this story to his reader in the form of the reported speech of someone who heard the story from the man who destroyed the boulder after the battle, which now seemed silly to him, since the Daleswood men all survived (with corresponding losses instead being inflicted on the other side).

This is one of the most realistic stories Dunsany ever wrote, but as we read through the collection, Dunsany begins to combine fantastic reference with propaganda. For instance, in writing of the devastation of the blasted natural landscape in "The Nightmare Countries" Dunsany searches for equivalents in prior literature, citing Coleridge, Poe, and Swinburne in attempting to convey to the reader a sense of a mad landscape dreamt by the kaiser. Two stories in particular, "A Deed of Mercy" and "Last Scene of All," use the symbolic resources of the weird tale to depict events in the war (the sinking of the *Lusitania*) as strange and uncanny. One story even uses the phantoms of supernatural literature in allegorical fashion to bring about a realization of war trauma in the kaiser's consciousness ("The Punishment"). Although clearly a piece of anti-German propaganda that blames Germany for starting the war, this story does show the suffering on both sides.

Dunsany patriotically supported the British war effort in writing such fiction tinged with propaganda, but nonetheless he, like many of his generation, found his wartime experience to be a riddle with no answer, fragmented to such an extent that he was left with only the middle of stories, but not their beginnings or ends.[85] Indeed, in certain stories collected in *Unhappy Far-Off Things* (1919), which examine in detail his experiences on returning to the front four years after the actual battles, Dunsany, his symbolic and allegorical resources exhausted, touches upon what Fredric Jameson calls the experience of the Real, as something that resists symbolization entirely.[86]

In these stories Dunsany visits the towns of Arras, Albert, and Bethune, nearly obliterated by the early campaigns of the war. Faced with the debris of towns and the surrounding natural devastation, he tries to imagine nature returning to the landscape in the future, bringing with it the old forms of romance, trying to reconstruct the cathedral of Arras from his memories of it. However, in the story "On an Old Battlefield" we find Dunsany, searching the debris of an unknown village, reaching the bottom of these reconstructive efforts as he realizes that it is not even a ruin (i.e., something that he or others could symbolically name and mourn for) that he is experiencing, but something far more radical, utterly stripped of splendor, which he calls rubbish, extending for hundreds and hundreds of miles. In these stories Dunsany tries to read the fragments of civilization in terms of a meaningful past, considering briefly the symbolic trade in war souvenirs, but concludes that things are so jumbled together that the very origins of things are in doubt.

The crisis of experience Dunsany expresses in these stories became well known to Marxist critics like Benjamin and Adorno, who examined the literature produced in Germany in the decade following the Great War. They linked the origins of European modernity and fragmentation in the arts to this crisis.[87] Although Dunsany was no modernist, and no supporter of German culture, his experience of industrialized warfare clearly had a deep impact on him, leaving him with a permanently dark view of mankind's future. Understandably, the period after the war was one of searching for him. The values of the old civilization had been swept away with seemingly nothing to replace them. Indeed, lost illusions and trauma became a theme of much British literature published about the Great War (see the poetry of Wilfred Owen, or Virginia Woolf's *Mrs. Dalloway*).

Yet like the natural world that Dunsany saw returning to the blasted gardens of the Somme, romance would again emerge in his writings, though without the naive consolations one would expect from the genre today. In his post—World War I novels, and well into the 1930s, Dunsany produced forms of romance that included the loss of illusions as part of their aesthetic. His realistic novels also provided an opportunity for him to critique his own adherence to romance. The sociology of the novel, which we must now consider, is of course very different from that of the traditional folktale or fairy tale, which Benjamin characterized as essentially an "artisanal form of communication."[88] Far from being tied to the milieu of work—rural, maritime, or urban—the birthplace of the novel was the individual in his isolation, read by people who were equally isolated. Furthermore, the figures inhabiting this form, like Don Quixote, seem perplexed about reality and are themselves often devoid of traditional wisdom. The sociology of the novel reveals a hero engaging in a degraded search for authentic values in a world that no longer seems to need him and that accepts the dominance of exchange value. The rise of the novel is thus tied to bourgeois society and becomes the very form of everyday life as experienced in the individualistic society created by market production.[89]

Now, in engaging with the novel as a form, Dunsany abandons by and large the oriental beauty and wisdom borne by the traveler's or wanderer's tale, but instead explores the other important area of traditional experience mentioned by Benjamin, that rooted in the lore of a specific place: Irish folklore or the rural English countryside.[90] Through his protagonists, who still encounter traditional stories told in the historical communities in which they originated, Dunsany preserves a strong and coherent relationship to memory and remembrance. At the same time, however, these forms and values are questioned by their contact with modernity in various ways. In the novelistic process of creating a modern character, Dunsany also introduces searching forms of self-consciousness, doubt, and anxiety in his protagonists that do not belong to the traditional tale, where meaning seems immanent and given in the narrative world. Thus Dunsany preserves the interior landscape of beauty provided by memory, but increasingly focuses on the quest for meaning in a degraded and inauthentic world.

An in-depth reading of Dunsany's dialectical relationship to the modern novel lies outside the scope of this study, but I would like to comment briefly on certain aspects of it. The reader may remember the discussion, above, of Dunsany's long story "The Journey of the King," where the spectral quest for the meaning of the afterlife leads to an impasse. What separates this material from a novel or novella is the absence of the interiority and open-endedness that we have come to associate with the central concerns of the modern novel. The king of that story experiences the clash of many different perspectives (a novelistic process), but does not reflect too deeply on them, and in the end is still subject to fate or doom. In the novel, by contrast, there is more of a contact with everyday life, where things have not yet entirely been determined.

In Dunsany's first novel, *The Chronicles of Rodriguez* (1922), set in Spain during the Golden Age (roughly the sixteenth century), we do find a continual tension or contrast between the epically distanced past of a remembered heroic age and the current fallen times (closer to us), in which the hero must gain glory and wealth through his adventures. The hero, Rodriguez, himself seldom considers the past but thinks mainly of the future, in which his fortunes seem to lie, but the narrator constantly reflects on this tension between the completed past and the open-ended future in a playful, pseudo-naive manner that refers anachronistically to institutions of modern times, like the London Stock Exchange. Often speaking in lengthy direct address to the reader, Dunsany echoes the ironic stance of Cervantes in *Don Quixote*, the acknowledged originator of the realistic novel.

These temporal tensions sometimes become an overt theme in the novel. For instance, in one of his adventures, the Third Chronicle, the House of Wonder, young Rodriguez and his gross companion Morāno encounter a magician who, through a magical-windowed room, shows them past and future wars. These blue windows are described by the narrator anachronistically as more beautiful than the Mediterranean as seen by Shelley, or like the sea round Western islands of fable seen by the fancy of Keats. Wars are something in which Rodriguez and Morāno hope to make their fortunes, but they are disillusioned when Dunsany's own memories of the Great War—the future for them—are displayed. They are appalled by the devastation machines can create.

This fantasy contrivance allows Dunsany to revisit his experience of the Real at Arras and other towns destroyed by the Somme offensive, giving him an anachronistic opportunity to reflect, while not wanting to offend the classical goddess of history, Clio, on how often official history is a construction tied to power. In this roundabout way fantasy art asserts its right to have an authentic relationship with the truth. In the following chronicle the magician sends Rodriguez and Morāno on a journey to the sun, which disillusions them about the value of gold and even brings up the terrifyingly heretical idea that creation itself may be evil.

The values of their quest thus critiqued, our heroes do not attain their goals by such gross and worldly means, though they still try. The hero, Rodriguez, rediscovers the old true values of romance in his love for a beautiful woman named Dona Sarafina of the Valley of Dawnlight (there are possible allegorical connotations to her name, and those of other characters in the novel). In the end they are granted their own kingdom and castle in Spain because they rescue the mysterious king of Shadow Valley from the clutches of the state police, la Garda. The description of the building of Castle Rodriguez out of the forest through the communal effort of the king's hundred green bowmen in the Twelfth Chronicle represents a Robin Hood–like fantasy of a non-dominating relationship to nature. It is told in relatively realistic terms, acknowledging the human labor and time it would take to construct such an edifice. The fortress is not so much made out of trees felled for its construction as it is carved out of the very woods themselves. Escaping the power of the Spanish king (Rodriguez later signs a treaty with him), it is built to last in relationship to both history and nature and will stand for centuries. Dunsany emphasizes the artisanal quality of the labor that goes into the fortress. The king himself is something of a magic craftsman, who defaces the royal currency with his own image in an earlier chapter (the Fifth Chronicle). The construction ends with the crafting of fabulous animals that stand before the hearth, uniting the house with romantic fables and with tales told in the wood, no doubt of hunting.

Despite some beautiful passages (the king of Shadow Valley's reveries in captivity in the Fifth Chronicle are particularly affecting), Dunsany's loosely constructed and episodic first novel is today all but forgotten; his second effort, however, is considered by many to be a classic of the genre, though it too has some problems integrating perhaps too many points of view. But nonetheless, *The King of Elfland's Daughter* (1924) brings together effectively many of Dunsany's concerns about the fate of beauty in the modern world and examines them through a series of perspectives assigned to different characters and social groups, which creates a series of critical perspectives on the ideological limitations of each group.

The story is set in motion when the Parliament of Erl, made up of artisan workers and farmers who represent the modern world and its materialistic desire for new things, decide that they want a magical king to increase the value of their produce at market. Alveric, the crown prince, sets out to find Lirazel, the storied king of Elfland's daughter. At approximately the same time as Alveric crosses the barrier into Elfland, a grotesque and ugly troll named Lurulu begins to make incursions into our world, astonished at the natural wealth of earth. His perspectives on mankind's experience of time are given in chapters twenty-three and twenty-four. Indeed, he becomes something of a celebrity among the trolls of Elfland for his amusing tales of human time, which bring them much laughter.

The main perspectives and experiences, however, belong to Alveric, Lirazel, Orion their son, and the king of Elfland. Although Alveric does produce a son for Erl, as is his duty, Orion is not pleasing to the Parliament of Erl because he does not apparently command magic as they understand it (i.e., as a utilitarian means to an end). Also, Lirazel cannot adjust herself or conform to human standards, and especially to the values of the Christian religion, as her husband demands. She becomes unhappy, and eventually her father sends a magic rune to bring her back to Elfland. When the king of Elfland calls his daughter back, he withdraws the boundaries of Elfland too, creating a desolate wasteland in which Alveric wanders for many years searching for Lirazel. Meanwhile, Orion is brought up by the potent witch Ziroonderel, who possesses much lore of the earth. He becomes a skilled hunter, as his name suggests, and his life becomes full of the rich craft and lore of hunting. After killing and beheading a unicorn with his hounds, he eventually subjugates Lurulu and with him makes plans to hunt and kill more of these fabulously rare creatures.

It is Lirazel's impossible desire to live in two social places at once that in the main shapes the political unconscious of this text. The novel provides a fantasy resolution to its many perspectives when the king, seeing that his daughter is unhappy without her husband and son, does a very human thing and releases his last master rune and extends the realm of Elfland over Erl. This rune is a kind of defensive weapon, held in readiness against the materialism of the human world, but the description of its effect on the real world, as the shining line rolls ever forward like a wave of idealization over the land, is not destructive. Made up of the murmur of many old songs, old music, and lost voices, it sweeps back again to our fields what time has driven from earth. It is saturated with a feeling of reconciliation with nature, and different temporal rhythms, transforming everything in Erl except for the Christian enclave of the freer (friar) and those humans who curse magic.

In addition to this dialectical interplay of character perspectives, there are specific locations and landscapes, both natural and supernatural, which also figure prominently in constructing the political unconscious of this text. To begin with, although Elfland lies far away to the east beyond the little human hamlet of Erl (the name means "elf") where the story begins, Dunsany does not orientalize either location to any marked degree. In its means of production, Erl seems much like a late medieval village with its fields and kings and a small parliament. The parliament is not made up of aristocrats, but of an artisanal class not taken with the romantic tales of the aristocracy. Beyond the hamlet stands the wild woods, full of seasonal imagery, where Orion hunts. By contrast, the enchanted beauty of Elfland is rather an intensification and deepening of natural beauty, especially as revealed in colors, already known to us, but unaffected by time. Dunsany compares the colors of Elfland to the seaweeds of the Mediterranean, a personal image that stayed with him throughout his life (chapter three).[91]

Much of the authentic beauty of this novel comes from the human desire to escape the ravages of the ebb and flow of time. In our world natural beauty is always tinged with the glory of its passing; however, the constant twilight boundary between blue mountainous Elfland and our world confronts our imagination with a fascinating opalescent object. As an aesthetic experience composed of many different twilights, it takes Dunsany an entire chapter to describe its effect (chapter twenty-one, "On the Verge of Earth").

With this iridescent and enchanted barrier—a horizon of meaning, really[92]—Dunsany raises romance to the ontological level. His hero Orion, who has both elfin and human blood, feels the emotional pull of both worlds.[93] He seems to want to slay the unicorns that have strayed into our world in search of sweet grass, precisely because they are beautiful, haughty, and powerfully aloof from human concerns. In Dunsany's account of this fabulous animal they are stripped of many centuries of Christian allegorical interpretation (though not of real history; see chapter twenty) and returned to the primal human desire of the communal hunt. Orion tracks them at night mainly from their pungent aroma, which is a reversal of traditional holy hunt unicorn lore.[94]

Another area of the political unconscious is revealed by the withdrawal or ebbing of Elfland itself. This is experienced ontologically by Orion's wandering father, Alveric, as a kind of fragmented desolation, like Dunsany's mournful experience of the Real in World War I. Interestingly, Alveric rediscovers in this wasteland bits and pieces of a coherent story, the lost and broken toys of his childhood mysteriously transfigured and restored, as if tossed up by the sea. Perhaps they are the transitional objects the psychoanalyst D. W. Winnicott speaks of as the beginnings of symbolization.[95] But in any case the immense withdrawal of Elfland poignantly brings home to us the loss of romance in the modern world.

Throughout this chapter we have seen how romance for Dunsany comes to be felt in the political unconscious as the true place of narrative heterogeneity and freedom from the confines of an all too dominant realism set in place by industrial capitalism. In *The King of Elfland's Daughter* romance and magic give us the experience of other temporal rhythms and social modes of being, suggesting that our social situation is not unalterable. Indeed, when the whole of reality is transformed and contained by the king of Elfland's last rune, Dunsany's fantasy manifests some of the apocalyptic and salvational values ascribed to romance by Northrop Frye. In Dunsany's next novel, *The Charwoman's Shadow* (1926), we witness, however, a sad farewell to these powers of magic, and then a gradual descent into the low mimetic and ironic modes, where the hero's powers are far less than those of nature.

Like *The King of Elfland's Daughter*, *The Charwoman's Shadow* is still read today, kept in print by the post-Tolkien demand for high fantasy. Indeed, both books have been given admiring introductions by today's fantasy authors (Neil Gaiman and Peter S. Beagle, respectively). With its enchantments and disenchantments, and its emphasis on narrative contracts such as dowries and evil bargains, the latter book is more like a fairy tale than high romance, but nonetheless it contains many passages of great beauty. The novel approaches the theme of beauty and the political unconscious through our natural relationship with shadows. In Dunsany's hands they further become images and metaphors for the ontological uselessness of artistic illusion (in the dialectical sense given by Adorno in the quote above). In the novel, set in a pseudo-medieval Spain that is linked with *The Chronicles of Rodriguez*, once again the motives for the quest are economic. Young Ramon Alonzo must gain a dowry for his sister, Mirandola, by apprenticing himself to a magician acquainted with his father, Gonsalvo (the result of a hunting expedition), and thereby learn the secret of creating gold from base metals.

The magician's price for such knowledge, which actually he regards as trivial and degrading when compared to his other areas of knowledge and power, is Ramon Alonzo's shadow, which will become a servant to the magician. Ramon at first resists, studying only lower things, but finally agrees. The magician snips off his shadow and puts it in a magic box. Now Ramon is like the old and ugly charwoman, Anemone, whom he has seen cleaning the magician's house. Anemone sustains herself by remembering the beauty of her hometown, Aragona, and it is suggested that she was once herself beautiful, which Ramon finds hard to believe. Nonetheless, out of chivalry, he vows to free her from the magician when he learns that he has enslaved her shadow, too, in the box. Eventually he solves the problem of unlocking the box by guessing at a series of Chinese characters (the magician has also taught him the magic of reading letters). By means of a love potion, the current duke of Shadow Valley becomes enamored of Mirandola, and Anemone is reunited with her beautiful shadow; Ramon falls in love with her and they all live happily ever after, or so the books of the Golden Age say.

In this manner Dunsany creates a wonderful interplay of magical and alchemical themes—the philosopher's stone, the elixir vitae—throughout the novel. These are in turn linked with themes of wealth, power, and dominance, for the shadows are pretty clearly slaves. Furthermore, Dunsany adds to the archetypal lore of shadows by creating a distinction between good (i.e., innocent or natural) shadows and bad or false ones created by magic. Actually, the magicians in both of Dunsany's Spanish novels are greatly concerned with gaining knowledge of the cosmos. But however magical the journey, we know that we are no longer in a medieval world when this magician sends his captive shadows out into the dark and chilly depths of interstellar space among the planets. This fantasy astronautical theme of the novel may have been what drew Arthur C. Clarke to it (see below).

Several passages in the novel also reflect on the value of things, like shadows, that lie unnoticed around us and that we normally take to be absolutely useless in everyday life. Ramon learns the social value of shadows when the local village people, who regard him with superstitious dread, shun him and try to drive him out, even when the magician supplies him with a false shadow. In the figure of Anemone the novel resolves the ambivalent theme of the ugly and the beautiful, showing us how they can be present in the same person. In this manner the novel's political unconscious, figured in shadows, provides a moving critique of the intolerance, prejudice, and power that lie hidden behind normalcy. Moving also is Anemone's transformation from an old woman bound to an evil bargain (like Tennyson's Tithonus, she has immortality but ages) to a young lady of high social station, pardoned for her low birth by the king of Spain.

But by far the most moving passage occurs after the traditional happy endings are told, in the novel's closing pages. This remarkable passage, which so moved Arthur C. Clarke, stages Dunsany's seeming farewell to romance and magic.[96] Realizing that he has no one to be his disciple or successor in knowledge, and that true happiness for him lies in the lore of the boar hunt he gleaned from Gonsalvo, he picks up a magic flute of reed and summons all the children of Pan in the woods surrounding his house. Natural and supernatural creatures, those belonging to old tales of romance, such as elves and fairies, as well as old shadows, follow him across the beautiful landscape of Spain, traveling eastward until they reach the Country of the Moon's Rising, where the magician enters the magicians' enchanted castle that puts them beyond Christian damnation. Throughout the novel the magician has not been a likable figure, but this ending seems to transform our emotions in his favor. Here romance, instead of being spread over the real world and containing it, as in *The King of Elfland's Daughter*, is in the end itself contained in an imaginary fortress that lies outside of time. In preparation for the Machine Age, the Golden Age closes with the withdrawal of Pan and magic from the world.

The problem of experiencing other, more natural rhythms of time that might challenge the increasingly total horizon of industrial modernity remained a concern for Dunsany as his novels became more realistic. He seems to have found two broad solutions to the problem of where to locate the alternative cultural time and space of romance: romance and the supernatural can come from the outside and invade our world (the ironic mode of *The Blessing of Pan*, 1927), or romance can be contained in the consciousness of a character, a solution first discovered, as Frye indicates, in the low mimetic period by the romantic poets. This latter solution is expressed and critiqued in two of Dunsany's finest novels of Ireland, *The Curse of the Wise Woman* (1933) and *The Story of Mona Sheehy* (1939). In all the realistic novels, as we might well expect, social types replace allegorical figures, and nature itself becomes an allegory of romance.

The Blessing of Pan tells the story of Elderick Anwrel, vicar of Wolding, as he tries to deal with the revival of worship of the pagan god Pan in his small rural village community at the end of the nineteenth century. In his religious duties, and especially in his preaching, he has been unable to eliminate entirely from the local people their belief in the folklore of an older time, and much of the novel has less to do with pagan beauty than with the cognitive struggle presented by things that come from "outside" his logical, reasonable, and even scientific frame of reference, his mind educated at Cambridge, a strategy for the political unconscious used to great effect by Lovecraft, whose writings we will consider in the next chapter.

The cause of the revival of Pan worship is Timmy Duffin, a seventeen-year-old local lad who has learned the language of Pan's pipes by listening to the wind in the reeds. The eerie music gradually takes over the whole town, drawing people from work that now seems weary into the dark primeval woods and to the old stone altar there. Despite his appeals, Anwrel is given no credence by his superiors in the church. And despite his vocation, religion itself gives him no answer to the purposes of nature, whose beauty and mystery he can increasingly feel around him. He senses transcendence in the autumnal harvest time of the year, but not in any language he can read. He collects eoliths and classifies them as information, but the Old Stones of Wolding mean nothing to him emotionally. Nature makes only furtive signs to him, like the unconscious in dreams, but he rather senses that nature means something that has no meaning. Dunsany's portrait of Anwrel's modern consciousness, governed by reason and enlightenment and distanced from nature, is complexly ironic: at the same time as he is afraid of the return of paganism, and struggles to defend Christianity against heresy, Anwrel is also a disconsolate antihero searching for authentic signs of meaning in a world that profoundly lacks them.

The old tales, however, are full of meaning to those who remember them. Gradually, and through encounters with such figures as Mrs. Tichener, the archetypal wise old woman of the novel, and Perkin, the wandering madman who talks to Anwrel about the need for illusions, we discover that Pan for Dunsany represents the unsettling and necessarily hidden idea that man and his modern consciousness are but a fable, or, as Dunsany puts it, that blend of fable and history that tells the story of man. Thus Dunsany gives to Pan a rather Nietzschean interpretation. The sexual seductiveness traditionally associated with this figure and seen elsewhere in earlier supernatural literature (Arthur Machen's *The Great God Pan*, 1890) is more hinted at than actually seen. For Dunsany, Pan is primarily a critique of the ills of machine civilization as he saw them.

There is more than a suggestion, though, that Pan represents the cyclical reappearance of romance in society, hiding away in stories known to the "proletariat" as civilization reaches its rational and scientific heights, but reappearing after people begin to experience the limitations civilization puts on human desire. Pan had disappeared from high culture at the end of the

Golden Age in *The Charwoman's Shadow*. He is repressed in the high religious culture known to Anwrel, but now he emerges again among rustic people. At any rate, after the vicar's own wife, Augusta, joins the other women of the town who are happy in their rediscovered oneness with nature, and, unable to resist the lure and awful power of the music any longer, he too joins them at the altar and sacrifices a bull. Thereafter the town becomes cut off from the world of cities, with their factories, machines, and need for exchange, producing fewer agricultural goods. As longevity comes to its inhabitants, death and modern commercialism forget the town of Wolding almost entirely, though the gypsies still tell tales of it.

The Blessing of Pan is an ironic novel of the supernatural intruding into the real world. In Dunsany's next two efforts the mode of internalized quest romance predominates. As previously mentioned, this internalization is usually accompanied by the character's abandonment of his or her illusions in the end, creating an aesthetic tension in which the author's irony or humor may be felt as an attempt to overcome the attractions of romance in his own consciousness.[97] This critique of illusions does indeed happen to both of Dunsany's protagonists as they proceed through an increasingly degraded world. However, Dunsany's own attachment to romance and traditional storytelling is not so much negated as it is dialectically transformed by irony and humor, as we will see.

In his 1911 essay on romance, Dunsany asserted that the culture of romance was still preserved among rural populations. This belief seems to be reflected in *The Story of Mona Sheehy*, the second of the Irish novels, whose action goes through World War I and into the postwar world financial crisis. I will come to that in a moment. In *The Curse of the Wise Woman* traditional Irish culture remains only in memory. Indeed, the story is told by the aging narrator as he looks back nostalgically at himself as a sixteen-year-old enrolled at Eton and living on his father's estate in Ireland, High Gaut, which is near the red bog of Lisronagh. Despite the honor of his appointment—he is a minister of the Irish Free State, presumably in France—the narrator feels a sense of exile and is haunted by a loss of meaning in his current social life. As he searches his memories for what Ireland still means to him, there is a strong emotional evocation of a lost way of life. As we meet various figures from the past, especially the social types associated with the estate, Ryan the coachman, old Murphy, Finn, and Brophy, they function as mediators to their young master of traditional Irish life, especially the lore of hunting. Gradually, as he remembers these and other figures from the past, Dunsany draw us into the world of the Irish country estate, which by the narrator's own admission has long since fallen into decay.

The dominant culture of Dunsany's Ireland was (is) Catholicism, though he himself was Protestant. Ireland is felt ideologically in both novels to be a kind of theocracy, religion and politics being fused together. In this novel

Eamon de Valera, a real historical figure and leader of Ireland, makes a disguised appearance as a sinister figure in a long black coat who tries to murder the narrator's father and continues to shadow him throughout his young life. The only oppositional culture comes from Tommy Marlin and his mother, who live on the boundaries of the bog. Tommy is taken with the pagan myths of youth and ageless beauty of the legendary land of Tir-nan-Og, and fears he has lost heaven; because of her extensive knowledge of nature the locals fear his mother as a witch.

The narrator, Charles Peridore, is divided between these two groups. He loves hunting on the bog and the lore he can learn from Tommy, but he also understands that their belief in the romantic myths of Ireland are condemned by the church to which he and everyone else (except the Protestant Laura Lanley, a storyteller of traditional Irish myths and legends with whom he is in love) belongs. Charles is also integrated into his community by his proud participation in the social ritual of the Clonrue fox hunt, the longest and most vivid description of an Irish fox hunt in Dunsany (chapters twelve and thirteen). Interestingly, the fox hunt does not run through the wild territory of the bog, which serves to indicate that it represents the political unconscious of this novel, on the personal, social, and historical levels of interpretation. After participating in this quest, Charles feels he has come of age.

The real dialectical image at the heart of the novel is the red bog of Lisronagh, whose layered substrata reflect Marx's notion of different modes of production being simultaneously present in society.[98] A crisis ensues when an English company, The Peat Development (Ireland) Syndicate, having been sold a rental license by his father, moves in and threatens to destroy with wheels and rails and machinery the world of natural beauty Charles has come to know and love for its richly heterogeneous layering of bird cries and other natural voices. The syndicate plans to use the water running in the local streams, a clear instance of what ownership of the means of production entails in terms of class and legal power or the relations of production.

By way of contrast with industrialized labor, Dunsany describes the labor of traditional Irish turf cutters with their age-old tools in some detail so that we understand how destructive (like strip mining, really) the company's plan to build a factory and compress only the black lower strata into coal will be. In traditional turf cutting, the land is used up slowly but remains in Ireland, adding its fragrance and allure to the experience of Ireland when consumed and burned as a use value. The British company, however, will remove it and turn it into a commodity for sale in London. To Charles, this seems like selling Ireland piecemeal. In any case Dr. Rory, the local physician, indicates to Charles that the company will be out of business in a few years anyway, as soon as the supply of deep peat has run out.

Meanwhile, Mrs. Marlin, who had earlier given to Charles a utopian vision of Ireland emerging from hidden and legendary cities to become a powerful independent sea power, resists Progress by cursing the workers on the construction site and praying for nature to take revenge. Unnerved, many of the Irish laborers leave, but the British company struggles on until a great storm from the ocean brings enough water to the bog to cause a kind of ground swell that destroys the factory. Mrs. Marlin dies in the process, her son having previously disappeared into the bog. It is possible at times to entertain a supernatural explanation for these events, Marlin may have reached immortality and Tir-nan-Og, but the narrator, after much intense anxiety and doubt, consciously rejects the beliefs of Mrs. Marlin and her son. Not a little irony is provided by the fact that Charles never marries Laura because she is a Protestant, though he encounters her again as an old woman, still beautiful.

The Story of Mona Sheehy is altogether less melancholy and more humorous and satirical in intent than *The Curse of the Wise Woman*, which is often taken to be Dunsany's best novel. As such, it is populated by social types rather than by three-dimensional characters. Unlike Charles, Mona's consciousness and identity are more purely a creation of traditional Irish folklore. Named after a mountain where the queen of the Shee is said to roam, she grows up as the romance of Athroonagh, the village that both fears and harbors her imagined supernatural heritage. Mona believes almost to the concluding page of the novel that the queen is her mother, though we know from the start that she is the result of an encounter between Lady Mary Gurtrim and a local villager, Dennis O'Flanagan, who raises Mona with the help of his sister. This narrative situation, in which we know more than Mona about her origins, provides the reader with much humor at the expense of the other credulous characters in the novel (even the village priest, Father Kinnehy, is uncertain of her mortal nature) as the beautiful Mona grows up and tries to reconcile her firm belief in herself as a romantic figure with her attraction to Peter O'Creagh, the ordinary but honorable son of the local gamekeeper.

Mona's life as a young adult takes the form of a series of adventures. Her wandering fancies lead her to run off on a quest for the queen of the fairies at World's End. On the road she encounters a fox hunt in which both Lord and Lady Gurtrim are riding. The experience fills her with delight and wonder, for she sees nothing in it that is incompatible with her dreams of the Shee riding out of the West with storms over Slieve-na-mona. She occasionally meets a wandering tramp, and he also tells her encouraging tales of the Shee. Unfortunately, Lord Gurtrim, whom she had planned to ask for help, is killed in the hunt. She then falls in with a group of tinkers who initiate her into an alternative culture, providing her with an experience of home that is closer to natural cycles. Being a nomadic and communal society, they provide Mona with a very different experience of time and cultural space from the settled life she has known. Somewhat like the gypsies, the tinkers live on the boundaries of respectable culture, obeying their own laws. Besides mending pots and pans, the tinkers create counterfeit money, which Mona helps them exchange. This experience of money created directly by human hands as needed helps her later, in London, to deal with the enormous fetishism of money. Though she understands its social power, it does not rule her imagination or define her quest. After a man kills another man over her beauty, Mona is rescued, though she is quite happy to remain among the tinkers.

If the novel has a villain, it would be Charlie Peever, a local magistrate and friend of Lady Gurtrim, who dabbles in financial capital, usually at the expense of his friends. Through his offices, Mona is sent to London to work in an advertising agency, The World Improvement Publicity Company. In these chapters describing her lonely and individualized life in the city, Mona is shadowed by insidious store detectives when she walks in the streets window shopping, but this is still very far from the naturalism of Stephen Crane. Although she easily sees through the false claims of advertising, she is courted by the scheming Martin Snerooth, the son of the owner of the firm, who is obsessed with a plan to replace good honest English table mustard with a liquid spray version called Murabom. Taken to a variety of London plays by Snerooth for her entertainment, the only thing Mona responds to is the language of a Greek tragedy in revival (script by Sir Gilbert Murray), an oblique reference to Dunsany's own views on the theatre.

None of these people have anything like Mona's expansive imagination and soul. Though Mona does not work in a factory—her duties seem mainly secretarial—her work life is numbing and repetitive. Her story at this point seems to mirror the degraded situation of the Wild Thing in "The Kith of the Elf-Folk" discussed above. Ironically, the other women working in the agency envy Mona because she will marry the boss's son, fulfilling the stereotypical desires of the women known to them from commercialized romances. Mona, however, shrinks in despair from such a constricted fate. She is rescued from it by the death of her mother, Lady Gurtrim, in a car-racing accident. Having kept tabs on her daughter without revealing her identity, Lady Gurtrim is able to leave Mona a substantial sum of money. All seems resolved. Mona can return to the village life she so sorely misses and marry Peter.

But once returned there, it turns out that Mona has too much money for someone of Peter's social station. Her inheritance has created a social barrier impossible to overcome. She must marry someone equivalent to her wealth. The novel's true and "realistic" resolution comes when Mona, who does not care about the money anymore, or her belief in the Shee, allows Peever to invest it in a financial scheme, which fails. Dunsany clearly created Peever as a satirical portrait of the finance capitalist as confidence man. Mona loses her considerable inheritance, Peever blaming the loss on a recent downturn in world financial markets. She is now free to marry Peter and live happily ever after in the village in which she grew up, a beautiful natural woman divested of her belief in her supernatural origins. Unlike *The Curse of the Wise Woman*, however, the true organic community still exists at the end of the novel, and not just in memory.

The biographical reason for Dunsany's turn to realism seems to have been his desire to be understood as an Irish writer, though his support of the Irish renaissance as orchestrated by Yeats had been, as I have mentioned, rather fleeting. When in 1932 Yeats founded his Irish Academy of Letters, giving Dunsany only an associate membership, the perceived slight stung him deeply, and he was never friendly with Yeats again. According to his biographer, this provided the impetus for *The Curse of the Wise Woman*, which was a critical success, and later *The Story of Mona Sheehy*, which was also well received.[99] As I have indicated, though, both are novels that find much romantic beauty in the Irish landscape, as *The Blessing of Pan* found it in the Kentish countryside. However much they construct an Irish identity for Dunsany,[100] it should also be considered that in writing them he remained true to his larger project of bringing romance into the modern world. In both Irish novels Dunsany makes the emotional experience of romance palpable through his characters' immersion in the Irish landscape and in traditional storytelling, despite their eventual accommodation to the "real" world in the end.

Dunsany's two Irish novels enabled him to continue his quest to provide an artistic critique of the spread of industrial capitalism. In neither of these novels, nor in any of the fantasy novels for that matter, does he use the impersonal techniques of high realism, but instead reinvents the figure of the storyteller, re-creating in himself as narrator a face-to-face relationship with his readers. His narrative stance is more characteristic of Dickens than of Flaubert.[101] In this manner a modified realism became a part of Dunsany's search for the cultural location of romance, made ever more problematic for him as capitalism extended and consolidated its totalizing grasp on our world. Throughout his career, by progressing dialectically through Frye's historical sequence of modes, he explored the resources of the political unconscious to resist modernity, and to suggest that our current social situation is not unalterable. Although much of his work is today forgotten, perhaps no fantasy writer writing today can make us feel so strongly the need for romance in modern culture.

NOTES

1. Northrop Frye, *The Anatomy of Criticism* (Princeton: Princeton University Press, 1957), 184. Frye is discussing Shakespeare's romantic comedy.

2. The novel could be read as an example of critical realism, in the sense given that term by Georg Lukács in *Realism in Our Time: Literature and the Class Struggle* (New York: Harper Torchbooks, 1971). See discussion later in this chapter.

3. Frye, *The Anatomy of Criticism*, 186.
4. See S. T. Joshi's introduction to *The Pleasures of a Futuroscope* (New York: Hippocampus Press), 5–11.
5. For an account of the various ideals of beauty that the West has produced, see Umberto Eco, *History of Beauty* (New York: Rizzoli International, 2004).
6. Raymond Williams, *Problems in Materialism and Culture* (London: Verso, 1980), 83.
7. Williams, *Problems in Materialism and Culture*, 81–82.
8. Darrell Schweitzer, *Pathways to Elfland: The Writings of Lord Dunsany* (Philadelphia: Owlswick Press, 1989), 77. I'm indebted to Schweitzer for the allusion to Robin Hood.
9. For discussion, see Ernst Fischer, *The Necessity of Art: A Marxist Approach* (Harmondsworth, UK: Penguin, 1963), 14–58.
10. "Art has in common with magic the postulation of a special, self-contained sphere removed from the context of profane existence. Within it special laws prevail. . . . The work of art constantly reenacts the duplication by which the thing [religious object] appeared as something spiritual, a manifestation of *mana*. That constitutes its aura." Max Horkheimer and Theodor Adorno, *Dialectic of Enlightenment* (Stanford: Stanford University Press, 2002), 13–14.
11. Benjamin famously defined aura through a kind of logical impasse as "the unique apparition of a distance, however near it may be." Walter Benjamin, "The Work of Art in the Age of Its Technological Reproducibility," in Benjamin's *Selected Writings*, Volume 4, edited by Howard Eiland and Michael W. Jennings (Cambridge, MA: Harvard University Press, 2006), 255–56. The second, earlier version of this essay provides more discussion of beautiful semblance as an auratic reality in Goethe and Hegel: Walter Benjamin, "The Work of Art in the Age of Its Technological Reproducibility," in *Selected Writings*, Volume 3, edited by Howard Eiland and Michael W. Jennings (Cambridge, MA: Harvard University Press, 2006), 127, 137–38.
12. For a Marxist account (influenced by Frye) of the value of romance for creating moments of narrative heterogeneity and freedom no longer possible for realism today, see Fredric Jameson, *The Political Unconscious* (Princeton: Princeton University Press, 1981), 104. I find Jameson's notion of the political unconscious as involving three concentric layers of textual interpretation—the political, the social, and the historical—very helpful, but find that it needs to be supplemented with an account of man's domination of nature. Hence my recourse in this chapter to Adorno, who wrote extensively on such matters.
13. Sarah Kemp, Charlotte Mitchell, and David Trotter, *Edwardian Fiction: An Oxford Companion* (Oxford: Oxford University Press, 1997), xvi. The authors date the period from 1900 to 1914 and say that it was characterized not by continuity with the past Victorian era, but by "generic promiscuity, inventiveness in new genres and new authorial voices," citing Dunsany's acts of fabulation as typical of fantasy in the period (xvii).
14. Lord Dunsany, "Romance and the Modern Stage," *National Review* No. 341 (July 1911): 827–35. The article is largely a defense of his dramatic practice at the time, but Dunsany specifically mentions the role of the storyteller in restoring romance to the stage (829). To discuss the development of Dunsany's drama and its relationship to myth is beyond the scope of this study, but a later play such as *The Laughter of the Gods* (1917), a tragedy in three acts, clearly depicts a religious crisis created by decadence in which the old gods appear to be failing to guide culture toward higher goals. By decadence Dunsany here means also the production of adulterated goods for exchange value, not for their use value in sustaining life. He cites Tennyson's *Maud* (stanza x), as an example of a poet/dramatist protesting the adulteration of good English bread. A year later Dunsany published another article expressing the same contempt for commercial culture in much the same terms, only this time the context was poetry. Lord Dunsany, "Nowadays," *English Review* 12 (October 1912): 390–97.
15. Kemp et al., *Edwardian Fiction*, xvi.
16. Frye, *Anatomy of Criticism*, 49.
17. Jon Clute and John Grant, *The Encyclopedia of Fantasy* (New York: St. Martin's Griffin, 1997), 899–901. Clute calls this aspect of the structure of modern fantasy "the story-shaped world," 900. For Dunsany as a fabulator, see 303.
18. W. B. Yeats, introduction to *Selections from the Writings of Lord Dunsany* (Churchtown, Ireland: Cuala Press, 1912), 6–7.

19. For an account of the field of orientalism, see Edward Said, *Orientalism* (New York: Vintage, 1979), 63.

20. See his account of the cry of the curlew as the voice of Ireland in Lord Dunsany, *The Curse of the Wise Woman* (London: William Heinemann, 1933), 36–37. Even in this realistic novel, which recounts considerable local lore about the red bogs of Ireland, going to the bogs is imagined as a quest for a far-off beauty (23). Dunsany explains that the bog contains a lore that is not of our fields (33).

21. Lord Dunsany, *Patches of Sunlight* (New York: Reynal & Hitchcock, 1938), 86. Dunsany says that he cannot remember what story this image occurs in, but as I explain below, it is *The King of Elfland's Daughter* (1924).

22. This is the gist of a Donnellan lecture on poetry that Dunsany delivered at Trinity College in Dublin in 1943. Lord Dunsany, *The Donnellan Lectures, 1943* (London: William Heinemann, 1945), 22.

23. Dunsany, *Patches of Sunlight*, 95. Dunsany's examples of enchanted landscapes in other writers include Keats and especially Poe. Dunsany, *The Donnellan Lectures*, 23–24.

24. For discussion of the intellectual history of this notion, see Martin Jay, *Songs of Experience* (Berkeley: University of California Press, 2005), 312–60.

25. For a portrait of Dunsany in America in the 1950s, see Hazel Littlefield, *Lord Dunsany: King of Dreams* (New York: Exposition Press, 1959), 36, 92.

26. He parodied Eliot's style in a story called "A Fable for Moderns," collected in Lord Dunsany, *The Ghosts of the Heaviside Layer and Other Fantasms* (Philadelphia: Owlswick Press, 1980), 115–18 (originally published in the *New York Times Book Review*, 1 July 1951).

27. For discussion, see Elaine Scarry, *On Beauty and Being Just* (Princeton: Princeton University Press, 1999).

28. Theodor W. Adorno, *Aesthetic Theory*, translated by Robert Hullot-Kentor (Minneapolis: University of Minnesota Press, 1997), 225–26. In his brief discussion of Marxist views of literature, Northrop Frye also expressed the view that the modern artist must develop in the work an "inner verbal strength," an autonomy that is not an imitation of reality but "an emancipation of externality into image, nature into art." Frye, *Anatomy of Criticism*, 113.

29. Adorno, *Aesthetic Theory*, 79.

30. Northrop Frye thought that socially fox hunting was "a race memory of pre-agricultural nomadism which has always haunted the aristocracy," Michael Dolzani, *Northrop Frye's Notebooks on Romance* (Toronto: University of Toronto Press, 2004), 87–88. The ritual of the hunt remained important to Dunsany throughout his writing career as a way of creating community and symbolic continuity with the past. At first blush, the hunt might seem just another form of the dominance over nature, but in terms of the socius and desire, leaping over fences and private property, the nomadism of the fox hunt does not create a territorial machine that dominates and divides the earth. According to Engels, only states do that. For discussion, see Gilles Deleuze and Felix Guarrati, *Anti-Oedipus: Capitalism and Schizophrenia* (New York: Viking Press, 1977), 145.

31. Dunsany understood that the historical decline of the upper aristocratic classes and the rise of the bourgeoisie required new forms of art and new social content, but argued for the lasting artistic value of art produced by the upper classes in previous times. See "A Word for Fallen Grandeur," in Dunsany, *The Ghosts of the Heaviside Layer and Other Fantasms*, 224–29 (originally published in 1951).

32. The process of the dispossession of aristocratic land by the bourgeoisie took several centuries. See Karl Marx, *Capital*, Volume 1, translated by Ben Fowkes (New York: Vintage, 1977), 884–89.

33. Edward Hale Bierstadt, *Dunsany the Dramatist* (Boston: Little, Brown and Company, 1917), 145. Not long after this letter Dunsany wrote a one-act play called *Cheezo*, which is sharply critical of advertising and modern manufacturing. In this play a manufacturer plans to use soap scum as the main ingredient of an artificial food.

34. For a general account of this reform campaign, see A. W. Coats, "Political Economy and the Tariff Reform Campaign of 1903," *Journal of Law and Economics* 11 (April 1968): 181–229. The basic idea behind the campaign was to limit free trade by establishing imperial "preferences" (i.e., trade within the empire and its colonies only) for certain products.

35. For a survey of oriental fantasy mentioning Dunsany, see Clute and Grant, *The Encyclopedia of Fantasy*, 734–35. The entry is by Mike Ashley.

36. Mark Amory, *Biography of Lord Dunsany* (London: Collins, 1972), 148–49. I follow Dunsany's spelling here. See *Patches of Sunlight*, 47.

37. For a recent account of Dunsany's relationship to imperialism, see Patrick Maume, "Dreams of Empire, Empire of Dreams: Lord Dunsany Plays the Game," *New Hibernia Review* 13, No. 4 (Winter 2009): 14–33. Maume considers the whole length of Dunsany's career, focusing on his relationship to imperialism as a kind of game. Maume correctly observes that for Dunsany, "the realm of story could not be defiled by modernity" (25), but feels that Dunsany was in the main an "irresponsible nostalgic" (33). My view is more focused on Dunsany as a writer who used fantasy to protest the radical impoverishment and constriction of modern life.

38. For the revolutionary quality of romance, see Northrop Frye, *The Secular Scripture* (Cambridge, MA: Harvard University Press, 1976), 139.

39. S. T. Joshi, *Lord Dunsany: Master of the Anglo-Irish Imagination* (Westport, CT: Greenwood Press, 1995).

40. See two essays, "Artist and Tradesman" and "The Carving of the Ivory," in Dunsany, *The Ghosts of the Heaviside Layer*, 176–81, 245–70.

41. Frye, *Anatomy of Criticism*, 57–58.

42. Frye's discussion of ghosts in different fictional tonalities is of help to any student of supernatural fiction. Frye, *Anatomy of Criticism*, 50.

43. For discussion, see Joshi, *Lord Dunsany*, 5–6.

44. Lord Dunsany, *The Gods of Pegāna* (London: Pegāna Press, 1911).

45. See Mircea Eliade, *Myth and Reality* (New York: Harper & Row, 1963), 93–98. Eliade discusses a Supreme God who has disappeared from cult and is more or less forgotten as the origin of the proliferating gods of many religions, and relates his discussion to Nietzsche's "death of God" experience.

46. Dunsany, *Patches of Sunlight*, 118–19. The birds were originally swans. S. H. Sime depicts Tragool as a sinister hooded figure with a starry double halo sitting beneath these birds in flight, reading his gigantic book. His head is a smoking volcano crater. The illustration contrasts fate and destiny with the flight of the imagination.

47. For a discussion of possible Nietzschean influences on Dunsany, see Joshi, *Lord Dunsany*, 20–21.

48. Jameson, *The Political Unconscious*, 74–76. The first level is the level of the individual literary work or utterance, which Jameson calls the political. As anxious as I am to include the social in all of the dimensions in the text, I still prefer the (bourgeois) term "personal" for this ground level of authorial reverie and experience, while recognizing that here too, as elsewhere in the literary text, the personal is ultimately political.

49. Kemp et al., *Edwardian Fiction*, xii.

50. For a recent account of Dunsany's poetics of naming, see Christopher L. Robin, "The Stuff of Which Names Are Made: A Look at the Colorful and Eclectic Namecraft of Lord Dunsany," *Names* 60, No. 1 (March 2012): 26–35. This essay shows how Dunsany cleverly disguised and displaced the origins of some of his words.

51. Walter Benjamin, "The Storyteller," in *Selected Writings*, Volume 3, 151, 166.

52. Eliade, *Myth and Reality*, 140–41.

53. For the boat of dreams as a utopian image, see Ernst Bloch, *The Principle of Hope* (Cambridge, MA: MIT Press, 1995), 24–25.

54. Lord Dunsany, *Time and the Gods* (London: William Heinemann, 1906).

55. The term "novelness" is not limited to actual fantasy novels, which often incorporate subgenres such as legends and fairy tales (see Tolkien's *The Lord of the Rings*), but signifies the spirit of the novel itself, the potential of the novel to resist and criticize all forms of absolute ideological authority. Dunsany's story about the king's journey seems to have "novelness" in this sense. For discussion, see Jørgen Bruhn and Jan Lundquist, eds., *The Novelness of Bakhtin* (Copenhagen: Museum Tusculanum Press, 2001), 42–45. For the distinctiveness of the novel among genres and further discussion of Bakhtin's notion of novelness, see Michael Holquist, *Dialogism: Bakhtin and His World* (London: Routledge, 1990), 72–74.

56. In German, *Erfahrung*, experience, is related the verb *fahren*, to journey. Another word for experience, *Erlebnis*, indicates the lived through quality of everyday life. In English, experience is related to the idea of risk or peril. *Erfahrung* is what Benjamin and Adorno argued is disappearing from the modern world. See Philippe Lacoue-Labarthe, *Poetry as Experience*, translated by Andrea Tarnowski (Stanford: Stanford University Press, 1986), 18, and the introduction to this volume.

57. According to his biographer, Dunsany read Nietzsche's *Thus Spoke Zarathustra* in 1903. Amory, *Lord Dunsany*, 40. In Nietzsche's book, Zarathustra as prophet of the overman is constantly urging his disciples to remain faithful to the earth as opposed to otherworldly concerns. The earth, and our bodies, have as yet undiscovered and unexhausted meanings. See Walter Kaufmann, *The Portable Nietzsche* (New York: Viking Penguin, 1968), 188–89.

58. Dunsany, *Time and the Gods*, 153.

59. Nietzsche often referred to his own texts as labyrinths, calling Zarathustra "this labyrinth of daring knowledge," and pictured his ideal reader as a monster of courage and curiosity. In listening to these dozen stories and in asking that the prophets remain faithful to the earth, Dunsany's King Ebalon does not lack courage. Keith Ansell Pearson and Duncan Large, *The Nietzsche Reader* (Malden, MA: Blackwell, 2006), 512.

60. Dunsany was later to claim that "The Journey of the King" was given to his publisher unfinished, to fill out the length of *Time and the Gods*. If so, this would explain the truncated and foreshortened feeling one gets from reading some of its embedded stories. Dunsany, *Patches of Sunlight*, 127.

61. Marx, *Capital*, Volume 1, 273.

62. Marx, *Capital*, Volume 1, 267.

63. Marx quotes extensively from Martin Luther. Marx, *Capital*, Volume 1, 740. See also Canto 45 of Ezra Pound's *The Cantos*.

64. Today this selling of experience is a growing sector of the economy. See Joseph Pine II and James H. Gilmore, *The Experience Economy: Work Is Theatre and Every Business a Stage* (Cambridge, MA: Harvard Business School Press, 1999), 164–65. The authors discuss how various companies commoditize experience in order to change people.

65. Clute and Grant, *The Encyclopedia of Fantasy*, 303.

66. In his autobiography Dunsany tells us that the name Babbulkund was a conflation of Babylon and the city of Orizund in Blake. I have been unable to find any reference to Orizund in Blake's writings. At any rate, he was not entirely happy with the name and later invented what he thought was a better one: Babdaroon. Dunsany, *Patches of Sunlight*, 33. The fact that there are slaves in the story, though they do not work on the creation of the city, and the reference to the pharaohs of Egypt, and the absence of any landed property, would seem to evoke the Asiatic mode of production in which the appropriation of surplus is through tribute. The control of water is also highly suggestive of oriental despotism. See discussion in Karl Marx, *Pre-Capitalist Economic Formations*, translated by Jack Cohen (New York: International Publishers, 1977), 77–79.

67. Marx, *Capital*, Volume 1, 548–49. Marx's account of the appalling conditions of factory workers was based on the experience of Manchester; in Birmingham the workers experienced ostensibly better living conditions because of bourgeois reformist movements. Nonetheless, Dunsany sees nothing but ugliness and grotesque mimicry of the classical world in the architecture of the houses of the town where Mary Jane lives. We know that Dunsany visited a wool factory in Ireland during his political campaign of 1906 to gather information for this story. Amory, *Lord Dunsany*, 44.

68. There are probably some echoes in this part of the story of Andersen's "The Nightingale," which is based on his adoration of Jenny Lind, a singer known as the Swedish Nightingale for her natural voice.

69. Marx, *Capital*, Volume 1, 284.

70. Adorno, *Aesthetic Theory*, 77.

71. Immanuel Kant, *Critique of Judgment*, translated by Werner S. Pluhar (Indianapolis: Hackett, 1987), 180. As Kant explains, ugliness that arouses disgust is another matter. Dunsany's play *Cheezo*, referred to above (fn33), would be a clear example of disgust used for the aesthetic purpose of criticizing industrial capitalism..

72. Dunsany, "Romance on the Modern Stage," 827.
73. Dunsany, *Patches of Sunlight*, 117. Dunsany was perhaps thinking of allegory here in a narrowly political sense.
74. Frye, *Anatomy of Criticism*, 53, 89–92. Frye observes that any interpretation of an image is already allegorical.
75. "Natural beauty is the trace of the nonidentical in things under the spell of universal identity." Adorno, *Aesthetic Theory*, 73.
76. Adorno, *Aesthetic Theory*, 136.
77. Frye, *Anatomy of Criticism*, 57.
78. Jorge Luis Borges, Silvinia Ocampo, and A. Bioy Casares, *The Book of Fantasy*, introduced by Ursula K. Le Guin (New York: Viking Press, 1988). Le Guin, herself influenced by Dunsany, thinks that this story is a miniature of the collection itself (11).
79. Lord Dunsany, *The Complete Pegāna*, edited and introduced by S. T. Joshi (Hayward, CA: Choasium Inc., 1998), xi–xii.
80. Dunsany, *The Complete Pegāna*, 203.
81. Frye, *Anatomy of Criticism*, 187–88, 193.
82. Dunsany would seem to reject Frye's vision of an ultimate allegorical coding by literature of man's destiny as containing nature: "Nature is now inside the mind of an infinite man who builds his cities out of the Milky Way." Frye, *Anatomy of Criticism*, 119.
83. The two sequels are "A Shop in Go-By Street" and "The Avenger of the Perdóndaris." They first appeared as a story cycle in the *Irish Review* in 1912, but the two stories were not collected until after World War I in *Tales of Three Hemispheres* (1919). See Joshi's discussion in *The Complete Pegāna*, xi. Because they both follow a different model of modern fantasy (similar to *Alice in Wonderland*) based on the reversal of narrative ground rules, I will not be discussing them in detail here. For analysis of this mode see Eric Rabkin, *The Fantastic in Literature* (Princeton: Princeton University Press, 1976). Basically, access to the dream world in these two stories is mediated through frustrating and tricky figures like the shopkeeper and the old witch, who represent the impossibility of exchange (a reversal of normality in the sense that you must ask for something that is out of stock for him to give you anything) and the negation of use value. Finally, the narrator tires of such nonsense games and affirms the world of normal exchange (another reversal) as preferable to the Land of Dreams.
84. Thus the sociality of this text calls upon an invisibly present third party. See discussion in M. M. Bakhtin, "The Problem of the Text," in *Speech Genres and Other Late Essays*, edited by Caryl Emerson and Michael Holquist (Austin: University of Texas Press, 1986), 126–27.
85. Dunsany, *Patches of Sunlight*, 307.
86. Jameson, *The Political Unconscious*, 35. Jameson here suggests that the Lacanian experience of The Real is that of history itself.
87. See Benjamin, "The Storyteller," in *Selected Writings*, Volume 3, 143–44, and Adorno, *Aesthetic Theory*, 34.
88. Benjamin, "The Storyteller," in *Selected Writings*, Volume 3, 149.
89. See discussion in Lucien Goldmann, *The Sociology of the Novel*, translated by Alan Sheridan (London: Tavistock, 1975), 4–5.
90. Benjamin, "The Storyteller," in *Selected Writings*, Volume 3, 144.
91. Dunsany, *Patches of Sunlight*, 86.
92. Jameson, *The Political Unconscious*, 75. Here Jameson distinguishes, using the concept of horizon from Gadamer, his three concentric frameworks for interpretation of the work: the political, the social, and the historical.
93. Brian McHale, *Postmodernist Fiction* (London: Methuen, 1987), 30–32. Relying on the analysis of the literary work of art provided by Roman Ingarden, McHale discusses how postmodern narrative worlds tend to oscillate between various possibilities, the question of which narrative world we are in being uppermost in the reader's mind. This aesthetic phenomenon is referred to as narrative "opalescence." Similarly, Dunsany uses opalescence to explain the lure and attraction of the magical twilight boundary between our world and the world of fantasy. For opalescence as used by other fantasy writers, see Dan Clore, *Weird Words: A Lovecraftian Lexicon* (New York: Hippocampus Press, 2009), 417–18. Unfortunately, Clore

does not mention Lovecraft's extensive use of this Dunsanian image in *At the Mountains of Madness*, which I discuss in the next chapter.

94. Odell Shepherd, *The Lore of the Unicorn* (New York: Avenel, 1982), 56–60. Unicorns are said to have a strong sense of smell, able to detect the odor of sanctity and virginity in weakened Christian allegorical versions of the hunt. For his part, Dunsany restores them as symbols of the Nietzschean beauty of power.

95. D. W. Winnicott, "The Location of Cultural Experience," in *Playing and Reality* (London: Tavistock, 1971), 95–103.

96. Keith Allen Daniels, *Arthur C. Clarke and Lord Dunsany: A Correspondence* (San Francisco: Anamnesis Press, 1998), 82. Clarke, profoundly moved, quotes the passage in full, calling it the finest example of pure magic in all of literature.

97. The position of the author in the novel according to Lukács and Girard, respectively. See the account given by Goldmann, *Sociology of the Novel*, 4. Building on these descriptions, Goldmann constructs a structural homology arguing that the degraded social experience of the problematic individual who does not accept the dominance of exchange value and who resists the values of bourgeois society in fact creates the critical consciousness necessary for the novel.

98. Jameson, *The Political Unconscious*, 94–95. These layers in turn reflect the generic discontinuities—between realism and romance—of Dunsany's novel, 144. The word "Progress" is capitalized throughout by Dunsany to indicate its allegorical stature in explaining man's fate in society according to the narrative of capitalism.

99. Amory, *Lord Dunsany*, 230–32.

100. See Maume, "Dreams of Empire, Empire of Dreams: Lord Dunsany Plays the Game," 26. Maume thinks that Dunsany's recourse to rural female figures as protagonists in these two novels allows him to resist modernity in defining himself as Irish.

101. Jameson, *The Political Unconscious*, 154–55.

H. P. Lovecraft, or Shock

The literary sociologist Lucien Goldmann, speculating on the origins of the novel's apparent focus on the hero's often demoniacal search for authentic values in a degraded world, its aesthetic form, argued that there must be a hidden class of people living on the fringes of society who rejected the predominance of exchange values in capitalist society in favor of use values:

> In view of this, there is nothing surprising about the creation of the novel as a literary genre. Its apparently extremely complex form is the one in which men live every day, when they are obliged to seek all quality, all use value in a mode degraded by the mediation of quantity, of exchange value—and this in a society in which any effort to orientate oneself *directly* towards use value can only produce individuals who are themselves degraded, but in a different mode, that of *the problematic individual*.[1]

Truly, if ever there were a concrete embodiment of such an individual, it would be Howard Phillips Lovecraft (1890–1937), who was born into a wealthy upper-class family in Providence, Rhode Island, in the last decade of the nineteenth century, when laissez-faire capitalism was still the dominant mode of production in America. Most of the wealth in the family stemmed from the industrial business investments of his maternal grandfather, Whipple Van Buren Phillips. Whipple Phillips was well traveled and cosmopolitan, and the only person in the family interested in supernatural fiction, which was destined to be Lovecraft's life-work (though not, as we will see, his vocation). He told the young Lovecraft stories based on traditional Gothic fiction. His mother, Sarah Susan, told him stories of his English ancestry, which could claim passage on the *Mayflower*. His father's family had emigrated from Devonshire, England, to Rochester, New York, in 1831. Winfield Scott Lovecraft, who made his living as a business representative for a

Providence silver company, consciously dressed and spoke as an English gentleman.[2]

Given this background in family stories, Lovecraft at a young age was attracted to the colonial past and felt increasingly drawn to the rural New England landscape that surrounded him. Eventually he claimed a lineage on his father's side going back to mid-sixteenth-century England. Learning to read at any early age, he absorbed *The Arabian Nights*, but also the New England *Farmers' Almanac* (of which he later amassed a large collection).[3] Thus it could be said with some justification that Lovecraft at an early age lived imaginatively in a doubly storied world, one part fantastic and the other part engaged with the real objective history of the New England colonies. As to why these different narrative worlds, one fantastic or marvelous, the other historical, should together have provided Lovecraft with the means for imaginative resistance to modernity in his writings he himself could never quite answer, but as he grew older he began to understand his nostalgic and melancholy moods increasingly in economic and objective terms.[4]

When Whipple Phillips died in 1904 the family, which then consisted of Lovecraft, his mother, and two maternal aunts, his father having died insane in a mental institution in 1898, began a slow financial decline into shabby-genteel circumstances. Heartbroken over the loss of his childhood home, Lovecraft vowed to return the family to its former social status, but unfortunately, though highly intelligent and an autodidact, he was ill equipped in personality and temperament to deal with any sort of wage-earning job that involved regular work. Lovecraft clearly understood that the society he lived in was based on exchange value, and that his authorship of supernatural fiction was not going to gain him a living. He realized he had nothing to exchange that society wanted, some commodity of genuine value.[5] Again and again in his correspondence, and especially after the stock market crash of 1929, Lovecraft railed against the machine civilization with its devotion to quantity as opposed to quality, as he himself became more and more impoverished.[6] His affective discontent with modern society is obvious in nearly everything he wrote. Furthermore, he tirelessly ridiculed the idea of measuring the magnitude of a work by its commercial reception or financial success as an illusion brought about by bourgeois civilization (placing the later word in scare quotes).[7] Yet when he came in contact with it in the 1930s, he scoffed at proletarian literature and the notion that the author should be politically committed to class struggle, blaming his unfortunate circumstances entirely on his own personal failings.

Lovecraft never sought to make his writing more commercial. He did not turn to realism in order to please an audience, as Dunsany did, but for purely aesthetic reasons. But as the spectral logic of his aesthetic evolved, he strove for greater length and added more and more layers of realistic detail and cosmic suggestion to his stories, effecting a kind of Copernican revolution in the field of the weird tale that been much discussed and admired.[8] Being a problematic individual who did not fit into society, Lovecraft in fact wanted to write a novel dealing with the hereditary mysteries and destinies of an ancient New England family, but died before he could begin the project.[9] It is then perhaps paradoxically fortunate that nearly all of his finest literary efforts went into the aesthetic perfecting of the weird tale, of which he is now an acknowledged master, despite some early detractors of his archaic style (another way in which he resisted commercialism). He would be astonished, I'm sure, to see his present-day iconic success as a popular author and the range of occult interest in his work.[10]

Not least among the paradoxes of this spectral writer was the fact that Lovecraft the materialist professed not to believe in the supernatural, or in romance (the world shaped according to our desires), the opposition between these literary modes being a product of bourgeois society and therefore having little force for him. In fact, he subverted the distinction between romance and realism that structures much of Dunsany's fiction by locating his work in a field that he called imaginative fiction, which is perhaps an attempt at the dialectical synthesis of them both. In rhetoric typical of the autonomous artist, Lovecraft argued that all moods were his to reproduce, the only limitation being the talent of the writer. If the imaginative writer is genuine in his mood, then he will create an authentic story through atmosphere.[11]

The term "aura" or atmosphere certainly had occultist and mystical connotations, but Lovecraft would have repudiated any occultist connotations of the concept, since he despised occultism and spiritualism. By the 1920s it had taken on the primary meaning of historical authenticity in Lovecraft's aesthetics.[12] For Lovecraft the function of the artist was to paint a picture of a *mood*. Aura, the medium that conveyed mood to the reader, provided an experience of *quality* that the society around him had suppressed. Throughout this chapter I hope to weave a thread of discussion around Lovecraft's complex aesthetics of the aura. Unfortunately, his comments on the aura are not set forth entirely in any one document, but appear scattered in his voluminous correspondence whenever he was moved to comment on aesthetic matters at different times in his life, and in an essay that he published in defense of his aesthetics in the amateur press.

His most concise discussion is in "Supernatural Horror in Literature" (1927), but that is only in the introduction to that essay. I will come to that essay momentarily. Suffice it to say for the moment that Lovecraft cautions us not to expect weird fiction to conform to any one theoretical model. The literature of the supernatural is a heterogeneous composite body made up of many intangible and fearful emotions. Nonetheless, the sensitive reader may detect and evaluate degrees of atmosphere, the only medium in which something as elusive and intangible as a human mood can be re-created.

But to continue with Lovecraft's life, his biographers assert that there was an unhealthy history of mental instability—probably paranoid schizophrenia coupled with depression—in the family, and at least one biographer called his personality "schizoid" and placed the blame for his inability to deal with the contingencies of life squarely on such a mental tendency.[13] However that may be, his family situation after his father's and grandfather's death seems not to have increased his sociability; he had no proximate male role models to follow except his uncles-in-law Franklin Chase Clark, a doctor and student of Oliver Wendell Holmes Sr., who wrote prolifically on medicine, natural history, and genealogy, and who died in 1915; and Edward F. Gamwell, a commercial editor and writer living in Boston, who inspired Lovecraft's own amateur astronomical journalism (1903–1909). Clark seems to have been the benevolent model for several likable and normalized doctor figures in Lovecraft's fiction. Coddled and overprotected by his widowed mother until she died in 1921 (she too suffered a nervous breakdown and had to be institutionalized), the teenage Lovecraft in fact had his own nervous breakdown and as a result did not graduate high school, largely shutting himself away from the modern world from 1908 to 1913.

Adulthood was a hell of emotional isolation for Lovecraft. For a time it looked as though he might commit suicide, having found no wider interest in society. Then, in 1914, he was invited to participate in the small world of amateur journalism. In becoming a member of the United Amateur Press Association, he found a broader and healthier, if often fiercely contentious and factional, social community with which to interact, editing and printing his own journal, *The Conservative*, from 1915 to 1923, thirteen issues in all. As one might guess from the title, Lovecraft's initial position was on the far right of the American political spectrum. He thought America was best kept for the elite descendants of the rich white landowners who colonized it, despised the bourgeoisie and working classes, and was an advocate of Aryan superiority in racial matters. In terms of class, Lovecraft throughout his life elaborated in his voluminous correspondence with others a compensatory fantasy of himself as an eighteenth-century gentleman, part of the landed gentry in colonial America.[14] In his fictional stories this ghostly (and ironic) pose of an autonomous gentlemanly writer from another time who wrote only for his own pleasure and that of others became central to the construction of his authorship.[15]

As I mentioned, Lovecraft's sense of his own authorship was problematic in Goldmann's sense because he knew he lived in the degraded world of bourgeois capitalism—what he described in no uncertain terms as the repulsive new culture of money, speed, quantity, novelty, and industrial slavery. Society based on the dominance of exchange value simply did not value what he felt to be the most important thing in life: the ability to express oneself freely and creatively as a unique individual. What complicates the picture of

Lovecraft's worldview is that he had accepted at an early age the scientific materialist view that the universe was an indifferent mechanism of cold deterministic horror without purpose, yet he felt drawn to the mood of *supernatural* fiction. Though he found himself opposed to capitalism and technological civilization, Lovecraft clearly needed to be deeply immersed in his own traditional cultural stream, as he called it, in order to write and in order for life to make sense to him. The parallels with Benjamin's discussion of the difference between traditional experience (*Erfahrung*) and immediate experience (*Erlebnis*) are striking.[16]

Understandably, Lovecraft had his melancholy moments in which he despised life as degraded and worthless. Indeed, his correspondence reveals that he felt himself to be an outsider in his own life, a spectator but never a participant. Life was a picture in which he had never been and would never be a part; he felt overwhelmed by a vast and terrible melancholy at the pain and futility of life in a blind and purposeless cosmos, proclaiming his inability to experience any pleasure except in mocking satire.[17] In fact, in his midtwenties he aspired to a kind of depersonalization in which nothing mattered. He believed he had succeeded in making himself into a kind of machine for the reception and classification of ideas (which he identified with the Epicurean experience of *ataraxia*).[18]

As the reader may have surmised, all this leads to a strong element of the grotesque in Lovecraft's fiction. "Nyarlathotep" and "From Beyond" (both written in 1920; see analysis below), to mention two of Lovecraft's most chilling and disorienting stories, do not so much attempt to create a fantastic world of their own, but are instead centrally concerned with the estrangement, deformation, or destruction of our world under the impact of fearful abysmal forces, which break it up and shatter its coherence. Indeed, the central experience of the grotesque is the feeling that our world has become strange and ominous, or even demonic.[19] One does not read very far in Lovecraft's fiction before encountering the grotesque, the source of shocks to normality. Indeed, either the word or the location ("grotesque" is derived from "grotto") is present in nearly every story Lovecraft wrote, beginning with "The Beast in the Cave" in 1905. The literary image of the grotto and the figure of the labyrinth are structuring elements of his entire work, suggesting a demonic world of underground fantasy.[20]

To Lovecraft human beings were ultimately just puppets, subject to the unconscious play of natural forces as Nietzsche's will to power had suggested. Furthermore, given the limitations of the human senses, human beings could not hope to completely comprehend the forces driving them. By his early twenties Lovecraft had absorbed and criticized most of the major thinkers in modern culture who had played a role in de-centering beliefs that supported man's pride of place in the universe: Darwin of man's difference from the animals, Nietzsche of God, and Freud of the ego. We should add to this list Lovecraft's considerable amateur knowledge of what modern astronomy had revealed about the vastness of the universe and our diminished place in it.

Lovecraft did not apparently discover Marx, who was in many ways the most radical de-centering thinker among those I have already mentioned, in any depth until the early 1930s, when he was not writing many stories, though he claimed to have read *The Communist Manifesto* earlier. He thought Marx to be right about the exhaustion of capitalism, and experienced firsthand the impoverishment brought on by the Great Depression. Unfortunately, yet understandably, he identified Marx, as did most people at the time, with what was happening in Russia after the revolution. The Russian model represented a cultural destruction of tradition too radical to be tolerated in America, in his view. Eventually he embraced a modified form of gradual state socialism (New Deal/Fabian Socialist) with some fascistic features as just right for America.[21]

In criticizing the shapers of modern thought I mentioned, Lovecraft came to formulate a philosophical worldview that was perhaps even more radically de-centered than other modern philosophies, which he called cosmic or scientific indifferentism. Its central tenet was the notion that nothing in life really mattered from a cosmic point of view. It's really an ethical position with regard to values. It ought therefore to be carefully distinguished from the central theme of cosmicism, which was the experience by Lovecraft's characters of the universe as inhabited by abyssal forces hostile to mankind, though it is not confined to Lovecraft's fiction alone.[22] The former is an ethical position about how to live, the latter an aesthetic experience. Yet if life was indifferent from a cosmic point of view, and human beings no better than lice, then why bother living or writing? When people pointed out the problematic nature of cosmic indifferentism as a philosophy of life—it seemed to destroy all value and choice—his argument in response was to say that it was *because* of mankind's de-centered status in modernity that the support of a traditional culture, in the form of continuous symbols and values, was a necessity.[23]

By 1918 Lovecraft was led to posit at the heart of his philosophical system a deep human desire, indeed a species-specific curiosity, to know absolute reality.[24] This is reflected directly in his early story "Dagon" (1917), in which the hero, shocked by his forced immersion in a grotesque world of black mire that has surfaced in the middle of the Pacific, nonetheless manages to find a (scientific) thrill and delight in the images of his horrific surroundings. Many, if not all, of Lovecraft's heroes, confronted with the horrors of a degraded world, experience to their peril the cost of cosmic knowledge. But they do not abandon the quest, even when madness or death ensues. Consider Crawford Tillinghast of "From Beyond" or Arthur Jermyn of "Facts Concerning the Late Arthur Jermyn and His Family" (both written in 1920). The latter, a person highly sensitive to beauty and to the aura of storytelling that surrounds his ancestor, Sir Wade Jermyn, immolates himself when he discovers the demoniacal truth that his ancestor had interbred with a white ape in Africa. Lovecraft may have been a cosmic indifferentist, but his stories involving scientists embody a curious paradox: they are always coming up against what limits reason: the terrifying experience of the Outside in its various forms accompanied by the threat of madness. And whilst warning us of the dangers of absolute knowledge, they nonetheless pursue it themselves at all costs, like William Dyer of *At the Mountains of Madness* (1931), or Nathaniel Peaslee of "The Shadow out of Time" (1934–1935), both, incidentally, professors—the latter of political economy—at Lovecraft's invented academic institution, Miskatonic University, which I will come to in a moment.

However Lovecraft's stories may be cognitively designed to horrify and estrange us, his images and myths also fascinate. Lovecraft found pleasure in such grotesque images of miscegenation and degeneration as the white ape, and such creatures as the shuggoths, and in the eerily beautiful ultraviolet images of "From Beyond," because they suggest the experience of what he came later to call the *absolute Outside*. Lovecraft understood the dialectical limits of enlightenment (demythologization) when he stated in the opening sentence of "Supernatural Horror in Literature" that the oldest and strongest emotion of mankind is fear of the unknown. "Enlightenment," said Theodor Adorno and Max Horkheimer, "is mythical fear radicalized. The pure immanence of positivism, its ultimate product, is nothing other than a form of universal taboo. Nothing is allowed to remain outside, since the mere idea of the "outside" is the source of fear."[25]

I am not implying that Lovecraft rejected scientific positivism, for as he created a new mythology, he also demythologized it. But he was clearly uncomfortable living in the world as revealed by science alone. And as far as aesthetic experience is concerned, without the experience of the outside, art (and more narrowly supernatural fiction) could not come into being in his view. That seems to be the point of his story "The Outsider" (1921), which I discuss below. The dream world, however, is never entirely adequate in Lovecraft either. Many of Lovecraft's stories are based on his own dreams, but that spectral experience had to be seen from the outside in aesthetic form to have aesthetic autonomy and validity. That is why his stories are full of dialectical images and shocking reversals that suggest the possibility that wider experience, no matter how horrific, might bring with it the overturning, or at least the momentary suspension, of the laws of the universe currently known to science.[26] The world as revealed by scientific rationalism was what he believed in, and he felt constrained to acknowledge it in his stories, but he found objective reality as revealed by science (endless and predictable repetitions of the same) inadequate nourishment for life.[27] Only subjective imaginative experience—the creation of the literary image—seemed to offer a pleasurable refuge, and could make the toilsome burden of consciousness bearable. Give me an inexhaustible faculty of creating literary images, he said, and I will be happy as a prince.[28]

Reflecting on the problematic nature of modern individuality in a letter to August Derleth in December of 1930, Lovecraft suggested why he had not chosen to commit suicide, given the loneliness of modern society, and the virtual impossibility of true communication. His reasons, which he did not expect anyone to understand, were strongly linked to his experience of architecture, scenery, and the folkways that surrounded him, and above all to *atmosphere* (i.e., aura). His response to modernity was to create an aesthetic refuge, and the experience he sought to create in his stories involved a sense of adventurous expectancy coupled with elusive memory that suggested a movement back in time.[29]

This letter also makes us aware of the deeper relationship Lovecraft's literary creations have with his life, his biography with the questing of his heroes. To be sure, like his heroes Lovecraft sought to achieve coherence in a world that seemed to lack inherent meaning, but that nonetheless appeared to have possibilities for the realization of both beauty and horror. Superimposed then on the inner form, on the experience of his heroes, who are problematic individuals, is Lovecraft's own search for meaning in the supernatural tale and in folkways that surrounded him, his quest for a *hauntology* that could conjure the spirit of modern technological inventions.[30] In this regard he even describes himself as a kind of "mystic" in a world without God. His was a difficult and problematic aesthetic, and he was often dissatisfied with the results. His atmospheric stories required a balanced tactfulness, their form achieved most often through large doses of irony, occasional black humor, and always with the evocation of the demonic and the grotesque.[31]

As I mentioned, there is in Lovecraft a drive for greater narrative length, and this involved a certain change of consciousness. His earlier short stories reflect the narrative stance and style of the Dunsanian storyteller, their heroes having a limited interiority due to their imitation of oral stories and legend. But by 1927 he was trying to achieve greater length through such short novels as *The Dream-Quest of Unknown Kadath* and *The Case of Charles Dexter Ward*. The former has many Dunsanian moments and oral-formulaic adventure characteristics but ends with a return to social reality, while the latter embraces from the outset a much more socially realistic world through the inclusion of written historical documents and the clashing of different professional opinions concerning the madness of the title character. This appropriation of madness as a limit experience reaches its apotheosis in *At the Mountains of Madness*, where it, in the guise of scientific rationalism, bids a final farewell to Dunsanian aura.

This search for the meaning of his characters' lives through their experience of the supernatural is evidence of the increasingly problematic nature of Lovecraft's writings, which end in "The Haunter of the Dark" (1935), a story that is all about the experience of being haunted by the demonic possibility of destructive non-meaning (figured ironically in the text as a religion, the Church of Starry Wisdom). In a letter that I will examine in a moment, Lovecraft acknowledged that his mind was paradoxically divided between the image and the scientific concept, a situation reflecting the two cultures of modern society.[32] I think we can agree with Gaston Bachelard, a philosopher of science who also studied the literary image, that the imagination provides us with a flood of sensations emanating from an admired object, an aura, but the scientific mind must create an epistemological break with the lure of sensation and constitute a theoretical object under the sway of concepts. Indeed, there is a constant threat from the imagination toward scientific concepts, which can become haunted by imaginary metaphors. For Lovecraft images play an important role in his stories and should first be experienced through admiring reverie, before any conceptual scheme explaining their origins in the political unconscious is imposed on them.[33] But human beings desire to know absolutely, no matter what fears the imagination may suggest, so there is a constant tension in Lovecraft's stories between the rational and what we may call the limit experience (i.e., madness).[34] Actually, as we will see, it is not so much the creation of the image as its suggestive deformation into the grotesque and arabesque that interests Lovecraft, as in *At the Mountains of Madness*, in which the reader is confronted with an almost constant imaginative transformation of scientific perception into the weird and vice versa.

The longest and clearest explanation that Lovecraft ever gave to aesthetics and its relation to scientific rationalism is in letter #345, to Woodburn Harris, a man for whom he had done revising work on Prohibition tracts, written over the course of a week in February–March 1929.[35] In what follows I want to examine this letter for what it reveals about the experience of the aura (that is, *quality*) in Lovecraft's aesthetics. To touch only on the high points, Lovecraft, after a few pages describing the reasons for the cultural decline of the Roman Empire, opens his essay on aesthetics with a discussion of the aura of associative glamour, feeling, and imagery that the work of art creates in each person. Art is rooted in the response to nature, but because of cultural (and racial) differences, there is a great diversity of response to the aura. Nonetheless, authentic art, that is, art that expresses the artist's unique vision, gives us a glimpse of the absolute that lies hidden beyond appearance. The search for ultimate reality is the source of our pleasure in art. We are bound to take pleasure in discovering something new and unexpected in ourselves, and art as it turns out has great resources to evoke involuntary memory. Here Lovecraft's argument about the importance of aura overlaps with that of Benjamin (and with Proust).[36] The involuntary memory was never before consciously registered, so when experienced it has all the striking fascination of absolute newness (it constitutes the work of memory as *Erfahrung*, as opposed to simple conscious recollection). The work of art enlarges us, not only in memory, but also in our relationship to nature and in our feeling of participation in the cosmos. Paradoxically, art reveals more of a natural scene than that scene would itself. Science remains the great destroyer of beauty as uniqueness, but at least art offers us the momentary illusion of wider participation in the cosmos.

So far Lovecraft has said nothing about art produced by machine civilization, but he soon takes up the assertion made by Harris that things such as automobiles have a certain aura of beauty. Here Lovecraft's argument strikingly anticipates ideas Benjamin would articulate in "The Work of Art in the Age of Its Technological Reproducibility." For Benjamin the unique aura of a work of art is identical to its embeddedness in the context of tradition.[37] For his part, Lovecraft acknowledges that mass-produced items may still appear to have beauty, but although clearly designed for a purpose they are removed from the life of the artist by the process of widespread duplication, which lessens their hold on our aesthetic sense. He also asserts that the men who fashioned the automobile had no part in the joy of its creation (a reference to art's alienation under the capitalist mode of production).

Written in 1929, the year of the stock market crash, the letter does link aesthetics to politics, proclaiming the need to keep a cultivated class of people in power, but I must set aside for the moment Lovecraft's obvious political conservatism. The letter goes on for several pages to discuss the deleterious effects of machine culture on art and everyday life. Lovecraft's narrative of modernity tells the tale of how creation and craftsmanship give way to technology and loss of the aura. Material objects produced by a tradition of craftsmanship, however, while not directly aesthetic, have the capacity to evoke epic memory and, even when intrinsically unbeautiful, can form a springboard for the imagination. Lovecraft introduces several examples from his own experience, including the reading of an old farmers' almanac and colonial houses for their associational and symbolic value. Old colonial towns such as Marblehead, Massachusetts, which he first visited in 1922, became the source of a rapturous experience for Lovecraft not because of the individual houses, only a few of which were aesthetically distinctive, but because the collective effect was of overpowering beauty that included a "mystical" sense of cosmic identification and totality. Lovecraft would spend the rest of his life trying to recapture the aura of wonder he experienced in those five minutes in Marblehead on December 17, 1922.[38]

In my view Lovecraft's 1922 visit to Marblehead marked a subtle change in his understanding of the aura. Earlier that year he had visited New York City very much under the spell of Dunsany, seeing the New York skyline as beautiful in Dunsanian marvelous terms. However, at Marblehead (and Salem as well), Lovecraft experienced collective history, the trace and nearness of the past, not just possession by the object.[39] While this distinction between aura and trace is not absolute, and while Dunsany's influence was still strong, more and more of Lovecraft's stories after the Marblehead experience, such as "The Unnamable" and "The Festival," both written in 1923, began to reflect local historical traditions, legends, and folklore. He had begun to incorporate more and more elements of his antiquarian researches into his stories. Most importantly, he was no longer a spectator or outsider, but a participant engaged with the political unconscious of New England. The spectral experience of the supernatural was no longer just a fantasy of himself as a colonial subject. For Lovecraft, the preservation and reinvention of tradition in his stories were the lynchpin to countering a hated modernity.[40]

At any rate, Lovecraft ends his long letter to Harris with a discussion of the beauty of the cosmos. So much emphasis has been placed on Lovecraft's hatred of life and the cold horror of the universe in his writings that it's something of a surprise to discover these pages.[41] Lovecraft links his discussion of cosmic beauty to the experience of the *veil*: beauty is semblance or appearing and always hides ultimate reality.[42] He then describes the frosty February scene from the point of view of imagination, and then of the scientific mind. The suggestive and beautiful images created by frost disappear in the scientific mind, which pursues concepts and structures. He then ventures into astronomy, with the same effect—aesthetic pattern discovered in reverie vanishes when the aesthetic mood evaporates. But not before Lovecraft's cosmic reverie, in which the stars watch him and send him secret messages, reveals a very important aspect of the aura: in auratic experience, the gaze is returned from the object.[43]

In summary, I would have to say that while it is not incorrect to describe Lovecraft as a scientific rationalist, such an assertion would only be telling part of the story of experience in his writings. For Lovecraft *as author* took ironic and sometimes sardonic comfort in images of the supernatural and the horrific, and a special pleasure in the unique aura of historical objects. As I mentioned, the image of the grotto, linked to that of the labyrinth as place of refuge and repose, is pervasive in his writings. But as he took refuge in traditionalism, he was not primarily interested in repeating stories about werewolves, vampires, witches, ghosts, zombies, and other figures from folklore. In response to modernity he created an extension of what, as a critic, he had called the literature of cosmic fear, constructing a literary utopia that subtly distorted social reality, but did not openly contradict it. Centered on the "awakened" scholars of Arkham's Miskatonic University, it proved a lasting shared construct among horror writers for investigating his myth cycle, the Cthulhu Mythos.[44] Based in part on historical Salem, Massachusetts,

Arkham was a location in which centuries of dark brooding and whispered horror lurked, and in which the shadow of legendary tales could encroach on the disciplined rationalism of the university. New England then became the very landscape of fear and the seat of weirdness as the towns of Dunwich and Innsmouth were invented. Such haunted places began to give shape to a hauntology, and to an understanding of what might lie beyond the positivity of science.

Following Goldmann's understanding of how the problematic individual overcomes his social situation through artistic expression, I would suggest that Lovecraft managed to supersede his own personal anguish about human life as revealed by scientific rationalism through the tactful irony of his stories, which always generate forms of black humor in which the hero is relentlessly driven to uncover the ghastly, shocking, and unnamable truth at any cost. Indeed, experience itself becomes identified with shock in Lovecraft, and his narrators begin to resemble the decadent traumatophiles they describe, interested only in conveying the morbidity of their greatest shocks. "Herbert West—Reanimator" (1921-1922) is the most intensive example of cold scientific rationalism and the mechanistic view of life haunted by traumatic repetition, though many others could serve (in this story Lovecraft explicitly compares West's grave-robbing and experiments in reanimating corpses to Baudelaire's poetry).

Supernatural fiction as problematically constructed by Lovecraft is always connected with the fate of society and with mankind, and there may very well be a pun on West's decadence in this story, for Lovecraft grew increasingly concerned about the fate of Western civilization. From Lovecraft's class perspective, certain deteriorative agencies—mechanization and immigration in particular—seemed to be at work threatening the American culture stream. Civilization itself had become problematic. Unfortunately, Lovecraft tended to demonize other races, and had little patience with liberal democratic arguments about the blessings of human diversity.[45] Other races, particularly Asians and blacks, were the enemy. Though he doubted that there was anything that the individual alone could do to reverse such trends, he began to understand his writing as *anti-cultural*, in the sense that it was opposed to the dominant bourgeois culture of commercialism (what Marxist thinkers call *affirmative* culture). Dunsany had advocated the creation of beauty as an antidote to capitalism, but Lovecraft, while deeply sympathetic to such an ideal, could only see it in ironic terms. For example, his character Kuranes in "Celephaïs" (1920) seeks beauty in this world but finds that truth and experience fail to reveal it. His only recourse is drugs and illusion. In the end a millionaire brewer buys Trevor Towers, his hereditary estate, for its atmosphere of extinct nobility, and enjoys himself as the drowned body of Kuranes floats in on the tide.

As it happens, Lovecraft wrote several letters clarifying his relationship to Dunsanian beauty. He did not entirely abandon the idea, but felt he was not enough of a poet to sustain such a vision of loveliness as Dunsany could write. For Lovecraft the experience of beauty had to be tied to a sense of intellectual freedom (Kuranes is free, indeed he still rules in the court of Celephaïs). Only in connection with the gesture of intellectual liberation combined with the aura of mystery was beauty of any significance to him.[46]

Lovecraft's most productive period came after he had some contact with the realities of the middle-class life. In 1924 he married Sonia H. Greene, a friend and associate in amateur journalism who admired Lovecraft. He then lived, from 1924 to 1926, in New York City, but was appalled and shocked by the proximity of the surging immigrant population. When Sonia Greene (herself an assimilated Ukrainian Jew) lost her job and fell ill, Lovecraft tried to secure regular gainful employment, but failed miserably. When it was suggested in 1924 that he take on the editorship of *Weird Tales*, the only professional outlet for his weird fiction in which he had gained a singular reputation and a following, he declined to live in Chicago. At the invitation of his aunts, he joyfully returned to Providence in April of 1926, and he remained there for the rest of his life, which was largely reclusive, except for antiquarian tours in his summers. He divorced Sonia Greene in 1929. Lovecraft's most famous stories, such as "The Call of Cthulhu" and "The Dunwich Horror," and his longer fiction as well, all date from the period after his New York exile (1924–1926). During his lifetime he never published a collection of his stories; not motivated much by the world of commercial publishing, he circulated his manuscripts among his friends and made his living by ghostwriting. Though one of the figures he wrote for was Harry Houdini, his own popular fame and literary reputation are entirely posthumous.

In trying to understand Lovecraft as a problematic individual, one must also consider what he regarded as sources of quality in his life. In that regard, for all the disdain that he evidently felt toward the lower classes, Lovecraft regarded himself as a craftsman, and penned many a technical note on how to write weird fiction.[47] As early as 1927, before his thinking turned at full length to a consideration of the role of economics in society, he was lamenting the disappearance of craftsmanship and local production in the dominance of universal exchange.[48] When Lovecraft spoke of the art of storytelling in terms of work, he referred to *style* as the mark of craftsmanship in which the creator had a personal involvement with his product, and perhaps left a trace of his mood.[49] Like the other writers considered in this study, Lovecraft strove to express himself in the craftsman-like tradition of storytelling.

Lovecraft's problematic experience of modernity and the decay of the aura was mediated and given direction by the writers in the spectral tradition that he admired and respected. Among those writers were, especially, Edgar

Allan Poe, Lord Dunsany, and Arthur Machen. Their stories were also experiences of quality. A consideration of Poe and Machen as influences on Lovecraft is beyond the scope of this study, but in the previous chapter we saw how Dunsany experienced modernity through a kind of elegiac mourning for beautiful semblance. The aura in his stories is centrally involved with the storyteller, who typically brought from far-off lands tales of the distant destruction of marvelous cities. Thus distance and nearness, past and present, were intertwined in the experience of the aura (as Benjamin described it) with temporal loss and ruination. This mournful quality in Dunsany's stories lends them a certain authenticity that Yeats praised, and that I commented on as redeeming any escapist tendencies that might accrue to the narrative worlds we experience in reading them. Though he did strive for reconciliation with nature, the source and model of beauty in his aesthetic, we noted that Dunsany was not a particularly consoling writer of fantasy. We noted too that many of Dunsany's stories took place in narrative worlds that seem to withdraw from mechanical civilization and the capitalist mode of production and to reconstitute small, out-of-the-way, sometimes feudal or pseudo-medieval societies that may have markets and exchange but that are largely pre-capitalist formations. *The King of Elfland's Daughter* was the most salient example. Only in this integrated societal context withdrawn from the capitalist mode of production could the magical aura of storytelling thrive.

Dunsany was an enormous influence on Lovecraft throughout his career, becoming for him a living example of the ways in which the aristocratic *fantaisiste* could have a role in the world. Indeed, Lovecraft maintained Dunsany as a point of reference to his own authorship in his correspondence from the time he first read "Poltarnees, Beholder of Ocean" (collected in *A Dreamer's Tales*, 1910) in the fall of 1919 and heard Dunsany lecture to almost the last year of his life.[50] What it was exactly in Dunsany's story that first so electrified Lovecraft we do not know for certain, but it undoubtedly had to do with Dunsany's *aura*, his rare capacity to evoke the atmosphere of the cosmically weird.

The reader may recall that in Dunsany's story Poltarnees is a mountain that forms the western border of the Inner Lands, comprised of three small utopian cities living in harmony with nature where everyone knows everyone else (a traditional *Gemeinschaft* community, based on shared mores and religious values and having a common fate). The story concerns a young hunter who crosses over the mountain on a quest to solve a mystery: why no one has returned to tell of the experience of the ocean. It turns out, however, that the ocean is not at all a pleasing or surpassingly beautiful phenomenon; indeed, it contains elements of pain and shock and dismay (figured as commercial shipwreck), and the hunter does not, indeed cannot, return to his naive community to relate his experiences.

In such stories Dunsany sharply criticized modern civil societies based on the pursuit of rational self-interest (*Gesellschaft*) because of their destruction of the fabric of tradition. In this story Lovecraft may have found an early model for everything he was looking for in a weird story: a secure, traditional home from which to pursue a mystery at any cost, followed by the authentic disclosure of the aura. At any rate, there is no question that Dunsany represented everything that the amateur Lovecraft wished to be, providing him an ego ideal, and was the inspiration for his early writings from 1919 to 1921, a brief period in which Lovecraft consciously imitated Dunsany's style, proclaiming after hearing him lecture in Boston that *Dunsany is myself*.[51]

It would not serve any purpose here for me to review the extent of Dunsany's influence on Lovecraft, which seems to be well understood and documented from Lovecraft's own writings and from the source-hunting efforts of scholars (those modern descendants of the hunter in Dunsany's story).[52] What I would emphasize is that, as previously mentioned, an ecstatic visit to Marblehead in the winter of 1922 provided Lovecraft with the experience of the trace, eventually leading him to a whole new aesthetic of the antiquarian traveler's tale. The tendency is already present in the richly atmospheric "The Picture in the House" (1920), in which he argues that the true epicure in the terrible can find his greatest thrill of utter ghastliness in the lonely farmhouses of backwoods New England. Aesthetically, Lovecraft would come to feel that his strength lay in shaping the aura and atmosphere of the weird tale in a realistic mode, as opposed to the exotic traveler's tale brought from very far off, though aura does require and preserve a certain distance in its essential structure in either mode. It is the breakdown of the aura in a kind of hideous proximity and intermingling that became Lovecraft's specialty, out of which he built the experience of the demonic grotesque in such stories as "From Beyond" (1920).

According to Lovecraft, there is a clear divide between his Dunsany-influenced pieces and the narrative pragmatics of a story like "The Call of Cthulhu" (1926), which depends on the "correlation" of isolated facts (really embedded stories) found in manuscripts, newspapers, and strange ritual objects, by a narrator who is not actively aspiring to immerse himself in cosmicity. The latter story launched the Cthulhu Mythos, and was written in a very different attitude, which Lovecraft called that of the hoax weaver. The method involved creating a believable lie, like a crooked witness at a trial.[53]

To widen verisimilitude, Lovecraft invented authoritative texts for occult traditions, like the infamous *Necronomicon*. Other authors of the weird, such as Robert E. Howard, Clark Ashton Smith, Frank Belknap Long, and Robert Bloch, followed suit, creating an intertextual archive that is still being used today. But Dunsany-influenced stories like "The White Ship" (1919), a reading of which I give below, were obviously not concerned with realistic verisimilitude in this sense, but rather with allegory, though Lovecraft thought that the principle of hoaxing would not have to be suspended even in dream-like narrations such as "The Music of Erich Zann" (1921) and the stories of the Randolph Carter cycle. The latter contains many features of pseudobiblia and weird archives.[54]

At any rate, without the connection to time past in a local place and the labyrinthine complex of associational traces offered by architecture and archaic survivals, he admitted to August Derleth, he could never have achieved the cosmic in the direct way that Dunsany and other writers could.[55] I have mentioned that the experience [*Erfahrung*] of the aura in all its fullness for Benjamin lay in the return of the gaze.[56] In Lovecraft's too the gaze is all-important, some of his most convincing emanations of the supernatural being composed entirely of mocking faces or translucent eyes, as in "The Shunned House" (1924). I tend to think that the gaze in such circumstances is Lovecraft's ironic reflection on his own work. But be that as it may, what if the gaze be not returned, or instead be found disintegrating or in decay? That is the question Lovecraft's stories endlessly try to answer, as experience of a traditional sort—the beauty felt by Dunsany—is found to be increasingly on the wane. Lovecraft's god Azathoth, who sits at the center of his pantheon as an agent of blind chaos, cannot return the gaze. This is no mere accident of descriptive detail. Lovecraft's cosmicism grew in grotesqueness well beyond the figures created by Dunsany, enabling him to represent allegorically the random and indifferent nature of modern existence. But cosmic fear, in which we experience the shock of the disintegration of the aura, is not the whole story in Lovecraft. It is also important to remember those sustaining moments of cosmic beauty or cosmic reverie in his writings.

Our shattering experience in confronting the blind eyes of inhuman and mindless Other gods who are indifferent to us seems to me an allegorical figuration of modernity.[57] Indeed, auratic experience of this inhuman sort inaugurates the transformation of looking relations in modernity, which Benjamin found in early daguerreotypes and in the writings of Baudelaire. A story such as "Pickman's Model" (1926) achieves its chilling effect of the supernatural by pointing up the difference between a painting, which is a unique human artifact, and a photograph, which is at once more reproducible and the product of a technological and inhuman gaze related more directly to the real (what Benjamin called the optical unconscious). The inhuman and grotesque qualities of the aura are concentrated in the limit experience of the *Outside*, where they create a fearfully distorted proximity that contrasts with the theme of proper auratic distance in Lovecraft.[58] We will see how these figures and themes combine in the interpretation of Lovecraft's stories.

Lastly, I must say a few words about aura in relationship to genre. Lovecraft wrote almost entirely in the tradition of the weird tale, with some science fiction that was published in pulp magazines such as *Amazing Stories* and *Astounding Stories*, so there is no question of a progression of modes such as we find in Dunsany. In fact, he seems to have applied the exact same aesthetic criteria to the writing of science fiction that he applied to the weird tale. The idea was to paint a picture of a human mood.[59] In a Lovecraft story the images would form *supplements*, rather than contradictions of reality.[60] Illustrating his point with examples from his own recent fiction, Lovecraft mentions "The Colour out of Space" and "The Whisperer in Darkness" (written in 1930, the latter features a professor of political economy at Miskatonic University as its hero), arguing for a new kind of weird tale in which images are weird in the sense of being outside the limits of known science or normal perception. Lovecraft was not therefore attempting to revisit extreme psychological horror or the violation of social taboos in the manner of Poe (what Tzvetan Todorov calls the uncanny) in the weird tale, though some of his narrators do indeed experience such extremes of alienation from the world and from themselves.[61]

Any discussion of Lovecraft as a problematic author would have to address "Supernatural Horror in Literature," first published in 1927.[62] In this treatise Lovecraft provides a broad historical account of weird fiction from its origins in religious myth and folklore, through Gothic fiction and the nineteenth century, and ending with sketches of then contemporary developments both in England and in America. Lovecraft opens his introduction with a defense of the existence of supernatural fiction, which is held in disregard by both the bourgeoisie, with its emphasis on materialistic satisfaction and external events, and others (idealists and holdovers from the mid-Victorian period) who deprecate the aesthetic motive in favor of didacticism. So the genre has already a problematic status. But the appeal of such a literature of cosmic fear is ultimately for those sensitive enough to appreciate it, those who can deeply experience an interior mood or emotion. Although he is clearly addressing a wider audience, in a restricted sense Lovecraft is writing his account for those who already have a sensitivity and attraction to supernatural fiction and want to know more about it.

In the last paragraph of the introduction he lays out his method of reading supernatural fiction. Just because supernatural fiction is such a heterogeneous body of writings, we cannot expect it to conform to any theoretical model. What can be compared in this diverse body of writings, however, is not authorial intent or the mechanics of plot but atmosphere (or aura; Lovecraft uses both words interchangeably), experienced as the creation of a given sensation. Stories can be compared and evaluated on a qualitative basis by the emotional level they attain at their least mundane point. Thus the one test of the truly weird is not the mere presence of supernatural events—many overtly "occultist" writings fail in Lovecraft's view because of undue familiarity with what should be felt as strange, while other, more realistic and stylistically suggestive and accomplished writers, such as Joseph Conrad and Henry James, succeed—but whether or not the story excites in the reader a feeling of dread and a subtle attitude of awed listening. In referring to awed listening, Lovecraft gives primary importance to the aura of the oral storyteller, but he does not neglect formal concerns of writing. The more unified a story, the better it is as a work of art, but without the high point of atmospheric intensity the story simply fails to meet Lovecraft's criteria.

The main body of the text, which for reasons of length I cannot summarize here, is written objectively and historically, but nonetheless one often gets the impression that we are in the presence of a spectral body of writings, inassimilable to any positive theory of literature. We are often treated, in fact, to Lovecraft's rich passages of indirect free style (especially in the section on Poe), which enable him to convey to us the impact on him of each writer's images and atmosphere, as if he himself were haunted by that writer's mood and style. The essay ends with the evocation of a beautiful artisanal image from antiquity: the treasured cup of the Ptolemies, which was carved of a solid piece of black onyx layered with golden chalcedony. This is Lovecraft's resonant symbol of fantastic art. The cup, which still exists today, celebrates the rites and sacrifices of Bacchus and contains many "hieroglyphic" representations of fantastic figures. The rites of Bacchus figure prominently in one of Lovecraft's earliest stories of supernatural agency, "The Tomb" (1917), in which the hero, Jervas Dudley, escapes from a lonely and isolated life in part through the eighteenth-century Bacchanalian mirth of his ghostly ancestors. The reference to handcraftsmanship then is not accidental, for Lovecraft intends us to see the connection between storytelling and work involving the hand (Lovecraft, as did Dunsany, always wrote out his stories in longhand).[63]

In summation, then, Lovecraft felt that the literature of the fantastic could not be treated as a single unit, because it was a composite resting on many different historical bases.[64] What mattered to Lovecraft, whether the end product was science fiction or the supernatural weird tale, was not mode but *mood*, not events or actions themselves but atmosphere (or aura), which was the medium that conveyed authentic mood to the reader and which had to be built up by the slow stylistic accumulation of detail.[65] The artist's function is to paint a picture of a mood.[66] In identifying atmosphere and aura with a medium, Lovecraft in his supernatural fiction was able increasingly to accommodate modern media—radio, telephone, phonogram—to the experience of being haunted, and to storytelling, a point I will take up in discussion of the stories.[67]

One final note about mood. In a 1930 letter to Clark Ashton Smith, Lovecraft further distinguished between two moods leading to the production of the weird tale, one cognitive and scientifically realistic and the other having the nebulous uncertainty of a dream. Lovecraft set aside his earlier infatuation with poetic suggestion in the manner of Dunsany, not because he did not admire this mode of writing, but because he thought himself not very good at it. Lovecraft acknowledged to Smith that the unconscious plays a role in both moods, the creation of an authentic weird tale being the result of a kind of *oneiroscopic* activity on the part of the author.[68] Thus whatever the status of scientific or cognitive thought in his writings, dream and reverie in Lovecraft should also be understood as among his primary experiences, i.e., ways of exploring new worlds, of contacting the marvelous Outside, and of personal sublimation.[69]

As I mentioned, Lovecraft in his aesthetic writings about the weird tale and science fiction was insistent that the purpose of the story was not to relay *events*, but to create atmosphere, or aura, which conveys mood. Little purpose then would be served by my providing a detailed account of what happens in a particular story. However, Lovecraft as a storyteller was well aware of the narratologist's formal distinction between story (the events in chronological and causal order) and discourse (how we learn about those events through the artistic manipulation of frequency, order, and duration), not to mention issues involving the narrator and point of view. Clearly too he understood the artistic question of focalization—who is seeing and who is speaking—at a deep level, since the weird phenomenon has to be seen and spoken of to be conveyed to the reader. He even distinguished four basic types of weird tale based on how the phenomena are presented.[70] But the weird phenomenon and its aura must overshadow everything else—characters and events—in the story.

In Lovecraft's first decade of writing we find many interesting weird tales that work on the problems inherent in realizing his aesthetics of the aura in modernity. "Dagon" (1917) introduces us to a morphine-addicted, impoverished narrator *in extremis* who must have forgetfulness or death, due to the trauma he has suffered. Indeed, he threatens to throw himself out of his garret window into the squalid street below after he has finished his hastily scrawled manuscript. Right from the outset, tactile values—those associated with the unique trace of the storyteller—are very prominent in the story's creation of aura. The manuscript mentioned in the first paragraph introduces the theme of the hand, which will be transformed into a monstrous hand in the last words of the story. Thus the human handwritten trace comes to have a spectral quality, haunted by a monster given the name "Dagon" in the story's title. As the traveler tells of his journey and experience, we learn of his wartime escape from a German sea raider (the story is set during World War I) and his awakening to an immense world of black slime cast up from the depths of the ocean. The main weird phenomena of the story are the primeval landscape through which he wanders, with its remains of creatures unknown to the world of science, and a large stone monolith carved with grotesque hieroglyphics based on the sea creatures. The monolith has aura because of its immense age, and the fact that it has known the workmanship of unique living and thinking creatures. The hieroglyphics also guarantee a sacred, as opposed to a profane, meaning, and suggest allegory (see footnote 73).

The story amplifies this aura through combining awe (the prospect of scientific knowledge) with literary references to the epic distances of the past, and partly through suggestions of allegory as objects are turned into images or pictographs. Climbing a hill and descending into a dark valley where the monolith sits, which because of its black waters he does not hesitate to call Stygian, the narrator recalls Satan's journey through space in Milton's *Paradise Lost* (one assumes that Lovecraft is alluding to Satan's escape from Hell at the end of Book Two). The allusions (and there are more to Poe and Gustav Doré) help the reader construct allegorical images.

At any rate, he realizes that he has been given a glimpse into the past that even the most daring anthropologist has never had before. For a while, he believes the human figures with fish-like features depicted in the bas-reliefs to be imaginary gods of some primitive fishing tribe (historical allegory), but when he sees a vast, loathsome creature—compared to Homer's cannibalistic giant Polyphemus—approach the monolith and wrap his scaly arms around it in worship, he goes mad, realizing that he is witnessing an inhuman spectacle much older than mankind. In Marxist allegory, Polyphemus is supposed to correspond to a primitive state of society, prior to agriculture, in which individual identity has not yet crystallized.[71] Be that as it may, there is no corresponding attempt to defeat the monster with the ruses of language. Later attempts to understand or integrate this shocking experience in terms of ethnology—as perhaps an expression of the Philistine fish-god, Dagon—seem unsatisfactory and conventional.[72] The narrator anticipates bitterly the contemptuous amusement that his story will provide for others, and he himself is sometimes not sure that the events actually happened. But the story ends with the approach of that real monster whose hand(s) touched the monolith in worship, and with the narrator's presumed defenestration.

"Beyond the Wall of Sleep" (1919) is one of Lovecraft's earliest stories attempting to create aura through the experience of the dream. "Polaris," written in the previous year, is another, but instead of being trapped in a demonic world, the situation in that story, the narrator of this story finds a kind of liberation in the aura. Indeed it is the first of Lovecraft's stories to use the word "aura" explicitly in connection with a phenomenon that is central to it: the gaze of the other. The narrator, an intern at an insane asylum in the Catskills in the winter of 1900–1901, claims to be narrating a plain tale of science without rhetorical effect. He is interested in the visions and the strange linguistic behavior of one of the inmates, a murderer named Joe Slater, whose ethereal visions of cosmic beauty shockingly contrast with his degenerate personality. Slater raves about luminous beings and things that he could not possibly have experienced. One not too convincing explanation for these visions among the alienists is that they are the product of a paranoid mind working on crude hereditary folktales. But the narrator has the idea that the visions are the emanations of a being who inhabits the far less material realm of the dream, a realm as much spirit as matter. Accordingly, he contrives a kind of cosmic "radio"—the first of many haunted media in Lovecraft—to contact the being and begins receiving communications, or rather visions, from another plane of existence.

Now, as Slater begins to die, the narrator establishes contact with this new brother of light, as the narrator describes him, who is surrounded by a resplendent aura. For a while he holds a colloquy with the narrator in silent but perfect interchange of thought. It turns out that this being is a cosmic wanderer or traveler among the stars, so his story having to do with his imprisonment in a human body is really a marvelous traveler's tale. He tells the narrator that they share a similar nature, that his real self can be experienced in dreams, that they have been companions before, and will be again (he lists a fantastic catalogue of possible meeting places that seems to defeat time and space). As he dies, the degenerate man who was Joe Slater gazes at the narrator with luminous and expanded eyes. To make sure that we understand that this is an allegorical moment, he tells the narrator that he will return to the stars as a blazing Nemesis and wreak vengeance on the star Algol (which means "demon"), which is confirmed by the appearance of a new star in the heavens not far from Algol.

With regard to the catastrophic history of the twentieth century, it is perhaps too obvious an irony to point out here that one story of experience takes place in wartime and the other in an insane asylum. In terms of the problematical (i.e., demoniacal) hero, the narrator of "Dagon" is a prototype of all Lovecraft's mad heroes. His experience takes him through an utterly degraded world in which the human is completely displaced by the grotesque and the monstrous. The everyday world has become problematic for him, and there seems to be no escape, other than suicide. But "Beyond the Wall of Sleep" seems to satisfy all of the personal requirements Lovecraft needed in a weird tale, including the sense of cosmic beauty and the escape from the limitations of the world revealed by science. Yet it does not contradict science. Rather, the dream images supplement the world of reality. The rhetorical stance of the narrator is ironic: he is scientific in relating the "facts" of his experience in the insane asylum, and in claiming to have contrived no artificial climax as proof of his tale (the account of a real nova near Algol is taken verbatim from a book on astronomy), but at the same time the story dreams in images, and opens with a reverie in which the narrator attacks Freud's theory of the symbolism of dreams. There is something more in the experience conveyed by dreams, the narrator asserts, than mere symbolism can grasp, or than convention can understand (the experience of the narrator in "Dagon" is also one that reveals the limits of convention; "Dagon" is an ironic title). Indeed our experience of the story is not rooted in symbolism, but in allegory (Nemesis is clearly an allegorical figure), the allegory of Lovecraft's experience of modernity, which was based, as I explained above, on the relationship between reverie and science. The story opens with reverie, embraces the sensuousness fullness of dreams, goes through physical death and devaluation, and then elevates spiritual meaning to the even more abstract level of scientific truth or concepts, precisely the central action of allegory according to Benjamin.[73]

"The White Ship" (1919) is a Dunsanian-style traveler's tale with an allegorical structure. As such, it tells the story of Basil Elton, a lighthouse keeper who one night walks out on a bridge of moonbeams to board the White Ship, which takes him on a marvelous journey to a series of cities that represent different figurations of experience. The story follows Dunsany's poetics, at least initially, by having its hero grow up surrounded by various stories bearing the lore of faraway places. But Elton must discover for himself the deeper lore of the sea, his own experience. First comes the Land of Zar, where dwell all the dreams of beauty discovered by men and forgotten. The ship does not stop here, because to do so would mean forgetting the beauty of one's native land. The mighty city of Thalarion is demonic, fascinating yet repellent. The streets are filled with the bones of those who have gazed on the eidolon Lathi, who rules over the city. Dominated by images and phantoms, it probably represents the modern city with its idols of the marketplace. To remain in Thalarion would mean becoming no longer human. Xura, the Land of Pleasures Unattained, is a charnel landscape infested with plague.

But the ship eventually stops at Sona-Nyl, the Land of Fancy. Here we find no limitations, but only infinite distances, one experience of beauty leading to another, the very heart of Dunsany's orientalist aesthetics. Elton begins to feel unrest, however, when he hears of Cathuria, the Land of Hope lying to the west, which is signaled by the appearance of a celestial bird. Cathuria represents the Western metaphysical dream of a land where the perfect ideals of things we know only darkly in experience can be found, a land specifically imagined as hosting Greek gods, heroes, and kings who gaze upward at a living Olympus. But Cathuria is only imagined in the land of fancy, not experienced.

As I mentioned, there is always something negative or shocking in Lovecraft's account of experience, whether in the realistic or dreaming mode. Modern experience certainly allows for no such ideal, Platonic land as Cathuria, so it is not surprising that the perilous voyage ends in catastrophe, when the White Ship plunges into an abyss of nothingness. Elton returns to a world of beautiful fragments, to the dead azure body of the sea bird that led him on the quest for Cathuria, to a landscape where the (symbolic) light of the lighthouse has failed, and where a single shattered spar of the White Ship is all that remains, bearing a whiteness greater than that of natural waves or mountaintops. The fact that the useful work of the lighthouse has become abandoned during the narrator's journey also suggests something of the art's guilty ties with luxury and privilege in class society. These objects have now become allegorical signs of a loss of inherent meaning in the modern world.[74]

The authentic experience of allegory in "The White Ship," in which painful contradictions are left unresolved, ought clearly to be distinguished from the ideological use of political allegory in "The Street," which Lovecraft wrote soon afterward. Here Lovecraft provides meanings in a mechanical way as traditional American culture, which for Lovecraft was English, white, and conservative, is threatened by the influx of immigrants and their ideas, including references to a certain squalid Rifkin School of Modern Economics that establishes itself. Given the date of the story, 1919, and the references to strange writings, assassins, and terrorists, it is entirely possible that Lovecraft is thinking here of the aftermath of the Russian Revolution (in that unhappy frozen land from which most of them have come). The xenophobic depiction of various alien groups, sinister, swarthy, and furtive, fighting it out in the public street represents the classic notion of ideology as Marx understood it. Indeed, Lovecraft constructs a fantasy *ideologeme* of American class history.[75] Lovecraft's ideologeme constructs a historical narrative in which colonial ancestors and their descendants, through their labour (ever the Anglophile, Lovecraft uses the British spelling), fashion the blood and soul of the street. These new groups, escaping communism, are all motivated by greed and ambition, allowing the beautiful old houses to fall into ruin, yet certain ones among them—the ideologists—threaten to overthrow the American spirit of free market independence. But ideology works through making the historically conditioned seem natural and eternal. We know we are reading an ideological fantasy when the contradictions in Lovecraft's story are resolved by having the old, worn-down houses collapse during the night *of natural causes* (but the uniformity of the collapse suggests that something more is at work) on top of the conspirators. All seems in ruins, but a storytelling poet and traveler sees another, spectral picture above the ruins, one that contains fair houses and beautiful trees (planted by ancestors), in the moonlight.

"From Beyond" and "Nyarlathotep" (both November 1920) are centered on the experience of cosmic fear and are based on Lovecraft's actual dreams. For the former story Lovecraft offered his own analysis of the dream in terms of what he had recently been reading, Mary Shelley's *Frankenstein* and Ambrose Bierce.[76] Not based, ostensibly, on supernatural events, "From Beyond" (1920) is nonetheless a story about violent and shocking changes in perception brought about by a scientific invention. But considered as an allegory of experience, it too centrally concerns the decay of aura, and in a horrible way. Crawford Tillinghast is a scientist who has devised a machine that will break down barriers that limit our perception of phenomena to the five senses. He shows the results of his experiments designed to reveal the absolute nature of things to his friend the narrator, who in turn describes the phenomena while making moral judgments on Tillinghast, another one of those characters in Lovecraft who go beyond conventional good and evil in their quest for knowledge. The story is carefully structured around increasingly horrifying phenomena, and makes clear the close association in English between experiment and experience. The narrator at first sees outré colors that Tillinghast says are ultraviolet. Tillinghast points to the existence of long-dormant sense organs (the pineal gland) that he has activated. Interestingly, during this discussion the narrator imagines that Tillinghast's attic laboratory is some immense temple of long-dead gods. This reference to a temple is enough to evoke the traditional associations of aura with the appearance of a god and the distance that must be maintained in such religious circumstances.

The temple effect continues as the narrator imagines the distorted image of Tillinghast's face as a new constellation in the sky. His machine, however, reveals not gods but jelly-like amorphous predatory creatures obscenely inhabiting the same space we do, who can in turn see and attack us, if we move. Lovecraft's narrator initially compares the effect of Tillinghast's apparatus to the experience of cinema projected on a screen, but soon learns that the experience of the gaze in this situation is not pleasurable but horrifying, for it abolishes distance, as the monstrous beings overlap with us in the real (a Lacanian nightmare). Trying to remain still as he takes all of this in, the narrator realizes that close to every known thing are disgusting alien creatures. Tillinghast allows that these creatures—demons from the stars— are not beautiful, but asserts that they have aesthetic standards that are *very different*. Claiming to have mastered the creatures, Tillinghast now threatens the narrator with disintegration, but the narrator fires his pistol into the machine, lapsing into unconsciousness. Doctors tell the narrator that he has been the victim of a madman (now dead), but he remains haunted by a hideous sense of pursuit, his perception of air and sky (i.e., atmosphere) changed forever into the spectral.

The ultimate meaning of "Nyarlathotep" (1920) is more elusive, but seems to have been shaped by ideological representations in its allegory. It can be understood on the three concentric levels of interpretation suggested by Fredric Jameson.[77] First, it can be understood on the personal level, as a dream, or nightmare, that Lovecraft had during a period of acute headaches and dizziness.[78] But even here the ocular discomfort that Lovecraft felt quickly takes on a feeling of vague universal terror. From the outset the body in question is not just Lovecraft's but the social body, as the gaze becomes increasingly alienated and terrifying. In the dream Lovecraft is reading a letter from Samuel Loveman, an amateur poet whose writings Lovecraft greatly admired, concerning a horrible yet wonderful experience he has had of a certain Nyarlathotep, an itinerant showman or lecturer. Loveman urges Lovecraft to attend one of his shows, which consists of a prophetic cinema reel and experiments with scientific and electrical equipment. This duality of prophecy and technology makes the meaning of Nyarlathotep—as god, as dream, as story—elusive. But primarily it is a proper name, that is, a unique personal sign. It may have been patterned, though, on a name in Dunsany.[79]

In any case, realizing that a shocking fear has already seized Providence because of Nyarlathotep, Lovecraft resolves to attend one his performances, joining crowds of people on their way to see him. The appearance of crowds announces the theme of mass perceptions, beyond the individual. From the letter it seems clear that the experience was one of real aura, and Lovecraft claims to have written the opening paragraph of the story while still half asleep in an attempt to preserve the atmosphere of unparalleled fright.

But what can we say regarding the experience of cosmic fear in social terms in the finished story, which is plainly an allegory? To create an atmosphere of cult value, Lovecraft has his character darkly descend from the pharaohs of mysterious ancient Egypt. However, Nyarlathotep is someone who speaks much of the sciences—particularly electricity and psychology. He may well bring with him the experience of new gods, but he is also someone who takes something from men, something that has never been taken before, from their eyes. Nyarlathotep brings a change in vision in the masses, in the whole experience of aura.

Now, Nyarlathotep's showmanship, at least in part, has to do with cinema, with projection on a screen—the equivalent of a dream. In Benjamin's account cinema really has no aura of its own, since it is only mechanically reproducing an actor's performance, unlike the unique stage actor. Aura is tied to presence; there can be no replica of it. The experience of authenticity would then seem to lie outside of the sphere of the technical. Of course, movie stars have aura, but that is the result of studio manipulation and the rhetoric of the culture industry. Cinema in Benjamin's account was tied technologically to the decay of the aura, which Lovecraft makes us feel in the "shadowy" and spectral projections on the screen.[80]

But Nyarlathotep is also a uniquely famous stage performer whose model may have been Nikola Tesla.[81] If that is so, and Tesla is the "real" historical source of Nyarlathotep's aura, then the story clearly points to the next level of interpretation, the capitalist mode of production, because Tesla's "magic" shows had to do with selling his invention of alternating current to the public, who had been made to think it dangerous by Edison, who was in turn trying to promote the viability of direct current, his invention, to J. P. Morgan in the contest for the electrification of New York City. Each of these men knew, as did the general public, that electricity was going to be a commodity immensely important to the future of the United States. Seeking to capture public attention with spectacle, Edison electrocuted an elephant, but Tesla countered by passing the alternating current through his body. Edison actually *filmed* this event and used it in his campaign against AC current and Westinghouse, which supported Tesla.[82] These public displays must have had something of the grotesque about them. No doubt the story points up the feverish phantasmagoria created by ruthless competition in the monopoly era of American finance capital in a way that would have appealed to the scathing humor of Karl Marx.

Lovecraft was at this time no admirer of industrial capitalism, but he had not yet pronounced it dead; that was not to happen until after the stock market crash of 1929, when capitalism entered a period of crisis. At any rate, the ideological implications enter the story through the description of Nyarlathotep as swarthy and sinister, exactly the same words used to describe the immigrant populations of "The Street." The cinema reel also represents and conveys the ideologeme of the yellow peril (mass immigration of Asians threatened white wages and standards of living and would eventually destroy Western civilization and its values). Interestingly, the narrator thinks of himself as a distanced expert, calling the electrical show grotesque (he claims to be older and to know more about static electricity and science than the average person). He labels Nyarlathotep's show an imposture, and protests that he is unafraid. But all this is, ironically, to no avail. Nyarlathotep's powers seem more than human, and he drives the audience out into the streets.

There follows an account of what seems to be the end of the world, as electric lights begin to fail in the city and columns of guilty, numbed people plod into a snowy abyss, the narrator among them. This is the "real" experience of the demonic grotesque, which Lovecraft offers us here in lieu of fear. I do not find the story to be in any way fear provoking; it seems to me that the fate of the narrator is too distanced and ironic to be fearful (he insists that he is *not* afraid). Allegorically the story signifies human beings adrift in a world defined by science, which reveals only a revolting graveyard of a universe. In the letter Loveman encourages Lovecraft to have a certain kind of experience, horrible and marvelous at the same time. The story achieves that much at least, but Nyarlathotep is primarily an allegorical figure of the unconscious optics of the story, of the decay of aura, and of the loss of individual uniqueness. Perhaps he exists in the real, too, paradoxically identified in the last sentence as the "soul" of the blind, voiceless, mindless gargoyles who are now the gods of the modern capitalist world. Nyarlathotep is the god of shock, both figuratively and literally, in Lovecraft's pantheon.

"The Nameless City" (1921) was also based on a dream, one suggested by the concluding phrase of Lord Dunsany's ironically titled "The Probable Adventure of the Three Literary Men" (*The Book of Wonder*, 1912). In Dunsany the quest is always for literary beauty, and in this Arabian

Nights–style story with comic overtones, a tribe of nomads, having run out of stories, decides to hire thieves to steal a golden box reputed to contain literature of fabulous beauty. After some traveling through the allegorical landscape of the Dubious Land, the thieves find and open the box, which does contain beautiful literature beyond price, but they come to a bad end when the owner discovers their presence. The master thief Slith, leader of the quest, decides to leap into the black and *un*reverberate abyss rather than face the demonic owner of the box.

In Lovecraft's opinion, Dunsany with *The Book of Wonder* had entered into a period of doubt about his own solemnity and truth as an artist.[83] Perhaps as a consequence of this view of Dunsany, Lovecraft's spectral story of a nameless city that no man has seen or dared see has none of the comic overtones of Dunsany's story but only the chilling suggestiveness, the aura, of the last line about a fall into the abyss. Dunsany always gave beautiful and exotic names to his cities, but Lovecraft negates Dunsany's practice by not giving his ruined desert city a name. In his story the quest is for fear, not beauty. Lovecraft's abyss will be blacker than all blackness and full of reverberations, in the form of echoes of other writers of the supernatural, real and invented.

In the opening sequence, the wandering narrator comes upon the ancient moonlit city with its viewless aura (it is sunken beneath the sand; but pieces of it are sticking out, like the parts of a poorly buried corpse). At first the aura repels him, but as he recalls the stories of the nameless city, and especially the lines written about it by Abdul Alhazred, the mad poet, he decides to explore the ruins at dawn. Already the city has supernatural reverberations, and he feels it looking at him. He returns the gaze, establishing eye contact with the city. In Dunsany the experience of beauty is always held at a romantic distance. But two aesthetic factors develop and guide the experience of the aura of fear in this densely associative story and make it more proximate.

First of all, there is the narrator's feeling that the stones of the city are haunted by a spectral presence, embodied in the wind that blows out of the black orifice of a buried temple entrance. Aura and atmosphere are of course closely associated with the visual. But originally, aura was associated with emanations of the wind. The experience of aura is one of an atmosphere surrounding us, the medium that helps us breathe in a landscape (in other stories, like "The Shunned House," Lovecraft seems preoccupied with describing the odors of supernatural phenomena). Secondly, after the narrator has entered the temple and begun his descent into the abyss, he does so in total blackness after his lamp goes out, until he reaches the phosphorescent lower depths. He must experience this world through his sense of touch, which is a much more primal sense, one that underlies our contact with the world. His experience of the small, glass-and-wood coffins bearing the mummified bodies of the grotesque crocodile-like creatures is at first entirely haptic.

Furthermore, in this utter haptic blackness he begins to remember fragments of demoniac lore, including the phrase from Lord Dunsany's story, and recites a passage from the poet Thomas Moore describing the black reservoir of a witch's cauldron. Far from *un*reverberate, Lovecraft's black abyss has begun to reverberate and proliferate with meanings and sensations. Once the narrator reaches the visible areas, he is caught up in allegorical interpretation of the frescoed walls and ceilings. In brief, he interprets the crocodile-like creatures as allegorical figures representing the rise and decline of an ancient human civilization. I won't go into the details Lovecraft provides, but they make up almost half of Lovecraft's narrative. At any rate, aura and allegory begin to intertwine as we learn that the artists of the later period (i.e., the modern) have told (pictured) their story of the perfection of former times *spectrally*, that is, always by moonlight with a golden nimbus hovering over ruins. These decadent artists also had envisaged a strange new realm of paradise to which the race had hewn its way beyond the ruins. Just as in Benjamin's account, the aura appears as an important historical phenomenon in art only when it is beginning to recede.

After the narrator experiences as much lethal dread as he can stand in touching and viewing the relics of this (he thinks) lost human civilization, he begins to feel uneasy when he sees a puzzling picture of the historically decadent creatures engaging in human sacrifice. He soon begins to suspect that the creatures were real, not allegorical representations, and fancies that he too could become a sacrifice torn apart by nameless creatures, when a howling demonic wind comes of out the night and into the black abyss, slamming the great brazen door—which was figured in the pictures as the door to their paradise—that he has seen lying opened before him and from which the phosphorescent light emanated. Lovecraft's description of this wind, full of ghostly cursing and snarling, adds the final touches to the ironic experience of aura as horror, bringing it close to us. The last sentence of Lovecraft's spectral story, revising Dunsany's, tells of the reverberations swelling out into the world to hail the rising sun as the statue of the god Memnon, when broken, was said to do.

Modernity, as Benjamin pointed out, was busy creating new perceptions, if not new senses, through technology. He was particularly interested in the way in which modern architecture, while visual, relied also on the experience of the tactile to codify the social world and bring it into closer touch with human usages.[84] Among the changes Lovecraft was making in the aura of supernatural fiction was, as we saw in "The Nameless City," a shift away from the visual to the tactile and the aural (sound, voices, reverberation; there is no etymological connection between aura and aural, though music is perhaps the most atmospheric of all the arts). In Dunsany the distance guaranteed by vision preserves the aura of the beautiful object, and its position in the narrative world. But in Lovecraft touch can upset that order and create horror, as it does in "From Beyond." Although the experience of the aura in this story is still largely visual, what is seen nonetheless reveals a kind of obscene visual tactility, given the proximity to ordinary objects of the jelly-like creatures Tillinghast uncovers.

In Lovecraft's world of perceptions architectural images often supply the kind of visual tactility Benjamin is discussing, linking modern perception to antiquity, as is the case in "The Nameless City." In "The Outsider" (1921), a story based on escaping Gothic architectural spaces and the past, Lovecraft turns the allegorical gaze on himself. It's unclear exactly how autobiographical the hero of the story actually is intended to be, but this story has come to represent for many readers how Lovecraft saw himself. But the story has certain features having to do with the relationship between author and hero, self and other, that make any interpretation of it problematic. For the hero does not have, it seems, that excess of vision necessary for the creation of human identity. Living alone in a castle in which there are no mirrors, he cannot see himself from the outside, and since there are no others (except for a servant who is somewhat like him but distorted and decaying like the castle) for him to see, he cannot form or consummate the meaning of any other life. Until the shocking end of the story, he has no experience of what Bakhtin calls the *transgradient* moment in human relationships, in which we seek to see ourselves mirrored in others. Trying to imagine oneself from the outside without the help of others produces a peculiar emptiness and ghostliness in the experience of this outward image, and "an eerie frightening *solitariness*."[85]

The question then is not one of interpretation (Jungian archetype or Lacanian parable of the mirror stage or whatever) but whether or not Lovecraft as *author* creates a transgradient relationship to his hero, giving him enough "outside" experience to have a self, and I think it can be said that he does, in what way I will try to explain. Though that experience constitutes his hero as a horrifying outsider, it nonetheless gives him the gift of a self. The theme of spectrality is announced by the epigraph from Keats's *The Eve of St. Agnes*, in which the eloping hero and heroine glide away in an elfin storm, unseen and phantom-like, from the baron her father's castle, leaving him and his guests haunted. The problem of the other is mentioned (and italicized) at the end of the first paragraph. The hero still prefers his private and sere memories to any mention of otherness. What those memories are constitutes the subject matter of the story, which apparently Lovecraft wrote without a surplus of vision, only having the hero see himself in a mirror in the final version.

The hero tells his own story of his longing for light as he wanders in the dark moldering castle, which smells like a charnel house. He knows nothing of his origins, has never heard a human voice, and has learned what he knows of the human world from decaying books. More than anything else the hero desires to be a human among humans. Climbing up one of the castle towers, he finds a room full of what must be coffins, then sees the full moon shining in through a grating, an experience of luminosity that provides his first experience of auratic ecstasy. He experiences a reversal of perspective, however, when he discovers that he is not high up, as he had expected, but on level solid ground. As he explores this demonic world, he comes upon an ivied castle in a thickly wooded park. Hearing the sound of festive human voices, he enters through a low window, and is dismayed to find the others shocked by a noxious creature whose presence he sees beyond a gold-arched doorway. The others flee in horror, but he pursues the ghoulish shade of antiquity until he is in agonizing nearness to the carrion thing. He admits to being bewitched by the gaze of the other he pursues. As Lovecraft describes it, the arresting experience is specular and shocking. Recognition combines with misrecognition, for he does not fully realize that he is looking into a mirror at himself until he reaches out and *touches* the cold and unyielding polished surface, establishing contact with the alienated image.

This is the paradoxical and shocking moment when Lovecraft consummates his problematic hero, but perhaps not himself as author. In a situation in which author and hero are so intertwined, it is difficult to say exactly what Lovecraft's relationship to his hero is. But in the end Lovecraft is more than what we see in the mirror, just as his demonic hero is. For Bakhtin the mirror presents a spurious and spectral exterior; it does not encompass all of me; nor can it be the basis of authentic art, which requires the real experience of the social other to create an "outsidedness" of author and hero. As if to remind us of this fact, throughout the story Lovecraft denies his hero the experience of the social outside until this moment, and we have assumed, as he does, that he is human in appearance.

But in the end Lovecraft's hero is an outsider for us not so much because of his shocking ugliness in the mirror, the *other* that he refers to in the opening paragraph, but because he has finally been given the experience of the outside by spectral fictions, by the mocking yet friendly ghouls of Egyptian antiquity. The mocking implies a distance, while the friendliness implies a social closeness. It also implies a dialogic experience of language, one in which my words are given back to me in the tones and accents of another. At least in the narrator's account of his own experience, one notes a passage beyond the momentary traumatic shock effect of the mirror to a new duration or continuity of experience (*Erfahrung*) and also the romanticized wildness and freedom that he now feels among the ghouls, despite his continuing alienage from human beings. While the hero had a certain continuity in his quest for light before the shock of the mirror, this new continuity, mocking yet friendly, this broader freedom, can only be given by Lovecraft as the outside author/storyteller who was fascinated by ancient Egypt.[86]

"The Music of Erich Zann" (1921) is Lovecraft's attempt to create aura in verbal terms out of musical experience. At the time of writing the story, Lovecraft was apparently reading the pessimist philosopher Arthur Schopenhauer, whose account of experience asserted that "everything in life proclaims that earthly happiness is destined to be frustrated, or recognized as an illusion."[87] For Schopenhauer the enchantment of distance (i.e., aura) shows us paradises that only vanish like optical illusions, bringing disappointment. We become trapped, it seems, in false representations of the true nature of life, which is really just the endless blind striving of the will, maintaining itself by constant destruction. Music plays an important part in Schopenhauer's philosophy because it alone among the arts can give us a true and complete picture of the world through the emotions, not concepts or representations. Indeed, music acts directly on the will itself and can provide alteration of the emotions or even release from the will.[88]

Lovecraft found Schopenhauer's philosophy quite congenial to his own ideals, which at the time involved appreciating the world as an aesthetic object without too keenly feeling the pain of life.[89] His hero in this story experiences the pain of life, but not to the degree that Erich Zann the musician and artist does. There is sympathy for a fellow sufferer, but still distance. It's not clear how much of Schopenhauer's philosophy Lovecraft absorbed, and he claimed not to possess much musical knowledge (as the hero of his story does not), but the experiential pattern of the story uses both beautiful and weird (i.e., sublime or hostile) music in a Schopenhauerian fashion to give us a metaphysical glimpse of the way things really are. The narrator begins his story in frustration because he cannot find on any map the street in Paris where he once lived as an impoverished student of metaphysics. In his memory, which he admits was damaged by the environment in which he lived, the Rue d'Auseil was located in a neighborhood of industrial decay. Smoke from factories perpetually shut out the sun, and an evil-smelling river flowed through the area (creating Lovecraft's first industrial landscape). The street and the houses are themselves distorted and angular in an expressionistic way, and the inhabitants are all very old. Why would the narrator want to return to such a place? To hear again the music of Erich Zann, whose weirdness still haunts him.

Most of the story has to do with the difficult task of providing an atmospheric verbal account of Zann's haunting music, which as I mentioned has the double quality of both the beautiful and the sublime. Indeed, in Lovecraft's story our musical experience spans the entire range of the sublime Schopenhauer mentions, from a single mocking note far away to an up-close-and-personal screaming blackness.[90] The man himself turns out to be a small, grotesque, and satyr-like figure, a mute who plays a Renaissance viol like the cello in the upper apartment of the building in which the narrator lives. The narrator first imagines that Erich Zann's world of beauty must lie in some cosmos far from human suffering, but eventually discovers that the beautiful music is a defense against a deeper, infinitely distant but terribly demonic music that actually plays him as if he were a puppet, and which emanates, aura-like (a malevolent wind figures prominently in the story), from behind a curtained window. The narrator admits to an odd wish to open the curtain, and to look at what he expects to be a broad panorama of moonlit roofs and city lights. What he eventually discovers, however, is hardly visual at all, but the shock of black and limitless space. There is motion and music, but no semblance to anything on earth, an allegory perhaps of what the inhuman Schopenhauerian will would be like without the ruses of human art.

At 12,000 words, "Herbert West—Reanimator" (1921–1922) could with some justification be called a novelette. Although the circumstances of its publication were internalized into the form of the storytelling—it was published serially and thus contains materials summarizing the previous events in each of its six sections—it nonetheless approaches the form of the novel through its spirit of irony. Because of the length, I think it fair to call the story an early attempt by Lovecraft to explore the longer narrative possibilities of the weird tale.

As for the novel's difference from the short story, Benjamin remarks that the novel's concern with the "meaning of life" is focused on the death of the characters, either literal or figurative (the end of the novel). Indeed, meaning only emerges from their deaths, in remembrance. Novels are like logs in a fire. The reader wants to devour and consume the life of the characters contained within it, to share their experience of death, preferably their actual ones, and looks for clues from the characters as to how they understand death as waiting for them. As Benjamin puts it, "What draws a reader to a novel is the hope of warming his shivering life with a death he reads about."[91]

Now, both the hero's, West's, inner quest for meaning and the outer or biographical form of "Herbert West—Reanimator" given by the narrator are about death and the reanimation of the dead, so in Benjamin's terms of experience, this fact alone should make it at least a quasi-novel. But I am going to argue that because of Lovecraft's pervasive irony, his text, while offering lurid thrills, does not allow us to warm up to the deaths of the characters in quite the consumerist fashion Benjamin describes. Shock was central to Lovecraft's aesthetic, but I think it entirely possible, given the circumstances of composition, that in this story Lovecraft was working through some of his own concerns about being received as a commercial (and therefore decadent) purveyor of shocks.[92]

The narrator, a close friend and collaborator of West's at Miskatonic Medical School in Arkham and later, opens his biographical account of Herbert West by alluding to his death (which, to create atmosphere, he calls a sinister disappearance), and the whole nature of his life-work, which is shocking. These are clues that lead us deeper into the meaning of the story of Herbert West's life. Now that the spell of Herbert West's life has been broken, however, the narrator asserts that memories and possibilities are ever more hideous than reality. On second reading we realize that the narrator is alluding to the fact that West or some of the reanimated dead he created may still be lurking around, *at least in part*. At any rate, the narrator describes himself at the end of the story as either a madman or a murderer, so he too partakes of the problematic nature of the hero of the novel. I'm going to propose an allegorical reading in which Lovecraft uses both his narrator and his character to comment on the decadence of the West in supposing that science alone can give meaning to life.

West is soon described as someone completely opposed to the ideological and humanistic limitations of respectable medical science, as embodied by the dean of the medical school, Dr. Allan Halsey, who spends his time caring for the sick and the dying of the Arkham community. Among his intellectual sins are a streak of custom-bound Puritanism, anti-Darwinism, and anti-Nietzscheism. West, by contrast, is a zealous scientist who looks at human beings in purely mechanistic terms, and thinks it possible to reanimate a corpse if the proper chemistry can be discovered and he can get his hands on absolutely fresh specimens.

In terms of the experience of modernity, both West and the narrator as medical students are involved with what Benjamin would call the decay of the aura, in this case associated with the human body. The special aura that we feel in the presence of a dead body need not refer to anything supernatural; a realistic writer such as Norman Mailer could describe unforgettably, as in *The Naked and the Dead*, a cone of silence around the bodies of soldiers killed in combat. The narrator, while admiring West's strident materialism, admits to feeling certain remnants of the awe traditionally associated with corpses, but indicates he has none of the traditional fears of graveyards or grave robbing. Yet Lovecraft has them both rediscover those fears and become haunted by a spectral past as the story progresses in a series of six increasingly hideous instances of reanimation, ending in an attack staged from a graveyard.

Each of these episodes is a small masterpiece of Lovecraft's ghoulishly fertile imagination playing with his own materialism but describing it in supernatural terms, holding them both in ironic tension as the story rediscovers the deep connection in Western thought between scientific experiment and experience. Unlike the story based on mood or atmosphere, the events in this story seem to matter more to Lovecraft. Indeed, our experience is one in which nothing ever seems to turn out exactly as West had planned. To take just one example, the good Dr. Halsey is reanimated during a typhoid epidemic, which turns him into a monster that murders seventeen people before he is caught and confined to Sefton Asylum. But later he is rescued by West's nemesis, who, it turns out, is also another one of his victims. Traumatic repetition is the narrative model Lovecraft follows, but with grotesque and demonic overtones, as we will see.

Despite its basis in materialistic science, the story is nonetheless haunted by a widespread theme in supernatural fiction: the awe at what might be told by one returning from the dead. Indeed, as West's depredations continue, more and more of the reanimated dead continue to reappear in the narrative, accompanied by their stories. Even the narrator notes that one of West's wartime experiments was ironic because the victim, a certain Major Sir Eric Moreland Clapham-Lee, a great surgeon who helped West get his commission, ends up having his body reanimated separately from his head. He reappears later in the story as the military leader of the reanimated dead, carrying his head in a black box but wearing an expressionless wax face of radiant beauty, the embodiment of the grotesque deformation of our world by materialistic science. It is he who rescues Halsey (humanistic medicine) from the insane asylum.

As the story progresses, the narrator increasingly tends to cast the events of West's life in the language and rhetoric of the weird tale, so much so that the story takes on allegorical overtones. Early on, Halsey was described as the embodied demon-soul of the plague itself, and now the fate of Herbert West is defined in terms that suggest fate, as a nameless titan claw reaches out from the past to seize him. It isn't long before the narrator is calling West a decadent, and comparing him to Baudelaire, who was well known for his use of allegorical figures. West now lives in a Boston house, near a cemetery dating from the colonial period, Lovecraft's symbolic location of the continuous culture stream (*Erfahrung*). The narrator makes it clear that West lives near the cemetery not for practical reasons (the dead there would be too old to be used in his experiments anyway), but for symbolic and aesthetic reasons. He still maintains a laboratory, but now experiments with reanimating body parts for his own amusement (in clear contrast to the warnings of Mary Shelley's *Frankenstein* about science without responsibility). The narrator clearly links the growing fragmentation of West's work to his experiences/experiments in World War I as a surgeon. The description of West's wartime laboratory creates the limit experience of madness for the narrator, who notes the simultaneous presence of the classified charnel things produced by modern warfare and the bubbling witch's cauldron of West's chemicals.

In a final irony, West is judged a degenerate by his former friend because the fear of his specimens has gotten the best of him, he has forgotten his earlier zeal for prolonging life, and he has forgone the gruesome thrill he could have had in uncovering centuries-old grave secrets by ordering the basement masonry of his house left intact and plastered over. West's complex nature reflects Lovecraft's own. The world of science and the shocks of lived experience need to be met with continuous experience, which comes late or not at all to West (his name and character suggest the contradictions of Western culture in Lovecraft's view). The story ends as various reanimated bodies, in a grotesquely heterogeneous horde, dig their way into West's Boston home stone by stone, returning to tear him to pieces. These charnel images of shocking fragmentation coming through the graveyard of the past constitute Lovecraft's allegorical response to a scientific modernity that has forgotten the long experience of the culture stream.

Many critics consider "The Rats in the Walls" (1923) to be the finest product of Lovecraft's first decade of writing. Certainly it combines the theme of hereditary degeneration and the haunted Gothic ruin beneath which lurks a subterranean grotto (source of the grotesque) with a narrator's descent into madness in ways that seem fully integrated. Indeed, despite some geographical and historical gaffs, everything seems aesthetically motivated by the language and history given in the story itself. In terms of experience, it makes especially effective use of atmospheric spectral sound that accompanies the movements of the rats in the walls—which only the narrator and his cat can hear—to create a sense of lurking cosmic fear. What is more, the story is densely embedded with allusions to English-American history, as well as to other stories, legends, and lore of the supernatural both real and invented, a technique that Lovecraft would use extensively in the novel-length *The Case of Charles Dexter Ward* (1927). Lovecraft also alludes to his other stories, such as "Nyarlathotep." We begin to feel that we are in the presence of a master storyteller weaving a tale of spectral horror, as Lovecraft very deftly sketches in the narrative background.

The story begins with the restoration by a man named Delapore of Exham Priory, his long abandoned ancestral home in England, in 1923. His first name is not given, but he describes himself as a stolid wealthy Yankee, a product of the grayness of business life in Massachusetts. Our narrator is a manufacturer, the first of Lovecraft's narrators to be from the capitalist class. The main reason or motivation for the restoration is the loss of family tradition, which happened during the Civil War. It turns out that an envelope containing the family history of the de la Poers, which had been handed down from father to son for generations, was burned in the destruction of Carfax (Lovecraft alludes to Bram Stoker's *Dracula*), their home on the banks of the James River in Virginia. The narrator was himself present at this burning, so we know that he is now elderly. Interestingly, Delapore's son Alfred reverses this order of family tradition by writing letters to his father from England while serving in aviation during World War I, telling him the wild legendary stories about the family that he learned from Captain Edward Norrys, who lived near the ancestral home. The son returns from the war a maimed invalid, and dies two years later.

As for Exham Priory itself, this ruin standing in picturesque desertion for centuries was much loved by architects and antiquarians for its unique combination of architectural styles, but hated by the local countryfolk, who suffered under the oppression of the de la Poers, who had a reputation for witchcraft, murder, and other cruelties. Indeed, the narrator has a difficult time collecting and piecing together village traditions since the locals still dread the aristocratic family. But Norrys helps him, and soon they have compiled a detailed history of the priory. I won't go into the details of these narratives (we learn too that a cousin of the narrator went among negroes and became a voodoo priest after he returned from the Mexican War of 1846–1848), but they begin to point toward a secret witch cult at the priory in existence since the time of the Druids. Most vivid is the epic story of the rats under the command of the de la Poers originating from medieval times, which Lovecraft derived from S. Baring-Gould's *Curious Myths of the Middle Ages* (1869).[93] A whole separate cycle of myths is associated with the rat army. Myths, ballads, legends, fireside tales—a veritable panoply of legendry—now surrounds the narrator, who as he pushes stubbornly on toward completing the restoration feels assailed by the lore he has collected in an attempt to fill in the gap left by the destroyed letter. Of course, as modern man he is completely skeptical of the spectral lore he has assembled in search of real family history. He find this lore exceedingly picturesque, a term that appears several times in the narrative, and whose connection to real class history I will comment on in a moment.

When de la Poer (who atavistically returns to the old spelling of his name) moves into the castle, the "supernatural" events begin to happen. His cats are extraordinarily sensitive to mood and pick up emanations (i.e., aura) from the old stonework. What is more, he begins to have terrifying dreams of a demon swineherd in a filthy subterranean world beneath the castle. Sensitive to atmosphere, he too hears the verminous slithering of the rats, now grown gigantic in imagination, but no one else does. In the design of the new tapestry hanging on the walls of his bedroom he sees, allegorically, a dance of death. The second half of the story is concerned with de la Poer's attempt, with the help of his friend Norrys and invited experts and eminent archaeologists, to get to the literal "bottom" of what is causing the noises. It takes the form of a descent into the subterranean world beneath the castle, but not before he has a dream of a Roman feast like that depicted in the *Satyricon* of Petronius.

In that story Trimalchio, a nouveau riche businessman, hosts a vulgarly lavish banquet for his many guests. Though fragmentary, the *Satyricon* is acknowledged as the first picaresque narrative and one of the sources of the modern satiric grotesque.[94] In picaresque narratives of the classical period a rogue character typically tells the story of his travels and adventures through a wide spectrum of society, conveying his experiences in the contemporary world.[95] I cannot help but think that Lovecraft, one of the finest writers of the modern grotesque, in alluding to Petronius in his character's dream, is inviting us to take up a satiric perspective on the efforts of this wealthy capitalist to restore the aristocratic past, and especially his efforts to assemble a group of savants (including a psychic named Thornton, who later faints at the sight of the grotto and real history; Lovecraft detested occultists). The capitalist, it may be recalled, had found the stories of real historical suffering under the oppression of the de la Poers picaresque (i.e., colorful lies not to be believed). In the end of the story, he gets his comeuppance, experiencing firsthand the remains of that demonic orgy the peasants will not forget.

The central features of the modern satiric grotesque are evident in the ending, and particularly in the degradation of the hero and in the dislocation of language. The shocking thing, of course, is that de la Poer's family banquet turns out to be a cannibalistic history of class predation on a previously unheard-of scale. The ghoulish grotto piles up horror upon horror until the narrator discovers among the bones a family signet ring that identifies the perpetrators of these atrocities as the de la Poers. The grotto is not fully explored, but before he goes mad, de la Poer claims that the eldritch scurrying of the rats is leading him on a quest for new horrors, and toward the deeper subterranean experience of Nyarlathotep, the mad faceless god.

The narrator, who is found eating the body of Norrys—a member of the landowner class—descends into madness in a passage moving backward through earlier and earlier historical periods of language, and from English to Latin to Celtic curses to subhuman noises, as it moves forward in time to the present. In one fragment of this delirium, the rats are finally identified with historical forces, as de la Poer wonders madly why the spectral rats should not eat him since the war ate his son (though Alfred was an aviator, rats were a well-known feature of life in the trenches during World War I). De la Poer is confined to an insane asylum, with Thornton in the next room. The last sentence is one of the most chilling endings to a horror story ever written, as the spectral and still unheard rats become real in the language of a madman, who tries to blame his cannibalism on them.

I mentioned above that Lovecraft's 1922 visit to Salem and Marblehead, and his experience of the historical trace, marked a turning point in his aesthetics. "The Unnamable" (1923) is largely a self-conscious working out of the historical and spectral implications of the trace. Although there is no clear dividing line between trace and aura, which still continued to be very important to him in his creation of atmosphere, Lovecraft develops in this story the implications of the trace as something that (we think) we can take possession of because of its nearness to us. By contrast, aura is always implicated in the experience of distance in time and space, and preserves, through the gaze, the position and elevated status of the aesthetic object in the world. Perhaps it is best to think of them as two poles of supernatural experience, one of distance, the other of a fearful proximity, between which Lovecraft moved.

These two poles of supernatural experience are represented in the story by two characters in debate with each other over the merits of supernatural fiction. One is a writer of supernatural fiction named Carter, who is the first-person narrator; the other is a high school principal named Joel Manton, who represents bourgeois insensitivity and unresponsiveness to supernatural fiction. Carter has recently published a story called "The Attic Window." Banned in the South but ironically underappreciated in New England, the story is the subject of their debate concerning the merits of supernatural fiction. As it happens, however, in this debate Carter is much less a believer in the supernatural and more of a materialist than Manton is, an irony that ideological analysis of the class contradictions in the story should not fail to note.

The debate takes place, appropriately enough, in the ancient graveyard of Arkham (based on Salem). Much of Lovecraft's own theory of the aura and of the trace, mixed with Arthur Machen's *Hieroglyphics* (1902), a revised collection of essays written in defense of the grotesque as a form of literary ecstasy that Lovecraft had been reading, finds its way into the story.[96] I cannot enumerate briefly all of the details of the debate, but with regard to ideological positions, Manton in stolid realist fashion claims that the writer has no proper business speculating about the suggestive and the unnamable, but must confine himself to facts and correct theological doctrines. To Carter's understanding the bourgeois mentality, with its ruling out of all that cannot be experienced by the average citizen (including dramatic recombinations of images that might have grown hackneyed), is a clear flaw in the logical, practical mind. Carter is quick to point out and mock the supernatural beliefs and superstitions Manton holds to be possible on the basis of religious belief in the spirit, which all have to do with aura or vision manifested in such afterlife spectral phenomena as the appearance of faces in windows long stared through or the appearance of the dead person in distant places. Here Lovecraft is probably satirizing the views of spiritualists regarding the presence of spectral substances on earth.

Lovecraft's account of Carter's story "The Attic Window" turns out to have grounding (if that is the word) in the historical trace. The story is linked to an actual story, of a supernatural beast with a blemished eye mentioned in the writings of Cotton Mather, but concerns a boy who went mad in 1793 after entering a shunned house to examine the traces of the supernatural suspected to be there. The boy had gone to look at the windows where the beast was confined because of the tales of things seen behind them. Is this not the apotheosis of the unnamable, the narrator asks? The beast, first of all, is given spectral reality in the tales told about it, which must be based on some experience. To add further verisimilitude Carter will claim to be in possession of a diary describing an attack of the beast leaving scars—traces—on one of his ancestors, as well as to actually have visited the house himself and disposed of the bones of a horned creature in the very graveyard in which they are sitting. The creature is in Lovecraft/Carter's materialist vision a creation of the human mind swept up in the historical witchcraft hysteria, but he asks us, are not these grotesque psychic emanations of the human brain in tales and legends the apotheosis of the unnamable? For they have taken on a spectral character of representation that still haunts us historically today.

As twilight descends on the graveyard, Manton becomes more and more distraught as the narrator tells him that he has already seen, but not recognized, the demonic glass window of his story, in a house near where they are sitting, though significantly it is now just a frame, the house having been windowless for a hundred years or more. Aura is that frame, the frame of the traditional supernatural story, together with the atmosphere of the historical graveyard surrounding them. Soon after this revelation an overpowering wind blows from the house, rendering them unconscious. They wake up in the hospital. Manton is covered with contusions and welts, and the print of a split hoof, traces of his contact with the beast. Significantly, however, when Carter asks him whether or not the experience *was like* the traces left on his body, Manton denies the connection with such a traditional representation of evil, claiming that although there was a blemished eye his experience was that of the *unnamable*, of a thousand shapes of horror.

Having discussed Lovecraft's fictionalized treatise on supernatural fiction, I must leave off my detailed account of individual stories and speak in more summary fashion of the experience of the supernatural in Lovecraft's later fiction.[97] It seems to me that much of what Lovecraft later wrote, as excellent as it often is, makes no dramatic changes to the aesthetic of aura and trace I have outlined here, but instead amplifies and plays these two poles of experience off of each other, trying to find extended ways to get them both to work in the same story. One of those ways, the most important one, is Lovecraft's increasing use of realistic techniques of description, which bears upon the experience of the historical trace. The traditional storyteller would have been able to use the tradition in which he was embedded, but Lovecraft, as a problematic individual with intellectual roots in modern science but whose real flair was for the fantastic, would have to discover his own narrative models. For Lovecraft, it's as if narrative had to be reinvented as one long, extended exercise in atmospheric effects and amplified shock.

"The Colour out of Space" (1927) is really a traveler's tale masquerading as science fiction. The narrator, a surveyor for a new reservoir to be built west of Arkham, relates the stories of those who experienced the deformation of natural images of the New England rural landscape by an unholy iridescence emanating from a fallen piece, itself vestigial, of the outside, which does not obey the known laws of science. Lovecraft creates a growing sense of unease at the transformation of Nature, as traces of the old remain beneath the new spectral phenomena (610). In addition to science fiction, the story has overtones of the dream world of the fairy tale and the ecological disaster story, something that J. G. Ballard would do again, to great effect, in *The Crystal World*.

The Case of Charles Dexter Ward (1927) has a hero who, like Lovecraft himself, in his youth is fond of dreamy meditation on the spectral qualities of the Providence landscape (496). His experience of the historical trace, however, which he thinks he possesses, turns out to be one in which an evil ancestor, the wizard Joseph Curwen, actually takes possession of his life, if not entirely his mind. The tale is masterfully told by a narrator who, detective-like, carefully weighs all of the various narrative accounts of Ward's increasingly bizarre behavior according to their relationship to the truth of the matter. It turns out that Curwen made the money for his alchemical experiments (once again in Lovecraft supernatural experience is closely linked with experiment) as a shipping entrepreneur during colonial times. Lovecraft vividly re-creates with historical materialist verisimilitude the period details of language and society based on trade, with attention to the economics of the period.

Lovecraft was uncertain about the aesthetic success and authenticity of *The Dream-Quest of Unknown Kadath* (1926–1927). Thematically it was an attempt by Lovecraft to combine the naive wonder of the fairy tale with Baudelairian decadence (i.e., the allegory of shock in Benjaminian terms). As someone who is arguing that the fantastic offers us a greater understanding of modernity—the experience of being modern—than realism allows, I should admire this text, and, despite its obvious aesthetic flaws and adolescent immaturities, I do. Lovecraft understood that the short story is the best form for fantasy, but nonetheless wrote what he called a picaresque chronicle of impossible adventures in dreamland, thereby acknowledging both its flaws and its strengths at the same time.[98] But to my mind the narrative has a quality of *Erfahrung* (the completed experience of the journey), despite the manner in which it rapidly piles up sensations and imagistic shock after imagistic shock: gugs, ghouls, night-gaunts (who never smile because they have no faces), and ghasts and gods as well, all appearing in prolific quantities, not to mention the obscene fungi that seem to sprout up everywhere in Lovecraft's universe. The dynamism of these images alone is enough to awaken oneiric reading.[99]

They constitute, I suppose, what Lovecraft meant by the decadence of the narrative. But in so doing he at least tries to extend in longer narrative form the fragmented experience of modernity. Lovecraft thought the narrative inauthentic, but the adventures of his problematic hero Randolph Carter (both a rogue decadent living among ghouls and a naive traveler open to wonder), searching for the gods whom he believes can give meaning to his life, reflect, as I said in the introduction to this study, the loss of aura in modernity in ways that seem to me authentic. Heavily saturated with Dunsany's experience of beautiful semblance, only made more poignant since it seems infinitely deferred (409–10), Carter's quest for Unknown Kadath is a dialectical quest through demonic realms for the meaning of his life. I say "dialectical" because he finds the concrete meaning of Kadath in his historical childhood in Boston only after a series of reversals, starting with a complex interpretive allegory given him by the messenger god Nyarlathotep.

This trickster god, full of capricious humor, tells Carter that in order for him to return to his real sunset city the gods must first leave it. That is why he has been unable to find the dream Kadath that he thought so full of immanent meanings, but which is actually a symbol and relic of bygone times. Clearly, he prefers allegory to symbolism. Further, Carter must tell the Great Ones a tale of their true home in dream Kadath, so that they will become homesick with nostalgia. In other words he must bring human modernity, i.e., homesickness, to earth's gods.[100] However, it ensues that Nyarlathotep pointed out to Carter the means of securing his marvelous sunset city only to mock him. Carter is barely rescued from the abyss of Azathoth by something the god had not anticipated: the strength of his memories reminds him that he is only dreaming.

It's hard to know exactly how this story fits in with Lovecraft's purported Cthulhu Mythos, or how seriously Lovecraft himself took his mythology. Not surprisingly, among Lovecraft's gods Nyarlathotep has been difficult to interpret, since he appears in so many different forms. But the internal coherence of the Cthulhu Mythos, which seems to have been a device Lovecraft invented under Dunsany's influence to introduce cosmic fear into his stories, is not my direct concern in this study anyway. To me Nyarlathotep is an embodiment of the author's irony toward his hero's subjective search for meaning, since in the novel irony is a force that counters subjectivity.[101] Likewise, Carter's outer biographical form is problematic and has had to be reconstructed from the stories in which he appears. At the time Lovecraft died, his hero was still alive, though not, it seems, in human form.[102]

At any rate, soon after the real shock of the stock market crash in October 1929, Lovecraft was announcing that prose realism paradoxically intertwined with fantastic vision was the basis for everything of importance he was now writing.[103] He had begun thinking too about the role of economic factors in culture and civilization, but still held that race and civilization were more important, at one point exploding angrily at "Marxolaters," who argued that changes in the economic base would necessarily (and immediately) create corresponding shifts in aesthetics.[104] He was apparently unaware of forms of Marxism other than the vulgar sort that affirm the relative autonomy of art (i.e., the Western tradition I am using here).

At the Mountains of Madness (1931) does not reflect the Depression directly, but it does "explain away" the Dunsanian aura of distance and beauty by revealing it to be produced by natural effects science could explain. Indeed, the whole of this lengthy story is about the unveiling of the materialist traces of an ancient alien civilization in Antarctica, and the fear that what was revealed there had great potential for cultural shock. The major shock in the story is Lovecraft's de-centering mention that these bio-shaping aliens created us as a kind of jest, and are also the source of other earth mythologies. But the spectral magic of Dunsanian conjuration is given its due in the story's title, and Dunsany haunts this story even as the city of marvels becomes a tortuous labyrinth.[105]

Indeed, when the explorers first fly over mountains, as if in homage to Dunsany, who is explicitly mentioned, they experience an ice mirage of opalescent beauty reflecting a Cyclopean city of unknown architecture (729), which at this point they have not verified as real. As we saw in the previous chapter, "opalescence" is a key word in Dunsany, associated with the magic aura of narrative possibility and the promise of adventurous expectancy. At greater length Lovecraft could afford to repeat the experience of opalescence several times (745–46, 756, 761, 778, 803).[106]

Contrasting with this experience of tantalizing distance is the actual reading of the historical traces left by the alien race in the pictorial murals of their homes and public structures. A lengthy interpretive experience accompanies the main armature of narrative action. It has some of the qualities of visual tactility that the narrator of "The Nameless City" experiences in reading the bas-reliefs of his sunken Dunsanian city, only on a much more epic scale, which gives the experience of continual shock duration and allegorical significance. The bas-reliefs tell the story of the degeneracy of a great alien civilization in artistic forms that postmodernity would recognize, that is, palimpsest and hybrid parody (795).

"The Shadow over Innsmouth" (1931) integrates the experience of aura and the historical trace with an account of the economic base. Written during the Great Depression, though set in 1927, Lovecraft's Innsmouth (inspired by visiting the town of Newburyport, Massachusetts), while once prosperous, has sunken into shabby decay. It is even shunned by its neighboring towns, especially Arkham, whence came the narrator's ancestors. The story revolves around the discovery by the narrator on his sightseeing tour of New England (motivated by genealogical and antiquarian interests as well) of lingering signs of fabulous wealth reputed to belong to the Marsh refinery in Innsmouth. His subsequent visit to the town reveals that everyone seems to have repulsive fish-like traits, called "the Innsmouth look" by outsiders, and soon he is hearing tales of what lingering alien (if not supernatural) forces still haunt the town.

In the narrative accounts of Innsmouth the narrator hears, one from an outsider, a ticket agent, and the other from a half-crazed but still human inhabitant of the town, Zadok Allen (whose story the narrator calls a crude allegory), there is a good deal of economic history of the town. This is not incidental, because just how the Marsh family acquired its wealth is the basis of the story. Indeed, Captain Obed Marsh and his demonic deal with fish-frog-like creatures of the South Seas in the mid-1840s, for their precious metal jewelry in exchange for human sacrifices and interbreeding rights with humans, supports our entire experience of the story. The economic narrative imbues everything we encounter in the story, objects and people, social relationships and religious institutions (the Esoteric Order of Dagon), with the aura of the weird. This integration of economic history into a tale marks the appearance of Lovecraft's new concern with the role of economic conditioning in aesthetic and ideological matters.

The first of these signs is a tiara held by the Newburyport Historical Society. Lovecraft describes with loving detail the aura of this object, and the mood of disturbing fascination it creates in the narrator (813). This encounter is a plainly auratic experience in Benjamin's terms, with the object enframed in museum-like perceptions, but with the addition of a strange trace of a tradition of manufacture that awakens the narrator's curiosity. As we get further into the story, we find the inevitable appearance of the grotesque in Lovecraft's description of Joe Sargent, the bus driver who takes the narrator to Newburyport on a rickety old bus (815–16). The narrator's experience of the town is beset by a persistent olfactory disgust at the fishy smells that permeate the atmosphere and his paranoid feeling that he is constantly being watched, both of these being aspects of the town's aura.

The high point of the narrative has to be the harrowing night spent in the local hotel, his perilous escape, and his eluding of the malignant saraband of creatures pursuing him (852–53). Once again Lovecraft provides us, in the duration of the parade of hybrid horrors, with an experience that lengthens out shock and that the narrator cannot resist looking at, until he faints. Aura and horror combine in this grotesque experience, which realizes Zadok's tale. The final shock, however, comes when we learn that the narrator is related, through his mother, to the Marsh family and to these very creatures. One of the clues or traces of that ancestry is the unbearably extravagant jewelry belonging to his mysterious great-grandmother bearing unmistakable signs of its origins in the Marsh horde. The narrator now has non-frightening dreams in which he is one of the hybrid creatures. In the mirror he notices that he has acquired the "Innsmouth look." This pleases him, and the story ends with him making plans to join the Deep Ones in their legendary city beneath the waves. Economics in the last instance does not determine the hero's fate, but heredity, race, and the culture stream do.

"The Shadow over Innsmouth" is simply one of the finest stories Lovecraft ever composed as a weird storyteller. It richly intertwines his interests in antiquarianism and family genealogy—those handmaidens of the trace—with mythical references to his other stories (Dagon, Cthulhu, among others). Realistic and localized in its economic details, it is still recognizably a traveler's tale of far-off marvelous realms (though in parodic form).

The final stories that Lovecraft composed are increasingly spectral and haunted, the word "shadow" in their titles giving us an indication of their haunted qualities. Among these, "The Shadow out of Time" (1934–1935) is perhaps the most significant in terms of Lovecraft's aesthetic of the aura. I mentioned above, in my outline of Lovecraft's aesthetics based on his letter to Woodburn Harris, that Lovecraft thought the experience of involuntary memory to be central to his notion of aura. Indeed, his characters, from "The Outsider" onward (and even Jervas Dudley in "The Tomb," 1917), always seem to find themselves tantalizingly reminded of something by an object in the present that stirs their inner depths, and they gradually begin to recall the memory (the tiara has this function for the narrator of "The Shadow Over Innsmouth"). Now, the experience of involuntary memory was central also to Benjamin's argument that Proust in his eight-volume work had restored the figure of the storyteller to modernity because of the overwhelming aura of continuous and full experience (*Erfahrung*), in which the gaze is returned from the object, these kinds of memories had for Proust, as opposed to the more static and detached gaze of the voluntary memory of things, which presented themselves more like photographs.[107]

I cannot say for certain that there was any direct influence of Proust on Lovecraft, but he thought Proust to be the greatest modern novelist, and by 1933 he had read *Within a Budding Grove* and had plans to read *The Guermantes Way*, which had just been published by the Modern Library.[108] At any rate, "The Shadow out of Time" deals with both amnesia and auratic memories experienced by its hero, Nathaniel Wingate Peaslee, a professor of political economy at Miskatonic University. The story is science fictional and involves aliens who have perfected a technique of mind exchange to study other cultures in different times, both past and present. The idea of *exchange* is central to the story. Ironically, one of these aliens takes over Peaslee's mind while he is lecturing on economics in 1908; his own personality and memories do not return until 1913, when he thinks he is still lecturing on economics. Of course the aliens have given him amnesia to protect their activities, but Peaslee begins to have involuntary memories of the time he spent in the archives of an alien world, writing of his own planet. It is the experience of these strange auratic memories that leads Peaslee on a quest in search of the aliens (called the Great Race), which ends in the archaeological discovery of their ancient base in Australia, where he finds proof of his experience in a document written in his own hand.

The basic mind-exchange scenario was a familiar theme of science fiction at the time, but what Lovecraft does with the theme, in using it to explode the ordinary limits of human time and in describing the incredibly rich and detailed range of uncanny mental phenomena—dreams, hallucinations, mnemonic constraints—produced by the exchange and now contained in Peaslee's disturbing memories, goes well beyond the limits of most pulp science fiction in the 1930s. Of course Peaslee, a true Lovecraftian hero in search of objective knowledge at all costs, becomes an avid reader of cosmic myths, legends, and tales, especially the ones that seem to convey experiences similar to his own. He is soon reading all of the various pseudobiblia invented by Lovecraft and contained in the library of Miskatonic University and elsewhere in the world (960–61).

There is perhaps no exact equivalent in Proust of Peaslee's experience of finding that his dreams and memories have a basis in shocking reality or, during the sequence involving the archaeological dig in Australia, of the trace as the *illusion of memory* (979). And the spectral shadow of these memories does seem to fall on him from fearful *outside sources* (949). But nonetheless Peaslee is a hero in search of duration, and in conclusion I would say that in these longer stories of the late 1920s and the 1930s Lovecraft found novelistic ways to extend his aesthetic of aura, shock, and the problematic hero to the cosmic level, by linking them to his ramifying mythology and by giving them the duration and aesthetic coherence of long experience (*Erfahrung*) that Benjamin associated with the storyteller.

NOTES

1. Lucien Goldmann, *Towards a Sociology of the Novel* (London: Tavistock, 1975), 8.
2. Kenneth W. Faig Jr., *The Parents of Howard Phillips Lovecraft* (West Warwick, RI: Necronomicon Press, 1990), 6–8.
3. For a historical account of Lovecraft's library, see S. T. Joshi, *Lovecraft's Library, A Catalogue*, 3rd ed. (New York: Hippocampus Press, 2012).
4. H. P. Lovecraft, *Selected Letters*, edited by August Derleth, Donald Wandrei, and James Turner (Sauk City, WI: Arkham House, 1965–1976), 3.366–70. In the early 1930s Lovecraft wrote several long autobiographical letters acknowledging the role that *economic decline* played in causing his melancholy moods. For his nostalgia, see 3.317–18, 405.
5. Lovecraft, *Selected Letters*, 3.189–90.
6. Lovecraft, *Selected Letters*, 3.64, 79–80.
7. Lovecraft, *Selected Letters*, 5.124.
8. See the essays collected in *H. P. Lovecraft: Four Decades of Criticism*, edited by S. T. Joshi (Athens: Ohio University Press, 1980), but especially Fritz Leiber, "A Literary Copernicus," 50–62.
9. L. Sprague de Camp, *Lovecraft: A Biography* (Garden City, NY: Doubleday, 1975), 423.
10. For Lovecraft and popular culture, see Andrew Migliore and John Strysik, *The Lurker in the Lobby: A Guide to the Cinema of H. P. Lovecraft* (Portland, OR: Night Shade, 2006), and Jason Colavito, *The Cult of Alien Gods: H. P. Lovecraft and Extraterrestrial Pop Culture* (Amherst, NY: Prometheus, 2005).

11. H. P. Lovecraft, "In Defence of Dagon," in *Miscellaneous Writings*, edited by S. T. Joshi (Sauk City, WI: Arkham House, 1995), 147–48.

12. Personal aura as a manifestation of the spiritual realm was one of the favorite topics of the theosophists, whose writings Lovecraft was familiar with, though of course he was not persuaded by their arguments. Similarly, it appears that Benjamin's materialistic definition of the aura as a widespread and changing phenomenon in modern culture was a direct attack on the theosophists and their more esoteric notions of clairvoyant vision. As opposed to the notion of emanating rays, Benjamin suggested that the aura could be found in a sort of ornamental halo. See Walter Benjamin, "Hashish, Beginning of 1930," in *Selected Writings*, Volume 2, Part 1, edited by Michael W. Jennings (Cambridge, MA: Harvard University Press, 1999), 327–28. Lovecraft, an avowed anti-modernist, was fond of the decorative in the arts for the associational and symbolic meanings it could provide. His stories are full of architectural bas-reliefs and other forms of pictorial carving, hieroglyphs and such, which provide a context of storytelling (see especially *At the Mountains of Madness*). For a non-spiritualist account of aura later taken over by spiritualists, see W. J. Kilner, *The Aura* (New York: Samuel Weiser, 1973), originally published in 1911, under the title *The Human Atmosphere*.

13. De Camp, *Lovecraft: A Biography*, 445–47. De Camp places the emphasis on Lovecraft's code of gentlemanly behavior as a defense against schizophrenia. For details of Lovecraft's difficult relations with his overbearing mother, see S. T. Joshi, *I Am Providence: The Life and Times of H. P. Lovecraft* (New York: Hippocampus Press, 2010), 65–67. I think that Lovecraft's racism in particular has paranoid and schizoid characteristics that constitute a political delirium in the sense that Gilles Deleuze and Felix Guattari give to it in another study of the political unconscious, *Anti-Oedipus: Capitalism and Schizophrenia*. I would rather say that Lovecraft's schizophrenic behavior, including his racism, is a decoding/recoding of capitalism that accompanies the breaking through of familial structures. I will come to this different view of the political unconscious in the next chapter, on Bradbury, who is writing at a later and more acute stage of capitalism.

14. R. Boerem, "The First Lewis Theobald," in *Discovering H. P. Lovecraft*, edited by Darrell Schweitzer (Holicong, PA: Wildside Press, 2001), 35–38.

15. R. Boerem, "Lovecraft and the Tradition of the Gentleman Narrator," in *An Epicure of the Terrible*, edited by David E. Schultz and S. T. Joshi (1991; New York: Hippocampus Press, 2011), 269–85.

16. The importance of the culture stream in relation to Lovecraft's general outlook on life is given its best concise definition in letter #438, written to James F. Morton in November 1930. Here Lovecraft makes it clear that without the culture stream around him, he felt absolutely adrift in a meaningless chaos. It is *because* of the meaninglessness of the cosmos that we must secure the illusion of a continuous cultural stream. This culture stream had many different layers of intensity and diversity, but other culture streams of non-European origin threatened to reshape the American culture stream in ways repulsive to Lovecraft. The culture stream represents what Benjamin called *Erfahrung*, or traditional, long and cumulative experience and is opposed to *Erlebnis*, or immediate experience, what Lovecraft calls uncorrelated experience. Lovecraft, *Selected Letters*, 3.207–10. Benjamin writes: "What distinguishes long experience from immediate experience is that the former is inseparable from the representation of a continuity, a sequence." Outsiders to a culture stream in Lovecraft and in Benjamin's view by definition cannot have long experience. Walter Benjamin, *The Arcades Project*, translated by Howard Eiland and Kevin McLaughlin (Cambridge, MA: Harvard University Press, 2002), 802.

17. Lovecraft, *Selected Letters*, 1.118, 130, 131–32, 156.

18. Lovecraft, *Selected Letters*, 1.112, 135. This type of depersonalization has clear overtones of schizophrenia.

19. For discussion of the grotesque as a modern worldview in tales of terror, see Wolfgang Kayser, *The Grotesque in Art and Literature* (New York: McGraw-Hill, 1966), 139–50, 183–85. For Keyser, the experience of the grotesque instills fear of life rather than fear of death. One of the basic experiences of the grotesque is the encounter with madness, and many of Lovecraft's narrators are at least thought to be mad, confined to asylums and such. For the

experience of the demonic grotesque, see the discussion of E. T. A. Hoffmann's characters, 105–6. In my reading, Lovecraft's Nyarlathotep is a figure of the demonic grotesque.

20. For an account of the modern cultural history of the grotto as a literary image of an underground world of dark fantasy in Kafka, Bruno Schulz, and Lovecraft, see Victoria Nelson, *The Secret Life of Puppets* (Cambridge, MA: Harvard University Press, 2001), 100–37. Nelson's account of the grotesque in Lovecraft largely follows Keyser's insight that the grotesque is a product of the fusion of the human with the inhuman. She also compares Lovecraft's experience of the grotesque with that of the psychotic breakdown of Daniel Paul Schreber.

21. Lovecraft, *Selected Letters*, 5.39–40.

22. S. T. Joshi, *A Subtler Magick: The Writings and Philosophy of H. P. Lovecraft* (1996; Berkeley Heights, NJ: Wildside Press, 1999), 260–65.

23. Lovecraft, *Selected Letters*, 3.208.

24. Lovecraft, *Selected Letters*, 1.61.

25. Max Horkheimer and Theodor Adorno, *Dialectic of Enlightenment*, edited by Gunzelin Schmid Noerr (Stanford: Stanford University Press, 2002), 11.

26. Lovecraft, *Selected Letters*, 3.123–24. "Arthur Jermyn" seems to suggest that all of humanity is the evolutionary product of miscegenation, and "From Beyond" presents the idea that certain human senses revealing a much different spectrum of experience that we once possessed have atrophied during evolution. The experience of the absolute Outside reaches its most archetypal expression in "Through the Gates of the Silver Key" (1932–1933).

27. Lovecraft, *Selected Letters*, 3.139–40. Lovecraft agrees with the assessment of scientific modernity robbing life of value given by Joseph Wood Krutch in *The Modern Temper* (1929), but suggests three refuges: drugs, religion, and art. His choice, art constructed in the Dunsanian manner, provides a *supplement* to objective reality.

28. Lovecraft, *Selected Letters,* 1.132.

29. Lovecraft, *Selected Letters*, 3.243.

30. Jacques Derrida, *Specters of Marx*, translated by Peggy Kamuf (New York: Routledge, 1994), 51. I used the word in the sense that Derrida gives it, the haunting of traditional ontology, which is based on presence, by the spectral.

31. Georg Lukács, *The Theory of the Novel* (Cambridge, MA: MIT Press, 1971). Written around the same time as Lovecraft's earliest stories (1914–1916), but published as a book in 1920, the same year he wrote "Nyarlothotep," this Hegel-influenced study examines the problematic individual's role in the rise of the novel form. The novel is "problematic" because modern social experience is not integrated. This situation affects both author and character in a dialectical process. Lukács asserts that, in a world abandoned by God, "the novel hero's psychology is demonic" (88) in the sense that his search for meaning can never penetrate reality. There are forces at work determining the nature of reality that the hero cannot know. The writer's irony must then assume the form of a "negative mysticism" about the ultimate meanings of his hero (90). However, contrasting the novel's focus on subjectivity with that short story, Lukács says that the short story is an objective yet abstract form that "expresses the ultimate meaning of all artistic creation as *mood*, as the very sense and content of the creative process" (51).

32. For instance, the traumatized hero of "The Horror at Red Hook" (1925), a New York police detective named Thomas F. Malone, unites scientific investigation with imagination in uncovering a weird cult operating in modern-day Brooklyn.

33. Gaston Bachelard, *The Poetics of Reverie*, translated by Daniel Russell (Boston: Beacon Press, 1971), 51–54.

34. Michel Foucault, *Essential Works of Foucault*, edited by Paul Rabinow, Volume 2, *Aesthetics, Method and Epistemology* (New York: New York University Press, 1998), 80–81.

35. Lovecraft, *Selected Letters*, 2.287–314.

36. Walter Benjamin, "On Some Motifs in Baudelaire," in *Selected Writings*, Volume 4, edited by Howard Eiland and Michael W. Jennings (Cambridge, MA: Harvard University Press, 2003), 338.

37. Walter Benjamin, "The Work of Art in the Age of Its Technological Reproducibility," in *Selected Writings*, Volume 4, 256.

38. The fullest account of that experience is in Lovecraft. *Selected Letters*, 3.126–27. Here Lovecraft identifies the aura with the experience of freedom and surprise.

39. In later writings, Benjamin distinguishes between the trace and the aura: "The trace is the appearance of a nearness, however far removed the thing that left it behind may be. The aura is the appearance of a distance, however close the thing which call it forth. In the trace, we gain possession of a thing; in the aura it takes possession of us." Benjamin, *The Arcades Project*, 447. In a startling analogy, Benjamin links the trace to the discontinuous experience of the hunt, and to literary study, "the fundamentally unfinishable collection of things worth knowing, whose utility depends on chance" (801–2). In Lovecraft the spectral experience of the trace can lead to ecstasy, as it did at Salem and Marblehead, or to madness, as it does in "The Unnamable."

40. See Timothy H. Evans, "A Last Defense against the Dark: Folklore, Horror, and the Uses of Tradition in the Works of H. P. Lovecraft," *Journal of Folklore Research* 42, No. 1 (January–April 2005): 99–135. Evans argues convincingly that in response to modernity Lovecraft created a new generic hybrid of horror, science fiction, and regionalism.

41. Michel Houellebecq, *H. P. Lovecraft: Against the World, against Life* (San Francisco: Believer Books, 2005), 25. Houellebecq cites a passage from "The Whisperer in Darkness" that called his attention to Lovecraft's beautiful style.

42. See the essay "Goethe's Elective Affinities," in Walter Benjamin, *Selected Writings*, Volume 1, edited by Marcus Bullock and Michael W. Jennings (Cambridge, MA: Harvard University Press, 1996), 350–51.

43. For a concise definition, see Walter Benjamin, *Walter Benjamin's Archive*, translated by Esther Leslie (London: Verso, 2007), 45. Benjamin affirms that words themselves have an aura and that the glance is full of poetry.

44. Leiber, "A Literary Copernicus," in *H. P. Lovecraft: Four Decades of Criticism*, 60.

45. For a brief yet highly suggestive account of Lovecraft's racism in the context of aesthetics, see Umberto Eco, *On Ugliness* (New York: Rizzoli, 2007), 200–1, 212, 239.

46. The comment about the aura and intellectual liberation is in letter #403, to James F. Morton, dated March 12, 1930, in H. P. Lovecraft, *Selected Letters*, 3.126. This letter practically defines the function of cosmic mood in Lovecraft. Lovecraft also lengthily comments about beauty and aura in a letter (#466) collected in the same volume, to Frank Belknap Long, dated February 27, 1931, 3.318–19. The comments on tradition as anti-culture are on 315.

47. H. P. Lovecraft, *Collected Essays*, edited by S. T. Joshi (New York: Hippocampus Press, 2004–2006), 2.153–82.

48. Lovecraft, *Selected Letters*, 2.131.

49. Lovecraft, *Selected Letters*, 2.309. This letter (#345) is centrally concerned with aesthetics and the aura and has been discussed above.

50. Lovecraft, *Selected Letters*, 2.328 and 5.353–54.

51. Lovecraft, *Selected Letters*, 1.234. Lovecraft experienced the electric shock of the aura in both the story and the storyteller (he could not understand why the newspaper accounts of the event did not mention Dunsany's handsome bearing).

52. Assessments of Dunsany's influence on Lovecraft vary depending on what you mean by influence, which can range from conscious imitation to unconscious suggestion. My own view is that Dunsany's *auratic* influence, both personally and in his stories, was deep and long lasting and that there is no decisive break with Dunsany in the Cthulhu Mythos, the inspiration for which Lovecraft himself attributed to Dunsany's pantheon of gods. There are however various "failed" attempts to synthesize Dunsany's essential experience of the aura as distance with other aspects of Lovecraft's aura of historical place (as in *The Dream-Quest of Unknown Kadath*, which Lovecraft repudiated). For concise discussion see Darrell Schweitzer, "Lovecraft and Lord Dunsany," in *Discovering H. P. Lovecraft*, 72–87, and Donald R. Burleson, *H. P. Lovecraft: A Critical Study* (Westport, CT: Greenwood Press, 1983), 221–27. See also footnote 39 on the experiential relationship between the hunt, a prominent theme in Dunsany, and the trace.

53. Lovecraft, *Selected Letters*, 3.193.

54. For Lovecraft's construction of a horrible text that would archive unspeakable otherness in response to modernity, see Leif Sorensen, "A Weird Modernist Archive: Pulp Fiction,

Pseudobiblia, H. P. Lovecraft," *Modernism/modernity* 17, No. 3 (September 2010): 501–22. Sorenson points out the temporal paradox involved in alluding to and citing such texts, which Lovecraft had yet to write.

55. Lovecraft, *Selected Letters*, 3.220–22.

56. Benjamin, "On Some Motifs in Baudelaire," in *Selected Writings*, Volume 4, 338.

57. See Miriam Bratu Hansen, "Benjamin's Aura," *Critical Inquiry* 34 (Winter 2008): 333–35.

58. See Lorenzo Mastropierro, "The Theme of Distance in the Tales of H. P. Lovecraft," *Lovecraft Annual* 3 (2009): 67–95, and Massimo Berruti, "Self, Other and the Evolution of Lovecraft's Treatment of Outsideness," *Lovecraft Annual* 3 (2009): 109–46.

59. See "Some Notes on Interplanetary Fiction," in H. P. Lovecraft, *Collected Essays*, 2.179.

60. Lovecraft, *Selected Letters*, 3.295–96.

61. Tzvetan Todorov, *The Fantastic* (Ithaca, NY: Cornell University Press, 1975), 47–48. Todorov points out that Poe's "The Fall of the House of Usher" is an example of the supernatural explained. Todorov mistakenly criticizes Lovecraft for basing his account of the fantastic on the emotion of fear in the reader, whereas Lovecraft had insisted that the commercial reader never be taken into account and that the authentic mood of the author was what mattered (34–35).

62. H. P. Lovecraft, *The Annotated Supernatural Horror in Literature*, edited by S. T. Joshi (New York: Hippocampus Press, 2000).

63. Walter Benjamin, "The Storyteller: Observations on the Works of Nikolai Leskov," in *Selected Writings*, Volume 3, edited by Howard Eiland and Michael W. Jennings (Cambridge, MA: Harvard University Press, 2002), 161–62. The word Benjamin uses (*Stimmung*), which is translated as "aura," can also be translated as "mood." Following a more directly Marxist analysis, Benjamin also exemplifies the art of storytelling with a story by Leskov involving the hand-carving of a semiprecious stone.

64. Lovecraft, *Selected Letters*, 3.293.

65. Lovecraft, *Selected Letters*, 3.427.

66. Lovecraft, *Selected Letters*, 3.139.

67. For a recent discussion of Lovecraft's use of modern media as haunted, see James Kneale, "Monstrous and Haunted Media: H. P. Lovecraft and Early Twentieth-Century Communications Technology," *Historical Geography* 38 (2010): 90–106. Kneale makes the very important observation that printed books themselves were a technological invention and were perceived in the eighteenth century (Lovecraft's spiritual home) as an occult means of communicating with the dead (3–4). We will take up this idea of printed books as haunted by consciousness in the next chapter, on Bradbury.

68. Lovecraft, *Selected Letters*, 3.212–13 (see also 2.120).

69. As has been suggested by Maurice Lévy, *Lovecraft: A Study in the Fantastic*, translated by S. T. Joshi (Detroit: Wayne State University Press, 1988), 99.

70. Lovecraft, *Collected Essays*, 2.177.

71. Horkheimer and Adorno, *Dialectic of Enlightenment*, 53.

72. Lovecraft does not mention it, but the educated reader may recognize that Dagon is the sea monster, part man and part fish, of *Paradise Lost* 1.462–46, and is of course used by Milton as the chief idol enemy of Samson's god in *Samson Agonistes*.

73. Walter Benjamin, *The Origin of German Tragic Drama*, translated by John Osborne (New York: Verso, 1998), 174–77. Interestingly in terms of writing systems, Benjamin associates allegory not with alphabetical script but with hieroglyphics, which in his view seek to guarantee a "spiritual complex."

74. For an account of shipwreck as a theme in modernity, see Thomas Pfau, "The Philosophy of Shipwreck, Gnosticism, Skepticism, and Coleridge's Catastrophic Modernity," *MLN* 122 (December 2007): 949–1004.

75. For the role of the ideologeme in narratives of class struggle, see Fredric Jameson, *The Political Unconscious* (Ithaca, NY: Cornell University Press, 1981), 87–88.

76. Lovecraft, *Selected Letters*, 1.102–3. The sardonically smiling Dr. Chester of Lovecraft's dream is a clear model for Tillinghast.

77. Jameson, *The Political Unconscious*, 75–76.
78. Lovecraft describes the experience in *Selected Letters*, 1.160–62.
79. Lovecraft claimed never to have heard the name before he experienced the dream, but he was beginning to allude to a pantheon of gods in such stories as "The Doom That Came to Sarnath" (1919) and "Dagon," though that name is already in Milton. Stories such as "The Temple" (1920), the longest story of Lovecraft's early career, and "The Tree" (1920) allude to the gods of Hellenic mythology. *Hotep*, meaning "at peace" or "at ease," is an Egyptian root used in the formation of proper names. On a personal level of meaning it's tempting to connect Loveman, Lovecraft, and Nyarlathotep to the love associated with the proper name. See discussion in Joshi, *I Am Providence*, 370.
80. Benjamin, *Selected Writings*, Volume 4, 259–63.
81. See the notes to the story in H. P. Lovecraft, *The Call of Cthulhu and Other Weird Stories*, edited by S. T. Joshi (New York: Penguin, 1999), 369.
82. http://en.wikipedia.org/wiki/Topsy_(elephant). This is a webpage containing an account of the famous elephant and a copy of Edison's 1903 film.
83. H. P. Lovecraft, "Lord Dunsany and His Work," *Miscellaneous Writings*, 107.
84. Benjamin, "The Work of Art in the Age of Its Technological Reproducibility," *Selected Writings*, Volume 3, 120.
85. M. M. Bakhtin, *Art and Answerability*, edited by Michael Holquist and Vadim Liapunov (Austin: University of Texas Press, 1990), 12, 30, 32. In Bakhtin's view the human body lends each of us a certain situatedness outside of all other human beings. Art too requires "outsidedness" in order to come into being. Once something has a body, the artist can be "outside" it and art is born.
86. See the many references to Egyptian art and culture in Lovecraft's letters, which sometimes contained hieroglyphics, in Joshi, *An Index to the Selected Letters of H. P. Lovecraft*, 17.
87. Arthur Schopenhauer, *The World as Will and Representation*, translated by E. F. J. Payne (New York: Dover, 1966), 2.573.
88. Schopenhauer, *The World as Will and Representation*, 2.448.
89. Lovecraft, *Selected Letters*, 1.215.
90. Schopenhauer, *The World as Will and Representation*. Schopenhauer writes, "The feeling of the sublime is distinguished from that of the beautiful only by the addition [of the direct experience of the Ideas] namely the exaltation beyond the known hostile relation of the contemplated object to the will in general. Thus there result several degrees of the sublime, in fact transitions from the beautiful to the sublime, according as this addition is strong, clamorous, urgent, and near, or only feeble, remote and merely suggested" (1.202).
91. Benjamin, "The Storyteller," in *Selected Writings*, Volume 3, 156.
92. Lovecraft, *Selected Letters*, 1.158.
93. Lovecraft, *The Call of Cthulhu and Other Weird Stories*, 381.
94. John R. Clark, *The Modern Satiric Grotesque and Its Traditions* (Lexington: University Press of Kentucky, 1991), 56–57. The modern satiric grotesque expresses itself through deadly laughter, degrading the hero, debunking the author, and dislocating language, all of which can be found in Lovecraft's story.
95. Robert Scholes, James Phelan, and Robert Kellogg, *The Nature of Narrative* (Oxford: Oxford University Press, 2006), 73–74. The authors note that the picaresque is a form of the traveler's tale whose main concern is with social satire.
96. See H. P. Lovecraft, *The Dreams in the Witch House and Other Weird Stories*, edited by S. T. Joshi (New York: Penguin, 2004), 414–15.
97. I have included in the text page locations for important passages in *H. P. Lovecraft: The Fiction* (New York: Barnes & Noble, 2009). This is the only anthology of Lovecraft's fiction that collects the stories in order of composition. Throughout this chapter, dates given in parentheses refer to the date of composition, not publication.
98. Lovecraft, *Selected Letters*, 2.95.
99. Lévy, *Lovecraft*, 108. While I can agree with Lévy that Carter's dream experience *in the story* seems to lack the "distance" necessary to constitute the fantastic, and so his hero remains in the marvelous world of the fairy tale, I think that the ending when Carter *does* become aware that he has been dreaming is a dialectical reversal of narrative ground rules. Lévy does not

consider the relationship of Lovecraft as problematic author to his character, which involves the distance created by humor and irony. We have already seen something of this distance toward Carter in "The Unnamable," and it recurs in other stories involving him. Carter is Lovecraft's most important searcher after the meaning of life in a demonic world. He actually ends up losing his human form, which is still not restored to him at the end of "Through the Gates of the Silver Key" (1932–1933; with E. Hoffmann Price).

100. For homesickness and homelessness as the condition of the novel, see Lukács, *The Theory of the Novel*, 29, 41.

101. Lukács, *The Theory of the Novel*, 74–75. Irony is a compositional strategy whereby the novelist splits his subjectivity in order to mediate the parts of his composition.

102. For discussion, see S. T. Joshi and David E. Schultz, *An H. P. Lovecraft Encyclopedia* (2001; New York: Hippocampus Press, 2004), 245. Carter exists in the form of an alien wizard whom he disguises on Earth as an Indian swami, Chandraputra. He now needs to crack the language of an ancient manuscript to recover the spell that can transform him.

103. Lovecraft, *Selected Letters*, 3.96.

104. Lovecraft, *Selected Letters*, 4.19, 210.

105. Lovecraft, *Selected Letters*, 3.139–40.

106. For opalescence in the weird fantasy tradition, see Dan Clore, *Weird Words: A Lovecraftian Lexicon* (New York: Hippocampus Press, 2009), 316, 418.

107. Benjamin, "On Some Motifs in Baudelaire," in *Selected Writings*, Volume 4, 316, 338.

108. Lovecraft, *Selected Letters*, 4.259.

Ray Bradbury, or Nostalgia

Few storytellers in the tradition of the fantasy have displayed so profound a kinship with the spirit of nostalgia as did Ray Bradbury (1920–2012), especially in his love of popular culture.[1] The personal origins of this nostalgia appear to lie in his idyllic childhood: he grew up in Waukegan, Illinois, during the Depression, and he was particularly drawn to traveling magic shows and carnivals. There are many sources of popular culture in Bradbury's texts, but actually only one origin story, which Bradbury told over and over again in different variations. When he was twelve, he came under the spell of a storyteller and performer, Mr. Electrico.[2] This man, who has not been identified, was a defrocked Presbyterian minister, who spoke to the young Bradbury in religious tones about living forever. But in listening to Mr. Electrico Bradbury realized not that his message was about salvation by God, but that he himself had died at the age of nine when he set aside his interest in Buck Rogers for fear of ridicule by classmates. He understood the need for the influence of Buck Rogers in shaping his future. Henceforth he resolved to live imaginatively through writing, feeding his mind with whatever imaginative stimulus it needed, without embarrassment, whether from high culture or low.

Bradbury's origin story is thus deeply imbued with nostalgia for a lost connection with a former life. It's often said that children are not really nostalgic because they have not yet lived, but the young Bradbury was deeply nostalgic for the future. Almost all of Bradbury's stories are marked by this primal nostalgia for popular culture. Many of his collections involve the special mood and atmosphere of carnival, but with autumnal overtones (Bradbury experienced the rituals of carnival in late September). His first collection of weird and supernatural stories was *Dark Carnival* (1947), which he reshaped into *The October Country* (1955), literal carnival being reshaped thereafter into a metaphor for the mood of modernity.[3] My own approach to these reshaped collections and other Bradbury stories is through the writings of the Russian scholar Mikhail Bakhtin, whose history of laughter tells the sad tale of the degradation of popular-festive celebrations in the seventeenth and eighteenth centuries, the centuries of absolute monarchy and rationalism in Europe.[4] Like other Marxist scholars (and Benjamin with the storyteller), Bakhtin was nostalgic for a more communal life in touch with the people, and he saw in the degradation and suppression of carnival laughter an extended literary history that needed to be written.

Much of what I have already written on Bradbury is an attempt to situate him in that proposed history of laughter. Moving on from preliminary articles and a short critical book, in 2004 I published an extended analysis of Bradbury's entire career up until that time in terms of carnival.[5] I won't repeat the details of that analysis here, but it had to do with Bradbury's nostalgia for the aura of another earlier chronotope, the freedom of carnival time and space, and his feeling that American popular culture had become degraded.[6] I was unable to get into that study much of a discussion of what in Bakhtinian studies has come to be called the experience of *bitter carnival*, which for Bradbury came to its height in the 1950s, just as he was becoming a recognized figure at home and abroad.[7] Since this study is focused more directly on the mood of modernity, I would like to give an account of bitter carnival in a recent Bradbury collection of stories dating from this period, *A Pleasure to Burn* (2011). Bitter carnival stems, as we will see, from the fear of not having a future.

The years during and especially immediately following the end of World War II, during which most of Bradbury's important stories were written, constitute a period of spiraling anxiety and paranoia in American cultural politics. The war had been won, America was becoming more and more affluent, but peace in the world seemed elusive. Fascism, which had condemned modernism in the arts as an international Jewish and Bolshevik conspiracy aimed at destroying the German *Volk*, had been defeated. But after 1946, our relations with our wartime ally the Soviet Union under Stalin became increasingly acrimonious. In debates in the Soviet Union over the path that art must follow under socialism, it was usual for Stalin to view the nonrepresentational character of modernism as a pathological fault of the capitalist West. Even Picasso, whose art had shown clear progressive tendencies in the fight against fascism, found himself condemned as "degrading, demoralizing, decadent, and degenerate."[8] It soon became clear that Stalin's intentions in Europe were expansionist, and the first stage of the Cold War culminated with the Berlin crisis of 1948–1949. Much closer to home for Bradbury, the House Committee on Un-American Activities came to Hollywood in 1947 in search of communist influences in the movies. Among the luminaries who appeared before the committee to testify about their activities was one of the founders of modern drama, Bertolt Brecht. Well aware of the irony of a Marxist intellectual trying to make it professionally in Hollywood, he scathingly observed that for him Los Angeles was a kind of modern hell, where cheap prettiness depraved everything—Tahiti in metropolitan form.[9] Brecht soon left America for communist East Berlin. Interestingly, Brecht's reflections on his time spent in Los Angeles have appeared in a recent Library of America volume that also includes Bradbury's "The Pedestrian."[10]

The times seemed ripe for satire, the commonest form of political literature, and indeed there was something of a revival of this literary mode in the postwar years, especially in science fiction, as we will see in a moment. Serious drama, Brechtian or otherwise, was of course protected under free speech in America, but it's worth noting in passing that carnivals and other "tawdry" entertainments from which Bradbury often drew his inspiration were then seen as common shows, and were not protected (movies were). Constitutional guarantees never stopped the mounting of attacks against modern art by politicians, however. Anyone wanting to become a writer and to think for himself now had to worry about the charge of being called un-American. In an inflammatory 1949 speech before the House of Representatives, Congressman George Dondero linked all of the "isms" of modern art—cubism, Dadaism, surrealism, et al.—to a plot launched by "germ-carrying art vermin" to undermine "plain American people" with subversive ideas.[11]

Perhaps in response to this, Bradbury's depictions of censorship always involved metaphors of antisepsis—his censors were always cleansers. To him the cultural situation was one in which art and literature were like a great twine of taffy being strung all about, twisted in braids and tied in knots, and thrown in all directions (an image from "Carnival of Madness"; see below). Soon the paranoia of the "red scare" and character assassination began in earnest with the McCarthyism of the 1950s. In these debates, modernism became identified with communist subversion of freedom and democratic values. Broader elements of American culture turned on the popular arts as well. Comics were investigated as contributing to juvenile delinquency. When the Space Age was inaugurated with the launching of Sputnik in 1957, fantasy books such as *The Wizard of Oz* were removed from library bookshelves on the basis that they were harmful, while the American educational system struggled to overcome the technological gap with the Russians.

To many observers of modern culture, the arts seemed to be in a permanent state of "crisis." High modern art, which earlier had rediscovered Mediterranean classical myths of sunlit pleasure in the paintings of Picasso and Matisse, had exhausted itself in the coldness of abstract impressionism, a largely American movement centered in New York.[12] The notion that the arts might provide pleasure and satisfaction in the experience of beauty, especially in the allure of a female model as the subject of a modern painting, as had been normal for previous centuries, was rejected. That art might be made a part of everyday domesticity was now seen by the avant-garde as a terrible inanity, hopelessly compromised by commodification. At the same time, advertising constructed a glittering world of consumer products (dominated by images of women), which promised happiness. The modern artist was above all someone male, someone involved in a heroic struggle to achieve the sublimity of pure form, eschewing any politics of desirable representation. Jackson Pollock, whose nonrepresentational action paintings were created by dripping paint on canvas, was considered the most "heroic" and original artist of the period, though his large paintings were often reproduced on the covers of chic fashion magazines with models standing in front of them.[13]

To the serious writer concerned about the fate of the arts in society there was the added threat of nuclear annihilation. The Soviets had exploded their first atomic bomb in 1949, starting a whole new era of cold war paranoia and secrecy. And, as the two postwar political systems developed, totalitarianism and government bureaucracy became an added burden. As early as 1946, George Orwell had argued that literature, which enshrines individual liberty—the mainstay of civilization since the Renaissance—might disappear entirely under the weight of bureaucracy and machine civilization if writers did not take a strong stand against these forces (the essay is ironically called "The Prevention of Literature"). Orwell argued that many writers were too blandly wrapped up in their own work to realize this growing threat to their profession or to take a stand against fashionable ideas. In this essay Orwell opined that at some future time "literature" would abandon any individual point of view and be churned out by mindless state bureaucracies. The literature of the past would have to be suppressed or elaborately rewritten. He went on to write a dystopian novel depicting just such a state of affairs—*1984*.

Orwell had been dead for three years when, in 1953, Bradbury published an article on science fiction in *The Nation* in which he pondered the question of "whether or not my ideas on censorship via the fire department [expressed in "The Fireman"] will be old hat this time next week. . . . When the wind is right, a faint odor of kerosene is exhaled from Senator McCarthy."[14] Like many people concerned about the increasing polarization of the world into a period of cold war, Bradbury saw himself as living between two books: Arthur Koestler's *Darkness at Noon* and Orwell's *1984*, and his times as poised between a dreadful reality and an unformed terror described in them. In this article, Bradbury linked modern science fiction with the great satire of the past—Swift, Rabelais. Yet satire is not often thought of as a serious literary form because often enough it is no more than a reflection of contemporary politics. By the end of the 1950s, though, critics were beginning to see Bradbury as a cartographer, skillfully drawing new maps of the conformist hell that had taken shape in American culture. To mention one prominent study of science fiction, originally given as a series of lectures at Princeton in 1959, Kingsley Amis, himself a gifted satirist, thought that he could detect in Bradbury's writings (he considered primarily "Usher II" and *Fahrenheit 451*) "a certain triumphant lugubriousness, a kind of proleptic *schadenfreude*," a relish and satisfaction in critiquing the deleterious effects of mass culture.[15] Amis thought of Bradbury as one of the finest literary writers of the group he was considering, though he noted also a penchant for sentimentalizing.

Eager to justify science fiction as a mature genre, Amis organized his discussion around the basic notion that the value of science fiction lay in a kind of utopian satire in which society criticized itself, though he did not go into precise detail about forms this satire took.[16] Nor did he have much to say about the roots of satire in carnival, which has had such a large influence on Bradbury's writings. Here I want to consider the artistic (i.e., carnivalesque) means by which Bradbury expressed his criticism of the 1950s, because the artistry of these stories enabled them to remain of interest long after the immediate political concerns abated. They are still of interest today. Now, the basic technique of satire, one of the "reduced" forms of laughter Bakhtin mentions in his proposed history of laughter, is one of reduction, "the degradation or devaluation of the victim by reducing his stature and dignity."[17] Throughout the texts considered here, the reader will find stories that expand on this basic technique (and to a lesser extent Socratic dialogue) by calling on the imagery of carnival and saturnalia, and the vast folk tradition lying behind satire.

Carnival is of central importance to the understanding of Bradbury's works as a whole, but it is especially important for understanding the imagery and symbolism of the censorship stories collected in *A Pleasure to Burn*. In medieval times, carnival was a period of license before the Lenten season, in which the rigid hierarchies of society were overturned and figures of power and authority could be mocked. Many forms of speech later incorporated into satire—travesty, parody, lampoon, profanity, invective, exaggeration—had their origins in this celebration, which in turn had its cultural roots in the Roman saturnalia and the Greek tradition of the satyr play. Carnival was a unique social event. There were no individual heroes and no spectators. Everyone participated. It took place in the marketplace square and celebrated things that were normally kept hidden in polite society, among them the maternal and reproductive body. If carnival had a hero, it would be the fool who was crowned king in its central ritual action, while the real figures of authority were debased, often in effigy. Because of the mockery directed at authority figures, one could say that carnival was a period when one learned the real meaning of "free and open" speech. Above all, carnival depended on the reversal of social norms and values, which became a favored technique of satirists.

As I mentioned, Bradbury experienced carnival firsthand as a child and has spoken about its profound influence on his writing many times. Although Bradbury imbibed the carnival spirit early in his life, he learned the techniques and themes of satire mostly by genre contact, by his readings in fantasy and science fiction, and through his personal friendships with other writers and editors in the field (Henry Kuttner and Anthony Boucher in particular), and not through any concerted study of the history of satire. In a sense one could say that the genre itself did the remembering for him. Of course, genre theorists understand that there never is an exact fit between "genre memory" and the concerns of the individual writer and his times. In fact, it is this very tension, between the inherent view of reality contained in genres—for carnival-based genres it is a kind of "joyful relativity" that laughs at absolutes in life—and the vision of an individual author, that renews the genre.[18]

Mikhail Bakhtin, the internationally renowned Soviet scholar, studied this process in Dostoevsky's writings. He also published a book, now widely influential in the West, exploring the influence of carnival on Rabelais, which scholars now understand is an oblique criticism of the Stalinist era.[19] For Bakhtin, carnival was always characterized by ritual actions leading to a festive perception of the world. If carnival was hostile to anything, it was to all that was absolute and completed. Death and degradation were only a phase, only the metaphorical grave for a new birth. Out of the destructive fires of carnival always came renewal and new life. I mentioned previously that I used Bakhtin's ideas about carnival to show how Bradbury created a host of life-affirming fictions throughout his career, but I only touched upon the notion of what might happen when the carnival turns bitter, and society cannot find the means for renewal.

The reader of the stories I am about to discuss will find a depth of anger and bitterness about the cultural situation of the 1950s—those attacks on the arts mentioned above—that may seem surprising to those who know only the later Bradbury of the 1960s and 1970s. But the fact that Bradbury's authorial voice might reveal a range of "anti-social" attitudes is instantiated by all of the stories the reader will encounter in this discussion. They offer a range of bitter antiheroes. Indeed, resistance appears positively only in the character of Clarisse, who appears first in the "Long After Midnight" typescript and who is developed later as the very spirit of "resisting" attitudes toward conformist culture in *Fahrenheit 451*. For it is she who is characterized as "anti-social" by the authorities. It is she who embodies that tenderness and sympathy toward the world that Bradbury felt was being eradicated by modernity. She disappears early in the narrative of that novel, and Montag's quest for meaning is largely a quest to recover her spirit. At any rate, these stories, both published and unpublished, tell us much about the difficult art of responding to modernity, which now contained the growing fear of nuclear annihilation ("Bonfire").

The thematic relationship of these stories to *Fahrenheit 451*, Bradbury's most influential work, will be touched on in the course of this chapter, but it must be stated at the outset that these stories do not simply "lead up" to *Fahrenheit 451* in a linear and unproblematic way. Rather, they explore along divergent paths the social force of a bitter carnival. As such, they construct a cultural politics in which the mocking laughter of carnival, which satirists have traditionally used to unmask the impostures of power and to alert us to dire forces and trends threatening to crush the human spirit, has turned inward, corroding the hero's faith in life and allowing a darker ethos of nihilism to emerge.

Looking back from the vantage point of the late 1950s, Amis established rather convincingly that Bradbury's postwar stories dealt with the dehumanizing effects of modernity—especially technological inventions, which seemed increasingly of global determination—on human consciousness. The environment of technology may have been full of new marvels to some, but to Bradbury it seemed to remove our ability to respond to life authentically and to remember the past, and even to threaten the very idea of a stable reality. While this concern with the impact of technology is a prominent theme in Bradbury's work during this period, what has not been previously noted is his creation of an abject hero (sometimes a major character or antagonist) who is driven by resentment and envy, a kind of demonic fool who parodies the role of the wise fool in traditional carnival. This character responds to society by taking part in a combative dialogue/debate with others in the story—often defenders of the status quo—in which the very values of civilization, threatened by mass culture, come under intense scrutiny.

But in its more extreme forms, the reader may be denied any vantage point from which to judge who has won the argument. We may feel that the abject figure is clearly a monster, yet still identify with him. For various reasons, he has come late to the life-affirming carnival, or missed it altogether ("The Reincarnate," "Pillar of Fire"). This type of antihero emerges particularly with the threat of apocalyptic social circumstances, when civilization is threatened with collapse:

"For them [the abject heroes of modern literature] the carnival was always marked by bitterness and that the licensed fool who jests . . . may already have shed his clown's motley and begun to rail in earnest."[20]

Bernstein's examples of the abject hero are Dostoevsky's underground man, Rameau's nephew, Céline's heroes, and, in American popular culture, Charles Manson. Now, the cultural catastrophe that Bradbury most often envisages in these stories is a descent into barbarity involving a total loss of the consolations of art and literacy, of the rich semantic depths of a usable past (the meaning of Benjamin's figure of the storyteller), and thereby the loss of any standard of excellence by which we might be able to judge the vulgarity of the present. To judge from the generous play of citations drawn from "great works" of the past, such as Matthew Arnold's "Dover Beach" (though modern art is referenced too, as we will see), Bradbury's own writings attest to a vision of culture in which art's role is to provide a criticism of life. Nor is there any doubt that Bradbury's stories argue the value of the literary imagination as essential to our humanity. Indeed, their primary function could be understood as helping us to inhabit the world in which we live, to show us how to "live on" in a postmodern world that is increasingly chaotic and meaningless, by evoking certain traditional structures of imagination (reveries) that create empathy with the Other.

It is always difficult for a writer, or indeed for anyone, to grasp fully the cultural ground on which he stands, or to predict which of his writings will have meaning for future generations. Jack Finney's *Invasion of the Body Snatchers*, for instance, became a metaphor for Cold War paranoia about communism, despite the fact that the author declared that he intended no such meanings. Being perceived as a "genre writer," as Bradbury was (and is), further complicates this problem. But genre is by no means to be despised, for it mediates between an author and his times, providing him the means for fame and fortune. Insofar as we now understand Bradbury's intentions as a writer during this formative period, he was struggling for recognition in the broader cultural world outside the field of science fiction (after 1950, Bradbury sought the public blessing of such modernist figures as Christopher Isherwood and Aldous Huxley, and got it). Soon after this initial recognition, Bradbury anthologized Isherwood ("I Am Waiting"), Franz Kafka ("In the Penal Colony"), and himself ("The Pedestrian") in *Timeless Stories for Today and Tomorrow* (1952), which with the exception of Henry Kuttner contained no regular genre writers.

Throughout the 1950s, Bradbury's stories expanded and "modernized" the genre potential of horror, fantasy, and science fiction, three of the oldest historical genres, by opening them up to the experience of modernity. The best of the stories of the postwar period, however, while reflecting the cultural politics of the period, also transcend it. "The Pedestrian," for instance, tells us much about the increasing militarization of city spaces and the concomitant disappearance of the reveries of a solitary walker from the urban landscape. The very idea of a leisurely reflective stroll on city sidewalks at night had become a fearful thing for most Americans, who now lived in urban areas. The cultural milieu in which Bradbury wrote these stories was complex and contradictory, but he concentrated on his special gift, his ability to evoke buried or marginalized emotions through the metaphors of otherness and difference these genres offered him. The suppression of fantasy and imagination by the conformist culture of the 1950s was, as Amis noted, a widespread concern among science fiction writers, but as a theme it soon came to be identified as Bradbury's own "specialty."[21]

Because of the prominence of this theme in his writings, Bradbury is often considered a liberal, and the term "liberal democratic humanism" probably does broadly describe Bradbury's ideological outlook at the time. We should beware of easy labels though. In the decade after World War II this was no longer an unproblematic intellectual position. Liberal democracies had failed in Europe, giving rise to fascism and communism. At home the whole project of democracy now seemed at risk. Though he would never claim to be an intellectual (or a sociologist), as a writer Bradbury was never quite as naive as some people took him to be. The threats of Nazi-like book burning and censorship were beginning to look to him like rearguard symbolic actions in a war that was now over, a war in which, for most people, unfortunately, the imagination and traditional humanism had already died under the pressures of mass culture. We must be careful to examine the artistic means by which Bradbury expressed his themes. Bradbury may have been a liberal democrat, but not every liberal democrat is a Bradbury.

The abject hero common to most of the censorship stories in *A Pleasure to Burn* makes his first appearance in "The Reincarnate," which dates from circa 1942–1943, when Hitler's Germany was not yet defeated. The plot of this story is fairly simple, but as a supernatural tale it is wonderfully rich in carnival symbolism (especially fire).[22] Motivated by desire, a man named Paul returns from the grave to visit with his lost love, Kim, in order to persuade her that they can in fact still "live" together, despite his decaying body and senses. That carnival sense of the collision of opposites normally kept far apart dominates the conversations that Paul and Kim have. She is the thing he most desires, while he is the thing she least desires—death. The potential for carnival debasement is evident (Paul discovers that he smells offensive to others and that his penis has shriveled to a twisted paint tube, a striking metaphor taken from the art of painting. But the overall tone, until the surprise ending (which is foreshadowed by Kim's pregnancy), is one of melancholy resentment at the enjoyments of the living, which can no longer be tasted and shared.

Philosophical debates between the dead and the living were a central theme of menippean satire. In these debates, stable and conventional ideas about dying and living were questioned. The clash of ideas emerges here as well, when Paul and Kim debate the possibilities of "life" together. These thematic opposites play off of each other throughout the story, creating a sense of how precious life is, and how "different" it is to be dead. Dead for Bradbury is really a category of "difference" and otherness, as the story makes clear. As usual, Bradbury's vivid metaphors invite us to imagine this sense of otherness (as when the narrator compares himself to a locust dreaming beneath the ground) and create a sense of empathy. It is interesting to note that here, as elsewhere in Bradbury's writings, otherness and alienation are questioned and overcome through an act that combines memory, sensation, and imagination with a female figure. Kim points out that they cannot have a life together because Paul can no longer have sensations, and thus cannot form shared memories. Paul really wants a kind of domestic bliss with Kim, but his desire is abstract. Kim points out the need for sensation. For her, Paul's memories are an illusion, a fire that needs constant tending.

We are also meant to wonder just who the "reincarnate" are. Why do they become reincarnated? And what possible "political" meanings could this story have? The story opens up to political meanings when Paul meets the Leader of the undead, who is attempting to organize them into a crowd by emphasizing their scapegoat status and appealing to the persecuted Jews of Germany. It's plain that he wants to destroy humanity, and it's equally plain that he is a kind of demagogue. Ironically, though, the dead in the end do not follow him. Since the Leader plans to appeal to the undead as a "persecuted minority," this may mean that Bradbury is rejecting minority group pressure politics (an argument later enunciated in *Fahrenheit 451*) as akin to censorship. But more likely he is just rejecting the bitter carnival of demagoguery.

Also, there is an important reference to the classical underworld in the Leader's setting of the rallying point for the undead at Elysian Park. The Elysian fields were a spectral place where the best of the Greek heroes waited to be reborn, a place of relative comfort and ease. This reference opens the story up to one of the three planes of the menippea: Olympus, the netherworld, and earth.[23] But the Leader is not going to be crowned there as a hero, and has to acknowledge his defeat. His path to a bitter carnival of destruction is clearly rejected. He ends in futility, his word having had no effect. He had wild plans, but now he is alone.

So the Leader is not, ultimately, one of the true "reincarnate" of which the story speaks. In fact it is the Leader's (failed) function in the story to encourage the hero to assume his own bitterness, the bitterness of embalming and suppression. But our hero is reborn not through paranoid politics, but by returning to the "satin womb" of the grave. This is the ambivalent carnival theme of pregnant death, in which mankind is reborn again through the earth.[24] Because he has followed the path of true carnival and returned to the grave—and not the path of abstract male desire—he rediscovers at the end of the story a sense of joy and triumph and laughter in being reborn as his own son, in the word that Kim utters in naming him: his name, Paul.

Fire is such a quintessential symbol of carnival ambivalence—it both destroys and renews—that we can easily find its presence in the imagery of "The Reincarnate": the corpse of Mrs. Hanlon seems a book burning, and so on (Bradbury was always personifying people as books and vice versa). And the firework festivities of the Fourth of July, during which Bradbury's real Uncle Bion used to set off a small cannon, is central to the "emotion of recapturence" [sic] that the dead hero seeks in being reborn. Looking around in recent zombiana for a point of comparison, something of the force of the genre memory of carnival can be seen in George A. Romero's *Land of the Dead* (2005), in which the living use fireworks explosions to attract and control the walking dead. When they are thus distracted by the memories of their past lives, they can more easily be attacked and destroyed. There is of course a very definite political message to Romero's film, which builds on the traditional depiction of zombies as inarticulate automatons, the subhuman slaves of others, but which reverses the notion that they are incapable of revolting. Bradbury, long before Romero ever contemplated doing so, enriched the horror genre by giving the zombie such a political dimension. But fire comes into its own as a major symbol in Bradbury's next exploration of the abject hero, "Pillar of Fire."

"Pillar of Fire" centers on another living dead character who also has wild plans, like that of the Leader of "The Reincarnate." Because of its greater length, however, it deploys a much more elaborate cultural politics in defense of the need for fantasy in culture. To begin with, Bradbury's abject hero has little of the glamour associated with the romantic outsider that Paul in part evokes in his renewed wooing of Kim in the earlier story; here he is a solitary representative of the walking dead, full of envy and anger. According to Bradbury, "Pillar of Fire" was a rehearsal for *Fahrenheit 451*. But the protagonists are reverse images of each other: Montag, who is trying to stop the burning of books, is a reversed image of Lantry, the last dead man "reborn" into an antiseptically clean, utopian society that has destroyed his grave and all other graveyards on earth. Lantry is obsessed to the point of extreme paranoia with burning down this society. The fact that both stories involve the suppression of works of fantastic fiction unites them thematically. Yet still, Bradbury's protagonist in "Pillar of Fire" realizes only belatedly that he is the last person remembering all the old books of fantasy and imagination, and that with his death they die also. In this respect he has much in common with the assassins material at the core of the *Ignorant Armies* fragments, which we will examine in a moment.

The story seems designed to make readers hesitate between a supernatural and a scientific explanation of the uncanny events that happen when William Lantry rises from the grave in the year 2349 AD. Is Lantry really one of the walking dead, or is he an extraordinary case of suspended animation? We suspect from the outset that he is undead and have our suspicions confirmed at the end. Appropriately, the story is set in Salem—prime Puritan (and Lovecraft) territory, with a history of persecution of witches—where the last graveyard has been preserved as a tourist attraction by the government as a reminder of a barbaric custom. But now this graveyard, and even alien tombs on Mars, is scheduled by the government for destruction. The State seeks thereby to make absolute its control over the world of darkness, death, and decay, and over all writers whose imaginations are attracted to it. We learn from Lantry's visit to a library that the Great Burning of 2265 destroyed all of the "unclean" writings of the past: Poe, Lovecraft, Bierce, among others. Lantry realizes with a shock that if he is destroyed, all memory of such literature will be destroyed as well, since he is the last person, or rather the last *dead* person, to remember them. Literature has indeed become spectral.

The society Lantry is reborn into could be described as an extreme Apollonian culture, as is evident from the symbolism it employs. It worships the sun of rationality, emblazoned everywhere on public buildings. The dead of this society are burned in a centralized rite, in "Incinerators," which are warm, cozy temples where soothing music plays and the fear of death is abolished through ceremonies that deify fire. As Lantry watches the operation of the Salem Incinerator, the golden coffins of the dead slowly roll in, covered with sun symbols, and after a brief ceremony they are cast into a flue. On the altar are written the words "We that are born of the sun return to the sun," a reversal of the words normally spoken at Christian burials, where the meaning of the earth is at least partially evoked.

It is these gigantic Incinerators, central to the mythology of an Apollonian culture, that Lantry wants to explode into a bitter carnival; he repeatedly compares his efforts to destroy them to reinaugurating the Fourth of July. Because deviant behavior is not expected, he manages to infiltrate the Salem Incinerator and to destroy it easily, killing hundreds of people in the surrounding towns. He hopes thereby to effect a revolution, to manufacture friends by creating more walking dead. But in this rationalized world the dead remain dead. Because they never imagined while living that the dead might walk, they cannot be resurrected by Lantry's magical procedures. He draws symbols of long-dead sorcerers on the floor of the makeshift morgue next to the bodies and chants his own magic formulas, to no avail. Eventually, he is picked up by the authorities and is interrogated by a man named McClure, who is this century's version of a psychoanalyst and something of a detective as well. McClure tries to analyze Lantry's mortified behavior, his paleness and lack of breath, as a self-induced psychosis, but is himself slowly unnerved when he finds that Lantry is the real thing, one of the walking dead.

Lantry is a logical impossibility to a mind such as McClure's. After a brief struggle in which Lantry tries to murder McClure, he is subdued and condemned to a second death by the State, a death that represents, as well, the death of every fantastic writer in history, since only Lantry remembers them. If this were a Christian fantasy in the mode of J. R. R. Tolkien or C. S. Lewis, the evident compassion of McClure for his victim would have resulted in his conversion to the imagination at the end, thereby saving the hero. But no, Bradbury really wants us to undergo the notion of the imagination dying forever, and on this level of response, the story is quite effective.

The second death, the death of the imagination, becomes more terrible than real death.

Since we are looking for traces of a cultural politics in these stories, it is relevant to ask here how a story like Bradbury's "Pillar of Fire" invests the social field, which is comprised of all those representations created by society that solicit our desires. Gilles Deleuze and Felix Guattari, two French thinkers who mention Bradbury in the context of a political discussion of madness and literature, link delirium to a carnivalesque cultural politics, and in what follows I make use of some of their ideas and terminology.[25] They see madness as the extreme experience of unconscious desire directly investing the social field. Madness is not so much a theatre of representations as it is "produced" by an oscillation from paranoia to schizophrenia. Deleuze and Guattari observe that real political figures often appear in the delirium of schizophrenics. These terrifying figures out to destroy us inhabit the paranoid pole of delirium. The schizophrenic pole (not to be understood entirely in the clincal sense) multiplies identities and masks in order to escape persecution.

Though Bradbury's fantasy is certainly theatrical—he turned this story into a successful play—when considered in terms of the investment of desire in culture, "Pillar of Fire" moves along similar political lines. Indeed, we can easily find investments of the first type, the paranoiac pole, which emerges from "the body without organs" (the term actually comes from the writings of Antonin Artaud). The body without organs is a kind of zero point of the social field, initially inhabited only by molecular desiring-machines on its surface. In Bradbury's story it is represented by dead bodies, which the State is attempting to eliminate. But the dead bodies are not just representations, they *embody* the hatred and the resentment of the social body under repression. Lantry's body is a social body, full of all kinds of wild experiences, which Bradbury lovingly describes in his description of the deep thoughts of a man buried in a coffin beneath the ground.

In terms of the political unconscious, these remarkable passages define the resentment and envy that mark the emergence of the abject hero. Lantry arises from the catatonic body without organs because a "fascisizing" (*fascisant*) and sovereign State apparatus has selected him and subjected him to its will. His delirium, which continues to intensify until he remarks that he is all that is left of H. P. Lovecraft and supernatural literature, is not so much a representation as a direct investment of the social field. Or at least we are meant to feel it as such. He was perfectly content to remain a body without organs himself, swarming with worms, bacilli, not feeling the ticking of the million insect watches (the desiring-machines) in the earth around him. But the fascisizing machine tears up the body of the earth, divides it up into new territories and structures. And so Lantry becomes a reactive paranoid, and this is exactly how Bradbury directs that the character should be played in the stage version of the story.[26]

As Deleuze and Guattari point out, the body without organs is the model of death; it is not death that serves as the model of catatonia. In their opinion horror authors have understood this very well.[27] They observe that there is no real death in the unconscious, only flows of desire between desiring machines. Lantry's behavior is the political behavior of the paranoid, which consists in the organizing of masses and crowds of people. The paranoid manipulates crowds; he opposes them to one another, maneuvers them (all these actions are investments of the social field implied by their verbal coinage, *fascisant*). This is clearly what Lantry intends to do, hanging around the makeshift morgue where the dead bodies have been laid out in rows on the surface of the earth, hoping to resurrect and to mobilize them into an army of the dead against the State, which has banished the word "dead" from the language.

In the end, Lantry realizes that his war machine had no hope of ever materializing. But when McClure tells him that he will die of loneliness anyway because he is a freak, one of a kind, we pass to the schizophrenic pole. Lantry realizes that he himself is a crowd of people, both fictional and real. The passage accompanying this schizophrenic "voyage out" is too lengthy to quote in full, but after saying that he is Poe and Bierce and a host of other fantastic creatures besides, Lantry goes on to add that he is a mask, a spectral figure, and all that is left of Dunsany and Machen. When he is destroyed, all of these writers will die with him.

The full list contains many names in the literary history of the fantastic, but ends with the name of the father, that is, Hamlet's father on the castle wall, which ends the delirium. Shakespeare's Hamlet was central to Derrida's discussion of spectrality in *pecters of Marx* because Marx loved Shakespeare and ghosts. Here Bradbury is "conjuring" the spirit of Shakespeare to make us feel the loss of masterpieces of the imagination that he loves. Through these names Bradbury and his antihero, Lantry, find a way to affirm a multiplicity of identities in the Dionysian manner, but there is little joy to be had in the notion that these authors will disappear forever.

Lantry's body is given to the Incinerators while he imagines being walled up in the catacomb of Poe's "The Cask of Amontillado." Poe's story of bitter revenge is set during carnival time, so Lantry's use of it is apt. His existence ends with a wild scream and "much laughter." Withdrawal—saying I am not of your kind, of the superior Apollonian race, but one who belongs eternally to the inferior race, the freaks—sweeps away social masks on leaving, or at least can cause a piece of the system to get lost in the shuffle. Lantry, the bitter hero, is an agent of fear, but that is entirely appropriate, since considered dialectically it is creative, the thing against which man has built all his lanterned cities and his many children. What matters is to break through the rigidity of social walls, to make society *afraid* again.

"Pillar of Fire" cries out with a certain desperation for the rights of dark fantasy in culture. In terms of style, this happens through a largely internalized polemic in which Lantry reflects with scorn on how much violence this supposedly utopian society has already done to creatures of the imagination, such as vampires, zombies, and ghosts. For the most part, Bradbury allows us to feel the bitterness of his hero instead of constructing overt intellectual arguments. We realize that, whereas Lantry is *physically* dead, the people who inhabit this utopia without imagination are spiritually dead, deader than he ever was, because they have lost the power of blackness. We detect a mocking tone in the drama of Lantry's last words. Lantry, the bitter hero, is an agent of fear, but that is entirely appropriate to the weird tradition, as noted by Lovecraft. What matters is to break through the rigidity of social walls, to make society *afraid* again.

The Amontillado bottle and fire symbolism reappear in "The Library," a short short story in which the library of a certain Mr. A (who perhaps lives in an apartment complex) has been discovered by the authorities. Mr. A is evidently dying, sick at heart perhaps, and his condition becomes more acute as he is being removed from his "catacomb" of books on a stretcher. At any rate, we are treated by Mr. A to a long memorial catalogue of book titles and intertextual references—typical of menippean prose or "anatomy"—that evokes the cultural past and what will be lost. The catalogue is reminiscent of Lantry's and has a similar function, to move us to a realization of what the death of the imagination might mean. This could easily have been a scene like the one in *Fahrenheit 451* in which the woman chooses to die burning with her books rather than live. But the "passivity" and fragility of works of the imagination—they only come alive when we read or remember them—are mirrored in Mr. A's situation. Here and elsewhere, juxtaposed health and sickness are representations of culture under attack. The images of fire used here, however, are perhaps more melancholy because we feel no promise of a rebirth through the fires of carnival.

"Bonfire" and "Bright Phoenix" also use carnival fire symbolism, the latter with a sense of renewal, the former without it. "Bonfire" sets up the expectation of carnival renewal in its title, but defeats it at the end by revealing that the fires are those of nuclear annihilation. Modern art is summed up by the reveries and sensations of the main character, William Peterson, a writer who is remembering his pleasures in literature, music, painting, sculpture, and film. Through his dialogue via telephone with a woman named Mary, we are given a menippean catalogue of what is still living from the past (Shakespeare and Plato heading the list) and what is good in the present (some Picasso and Dalí paintings are worthwhile, and some are not). The criterion seems to be whether or not these objects gave pleasure and the experience of beauty and satisfaction in an alienated world. Interestingly, Peterson remembers touching a nude female statue in the Museum of Modern Art. Although he can appreciate pure form in a sensuous line drawn by Matisse, it is touching this female statue that gives him the most pleasure. Such an art object at MOMA would of course have been rather hard to find at this time, since women and beauty were perceived by many male artists as threatening the whole project of modern art with cheap tawdriness. In fact, Bradbury has to invent a fictitious artist (Lembroocke) in order to discover this pleasure for his character. Toward the end a bitter tone of nihilism creeps in. What was it all for, this adventure in civilization? Was it all for nothing? Peterson reveals that he had thought that some remnants of culture might survive among "the Islanders" or "the Asiatics," but the coming destruction is total. Significantly, the last thing Peterson thinks of is women, but there is no possibility of rebirth through the fecundity of the earth, which itself burns for a thousand million centuries.

"Bright Phoenix" is much more obviously influenced by carnival modes of speech. Indeed, it is told from the mocking point of view of a librarian, whose name (we find out at the end) among these book people is Socrates. Now Socrates in the dialogues attributed to him by Plato proceeds to remove ignorance largely by a method of *anacrisis*—the provoking of the word by the word, which makes of the truth a matter not of dogma, but of dialogue. As Bakhtin points out, the heroes of the Socratic dialogue are all ideologists bent on seeking and *testing* truth.[28] And if you are not an ideologist in this sense, then Socrates would turn you into one. Bradbury's story, modeled on Socratic dialogue, stages a debate in which those who would censor and burn books are stymied because those who love books have made the commitment to memorizing them as part of a strategy of resistance. The fascist-like Jonathan Barnes, who is expecting crowds of people to show up for the book burning, is confronted and tested by people who, while allowing him to do his job of book burning, quote various books to him that throw into doubt his assertion that books are "full of double-talk" and therefore should be suppressed in the interests of plain speaking. Barnes does not want a reasoned debate, but he is forced into one. Bradbury uses quotes from both traditional sides of our Western culture, the Hellenic (with its tradition of debate and resistance to tyranny) and the Hebraic (with its emphasis on justice and ethical vision). The narrator twice describes "the great Baal machinery" of the censor, referring to an episode of the Bible in which the prophet Elijah confutes the priests of Baal, recalling that prophet's satiric taunting of them on Mount Carmel (1 Kings 18:27)—they are unable to make their sacrifices burn. Acting the fool, the narrator also uses fire by tearing a page from Demosthenes, rolling it into a cigar, and smoking it while he quotes from him, thereby claiming that he is helping the chief censor do his job. This last act of carnival defiance enrages Barnes, who, like Hitler, wants every human action to have a clear "nationalistic" and racial meaning. Fire, always the ambivalent symbol, is here used as an agent of resistance. At the end, Mr.

Barnes is seen dying slowly of a hidden seepage of fire and raging life. His dignity and stature have been considerably reduced, and by the very means he sought to use. The initial attack of the censors has been effectively resisted, at least in Green Town, Illinois.

The phoenix is used as a fire symbol of recurrence at the end of *Fahrenheit 451* to indicate the rebirth of humanity out of darkness, but the earliest reference to people becoming books in order to resist state censorship is not in that volume, but in a manuscript of Bradbury's that dates from around 1947, *Where Ignorant Armies Clash by Night*. It is less an achieved literary work than a series of drafts for one. We know nothing of what Bradbury thought his audience was in writing it (it's dedicated to his wife, Marguerite McClure, whom he married in 1947). However, in the folder with the manuscript discards is the draft of a brief paragraph describing his intentions to a certain Miss Gauss, a fiction editor at *Harper's*. In this paragraph Bradbury states that the story describes the "final breakdown of faith" in a world of anarchy and disillusion in which values have been completely reversed. *Ignorant Armies* has literally fallen out of history for over sixty years, except for "The Smile," which was revised from it and published in 1952. Nonetheless, it is an important document, for it represents the abject hero at his most bitter, when carnival itself has been perverted, and there is no doubt that it reflects the tensions of the postwar years. Here "genre memory" can help us in understanding its broad artistic intentions, even if Bradbury does not remember them.

This lost novel manuscript is evidence that Bradbury was thinking about a dystopian novel focused on an abject hero and a bitter carnival well before the publication of "The Fireman" (*Galaxy*, 1951). *Where Ignorant Armies Clash by Night* depicts a situation of near absolute nihilism and vulgarity.[29] The story is set in a barren post-apocalyptic United States two centuries in the future, in which cultural values have been profoundly inverted. Society is held together by ritualized Roman circus-like ceremonies in which people are murdered by the Assassins or Great Killers, a guild of honored warrior-killers, who also—and this is its thematic link with *Fahrenheit 451*—burn and mutilate books for the adoring crowds. The last copy of the Bible is scheduled to be destroyed during an upcoming carnival in New Orleans. Books have become the center and focus of the democratic crowd's hatred of "elite" culture such as Shakespeare. The plot in one version has the assassin Muerte, like Montag, begin reading the books he is destroying. This reading in turn provokes a profound crisis of values in which the hero revolts against the democratic masses, discovering "the violence of writing" as he tries to make a copy of the last Shakespeare text before it is destroyed. His story does not end happily. Because of these actions, he becomes one of society's outcasts, not touchable or killable. Finally a committee of elders comes to him offering death by suicide (poison), considered a highly dishonorable death, and he accepts. Before he dies, he makes a speech in which he identifies with the authors he knows—Byron, Poe, Plato—expressing the idea that when he dies, they too will die. This speech identifying a character with what he has read has thematic links with several of Bradbury's other stories, including "Pillar of Fire" and "The Library," where similar lists occur. Interestingly, Muerte has heard stories of "people who are the books" living somewhere in the world and thinks of organizing them together into one community.

The entire text of Arnold's "Dover Beach" is cited in this text, as if in this desperate situation a great poem remembered could still have the power to teach us how to feel. It is ironic, of course, that with this gesture toward Arnold, Bradbury is making Arnold's idea about the "touchstones" of the past (the best that has been said and thought) come true in an ironic way through his own poem.[30] Bradbury indicates on one page of the manuscript that he took the poem from Louis Untermeyer's *A Treasury of Great Poems*. As he was using it then, Arnold's poem provides a context for melancholy, and for an act of suicide committed by one of the assassins, William Klinger. Arnold's poem is about a spiritual crisis in culture when the "Sea of Faith" has withdrawn from the world, leaving only the detritus of civilization on the beach. Likewise in *Fahrenheit 451*, when "Dover Beach" is recited almost in full, it creates the emotion of melancholy among women who have forgotten about feelings, and any ideal of radiant literacy has long since been replaced by the culture industry.[31]

At the heart of this fragmented story lies a struggle with the modern crisis of values, with nihilism, which is explained in a speech by the "old man" (not named in the manuscript but a clear analog to many "wise old man" figures in utopian fiction) to the child he is educating. According to the old man, everything is futile, all effort is in the end worthless. A man may, of course, still pursue disconnected ends, money, fame, art, science, and may gain pleasure from them. But life is hollow at the center. Hence the dissatisfied, disillusioned, and restless spirit of modern man. It is clear that Muerte (Death) the assassin is an almost allegorical figure, and the perverted carnival over which he presides is an attempt to make a religion of meaninglessness. But the bitter carnival can never create new values, not even when it is later supported by all the efforts of mass media depicted in *Fahrenheit 451*. It remains a performance for spectators, even though it is considered an honor to die in such a spectacle.

The wise old man of *Where Ignorant Armies Clash by Night* sees no way out of nihilism, which goes in cycles, but thinks that this new religion of Death can at least offer certainty, if not hope, in the figure of William Donne (Muerte), who is like a god to the people. This "god," however, is himself infected with a weariness of spirit toward the wonderfully negative world of killing and being killed over which he presides. He sees everyone, including himself, as ignorant and stupid fools, rolling in the filth of human degradation, and desperately wants to smash the system of false entertainments, of banquets, feasts, and festivals, over which he presides. This is where Bradbury's nostalgic longing for the true rituals of folk culture is at its most intense. But Donne remains an abject hero, powerless to do anything about his situation. He is full of bitterness.

The names of the assassin characters vary in the discarded pages. But William Elliott was probably a developmental character concept—an assassin, himself, who took to reading books. It is he who reads "Dover Beach" to the crowd before giving it to them, burning it leaf by leaf, in a scene whose language looks forward to that of Beatty's nihilistic reading in *Fahrenheit 451*. But in *Where Ignorant Armies Clash by Night*, the burning pages are caught by the crowd and eaten in a ceremony that suggests a cannibalistic feast. All of the fragments are filled with these debased social rituals. Possibly what Bradbury is aiming at with this character is a way out of the system. Elliott nearly breaks down in front of the frenzied crowd, and in the fragments from a somewhat later draft or section of the novel he subverts the system by pleading with another assassin, William Kindler, to spare his life. Elliott as victim is given a long speech in a revised outline fragment (parts of which are recalled later by William Kindler). In his speech before Kindler he calls himself a flame in the wilderness, which can burn people clean of melancholy. But Kindler is apparently unable to affirm his own life, and slays Elliott, regretting it later. What is missing is the way out of nihilism, which is only briefly hinted at here—a rediscovery of the value and meaning of earthly life through imaginative reveries of purifying fire.

A story related to *Where Ignorant Armies Clash by Night* is "Of All Things—Never to Have Been Born Is Best," which creates a seriocomic travesty of the cycle of tragic nihilism (the title is taken from Sophocles's *Oedipus at Colonus*). The story takes place on a "planet of wild values," whose landscape of little white chess cities set beside dry sea bottoms lit by "unbelievable" red dawns and sunsets suggests the Mars of *The Martian Chronicles*. The fog that surrounds these "fog people" is symbolic of the confused state of values in their culture. In this story William Richard, the unhappy descendant of one of the Greatest Killers, is repeatedly urged to commit a ritual slaying by an old man whose belief is a nihilistic pun—there is nothing better than Nothingness—and who claims that it would be an honor to be killed by him. Richard abuses him throughout their satiric dialogue by viciously attacking various parts of the old man's body, protesting after each outrage that he still feels nothing. Clearly, this parodies the serious quest for the meaning of the earth as a way out of nihilism and bitterness, which is evoked in "The Tanami Couplets" that the old man recites to Richard, but only in order to enrage him more (because the meaning of that land is absent from the poems). Although the old man apparently falls down dead,

Richard's crisis of values continues. In the end we find out that the old name (i.e., meaning) of this planet really is Earth, but no one cares.

Another story from this lost manuscript is "The Smile," published in 1952. It is set on a festival day on which the common denizens—possibly farmers—of a post-apocalyptic world line up for a democratic day of marketing and art appreciation. One of these marketplace rituals involves spitting on works of high art, in this case the *Mona Lisa*. In one of the mocking gestures of Dada, Marcel Duchamp had drawn a moustache and goatee on her famous face—which had come to stand for the idea that the representation of a mysterious and seductive female beauty *is* art—but Bradbury's carnival debasement goes a long way past this humorous act of defacement (meant by Duchamp in part to suggest da Vinci's homosexuality). In the manuscript version she is covered with the accumulated spittle of boys who are anxious to degrade her gaze, which they think is "smirking" at them. In this manner Benjaminian aura is completely defiled. The "river of vileness" that finally covers her has clear sexual overtones.

By contrast, in the published version, the devastated landscape of bitter carnival (cities all junk, radioactive cornfields glowing at night) is more in evidence. The central character, Tom, is a young boy who remembers other festivals of hate (when everyone was "drunk and laughing") that destroyed books and other objects from the past. Indeed, these characters hate the past so much that they have no intention of rebuilding civilization like it was. They allow that someone with a soul for pretty things may accomplish it, however. At the chaotic destruction of the painting, Tom manages to tear a piece of the canvas containing her smile, that enigmatic smile that has puzzled art historians over the centuries, voicing many male anxieties over the representation of women in art (Walter Pater famously found the painting haunted by a female vampire). At the end of the story Tom, while probably an excellent expectorator, is one of those people with heart who can see the smile as "warm and gentle" and on whom the rebuilding of civilization will depend. The smile provides an experience of pleasure and satisfaction on which Tom can base his reveries of the moon (the female light that shines by reflection) as he falls asleep in a silo. In the earlier version found in *Ignorant Armies*, which was to have been the final chapter of the novel, the smile is more obviously a fetish object, a "fur-wrapped treasure," which is unwrapped slowly, fold by fold. Bradbury in both versions is hinting that the bitter carnival may be overcome, by bringing back Venus from exile.

Poe, who said that the death of a beautiful woman was the highest subject for poetry, is the subject of two stories in which Bradbury explores the politics of resistance. In "Carnival of Madness," antiseptic technology is turned against itself to create a replica of Poe's decaying House of Usher in a modern land. Constructed by technicians who are unconcerned about its meaning, it is nonetheless emphatically declared beautiful by its owner, Stendahl. Eventually the house kills, in hideous ways prescribed by Poe, the members of the Society for the Prevention of Fantasy, but the focus of the revenge is on Garrett, the investigator of moral climates. At first glance Stendahl seems a bitter hero, indeed a reactive victim of self-poisoning, having nursed his hatred and anger over the years until he can pay back tit for tat a government that sees fit to ban all escapes from reality. Both he and Pikes the horror-film actor have had their libraries and films destroyed and have spent many hours in "bitter brewings" of thought before they come up with the ruse of the House of Usher. I would argue, however, that though they are outcasts, and Pikes is described as impossible and defeated, Stendahl and Pikes are not entirely abject. Actually, their conduct is more in the nature of artistic self-defense. I'll explore this notion of aesthetic revenge as a part of the cultural politics of this story, in which fantasy is at war with realism, as we go along.

As in the saturnalia, Stendahl reverses values by having his guests mask themselves, "the very act of putting on a mask revoking their licenses to pick a quarrel with fantasy and horror," Bradbury says. Stendahl also ironically asks one of his guests before killing him if he does not have the feeling that "all this has happened before," testing his victim's knowledge of the fantasy books he has helped to burn. In the war against realism, Bradbury even drops an ironic reference to Sinclair Lewis's *Babbitt* (the very name "Babbitt" suggesting to the informed reader *the* model of American middle-class narrow-mindedness and self-satisfaction) when he tells Garrett that he'll be burning Babbitts next. Since Garrett has just declared his purpose to destroy *any* creature of the imagination, Stendahl's joke relies on our understanding that Babbitt (i.e., Garrett) is a literary creation (in fact a robot simulacrum, as we later discover) and thus equally a creature of the imagination.

The title "Carnival of Madness" amplifies Poe's "The Cask of Amontillado," which is set, Poe's narrator tells us, one evening during the supreme madness of the carnival season. What is more, Garrett, the investigator of moral climates, is killed by Stendahl in exactly the same way and with much of the same dialogue as Fortunato is in Poe's story. Thus, although the main instrument of Bradbury's revenge against those who would censor and repress fantasy is an artificial robotic incarnation of Poe's House of Usher, this story, like Poe's, has a deep connection to the thematic matrices of carnival. Poe's "The Masque of the Red Death" also provides the imagery for the costume ball in which the members of the Society for the Prevention of Fantasy are killed (and which is the source of the illustration used by *Thrilling Wonder Stories*, April 1950, when it published the story).

Bakhtin has in fact given us a very interesting reading of Poe's place in the history of carnivalization. Bakhtin argues that in romanticism and symbolism generally, the matrices of carnival are transformed from "the all-encompassing whole of triumphant life" to sharp static contrasts that are not resolved at all, but remain in tension, sealed off in the progression of an individual soul and life.[32] This can lead to the experience of bitter carnival, which is what "The Cask of Amontillado" in fact celebrates (if that is the right word). At the heart of Poe's story is a complex series of themes derived from the carnival matrix: death, the mask of the fool, laughter, entombment. But the story seems to have an intense inner focus. Psychoanalytic critics have argued that the story largely deals with Poe's own interior self. They see the victim, Fortunato, as a double of Montresor who is sealing off his own sexual impulses that are driving him toward returning to the womb of his mother (in Marie Bonaparte's famous reading, echoed by Daniel Hoffman). Bradbury's early critics, Anthony Boucher among them, were quick to seize on the return-to-the-womb fantasy in Bradbury's writings.[33]

In my opinion, Bradbury's second House of Usher, however personal, does not have this type of interior focus. His story is about political trends in the field of culture that were affecting his authorship, particularly censorship. Bradbury's house murders people who are types belonging to certain ideological and class positions, though the best revenge is taken individually, on Garrett, who has not read Poe but who could have escaped his fate had he done so. Furthermore, Bradbury gets the kind of revenge that Poe's narrator only wishes for: Montresor wants to be revenged at length and without the possibility of retribution overtaking its redresser. He wants to avenge himself with impunity. But if the psychoanalytic reading of the story is correct in terms of Poe's authorship, then Poe turns out in the end to be his own victim. Not so for Stendahl, who fulfills Poe's wish by destroying the House of Usher in the exact artistic way described in Poe's text and, in the process, destroys the evidence of murder. We are compelled to see the destruction of this second House of Usher as an exercise in the *art* of murder.

Though the aura of the Gothic house is restored together with its chronotope, this act of creation/destruction may not quite fulfill Bakhtin's nostalgic sense of carnival needing to return in modern culture, overcoming alienation and bringing people closer to one another. Its tone is too angry, one-sided, and bitter. But Bradbury's bitter carnival was an authentic response to the dominance of realism in American cultural politics at the time, though he was never entirely comfortable with its role in *The Martian Chronicles* (1950).[34] Incidentally, one of the many ironic jokes in this story involves not a fantasy writer but Hemingway. Stendahl reveals that Garrett's people had forced film producers to abandon the making of horror films (hence the end of Pikes's career) and to exclusively make and remake Hemingway in "realistic versions." As it turns out, Bakhtin, the Soviet scholar, in revising his book on Dostoevsky, thought Hemingway was a writer whose works were on the whole "deeply carnivalized" because of the presence of bullfights and other festivals of a carnival type in his writings.[35]

Now, Bradbury's understanding of Hemingway—a writer whom he truly admired and about whom he has written several stories—also goes beyond seeing him simply as a "realistic" writer, narrowly conceived. Carnival does not exclude realism. On the contrary, Bakhtin's very term for it as an aesthetic mode was *grotesque realism*. It's hard to resist plumbing the depths of irony in this story. Bradbury masks himself as Stendhal—a master of psychological realism in such novels as *Red and Black* —in order to unmask the stupid rigidity and narrow-minded seriousness of an official culture that cannot even discern the presence of the carnivalesque in the writer it picks to represent the status quo (chapter eighteen of *For Whom the Bell Tolls* is filled with carnival symbolism).

This ironic situation has its historical parallel in Bakhtin in the early decades of Soviet Russia, which under Stalin was "progressing" along the path of socialist realism. In terms of satiric technique, Stendahl in Bradbury's story double-voices many of Montresor's words in Poe's story in a way that subverts the authority of literary culture in America at the time. For instance, Stendahl requires Garrett to say the exact words of Fortunato in Poe's story, to put on the fool's cap and bells, remarking that the entombment of Fortunato/Garrett is indeed a "very good joke" (Montresor's very words in Poe's story). It's important to realize that at the time Bradbury was writing, Poe was not an accepted part of the literary canon, not in America anyway. He was acknowledged as the founder of popular forms such as detective fiction but was primarily thought of as a writer whose appeal depended on sensationalism and whose artistic integrity had been compromised by the commercial forces of magazine publication.

I said above that although this is a bitter carnival, Stendahl is not in the end an abject hero like Lantry of "Pillar of Fire" (though he too has felt abjection). This is so because the artistic techniques of satire—reduction—are directed primarily at the enemies of fantasy, like Garrett, and do not turn inward on the hero himself to create self-doubt or a stinging awareness of having missed the carnival of life. In building the second House of Usher, and in taking their "artistic" revenge, Stendahl and his factotum Pikes do not construct fantasy so much out of self-hatred and impotent anger as out of strength of the artistic will affirming itself in play. There is a great deal of play with robot simulacrums replacing real humans in the course of the narrative, and a deliberate confusion of the imitated with the real at some points. In order to pull off his murders, Stendahl has to convince everyone that he is in fact only murdering robots (i.e., aesthetic illusions). The story is a lesson in the *interestedness* of art, in how elements of ego and power mingle in all its aspects, as opposed to the Kantian notion of aesthetic experience as impersonality and disinterestedness, the aesthetic that has dominated modern art.[36] Stendahl is clearly an *author* in constructing Usher II, his "mechanical sanctuary." Although it is satire expressing some bitterness, the story's point of view is that of the creative artist, and it is full of evocative details about the robots, those desiring-machines, that inhabit the house so that we, too, are invited to revel in the creation and operation of the House of Usher.

A bitter carnival, we may remember, is basically "a dispute between culture and its discontented rejects."[37] This is the exact situation in "The Mad Wizards of Mars," where we see from alternating points of view both the ideological forces that are hostile to fantasy and the imaginary forces inhabiting the red planet, which is a fitting site for such a war to take place, since so many fantasies, scientific or otherwise, have historically been projected there. The tale begins after the mass burning of literature on Earth has sent the spirits of great authors and their famous characters into exile on Mars. As the first Earth expedition approaches Mars, the exiled ghosts begin to take revenge. Although "Shakespeare's army" is very much in evidence— the story opens with the weird sisters from *Macbeth* —the real leader of the exiles is Poe, who inhabits the House of Usher. Poe is romanticized in a Byronic fashion: as the Satan of some lost dark cause. But it is Poe who expresses the abject bitterness of all the "Others" who have mysteriously appeared on Mars (including the most abject of them all, Santa Claus). It seems that they were never given a fair trial before a company of literary critics, but were simply condemned. Because of their unjust repression on Earth, they have the spectral power to enter into dreams and cause havoc and hallucinations, as long as the books containing their works survive. Poe tries to recruit Hawthorne, who lives in his own land, in the hopes that he can negotiate with the invaders. But Hawthorne demurs, feeling that he does not belong among the outcasts. After all, he has only written one supernatural story, "Rappaccini's Daughter." Poe points out that this is the way censorship works. Once censoring begins, it is a quick slide to removing the entire oeuvre of a writer, whether fantasy or not. This has not happened with Dickens, however, because, ironically, he wrote such a wealth of uncensorable material. Hawthorne agrees to help, but it is too late for negotiations.[38] The rocket ship arrives with the last collection of banned books, and the captain promptly burns them in the spirit of technological modernism. Fire symbolism is once again used to point toward a bitter carnival. Poe's army too has fire, and strikes back, hearts bursting in bloody fireworks on the singed air, but it is ineffective, imaginary. The authors disappear together with their creations, as the bonfire consumes the ancient books with their blasphemous names.

Both of these stories create through the techniques of bitter carnival sites of potential resistance to the authority of mainstream cultural politics in 1950s literary culture. However, the great satirists of the Western tradition— Rabelais, Swift—attacked not just people or ideologies that they thought were bad, they also created dream worlds in which the real world is fantastically inverted. In the more recent history of utopian fiction, we could mention George Orwell's *1984* (where freedom is slavery) and Aldous Huxley's *Brave New World*, whose referencing of Shakespeare (in its title and in its main character, the Savage) Bradbury certainly knew. In the last two stories of this collection that I will consider, Bradbury's inversions all have to do with the real world suddenly being transformed into a nightmare world of abjection. It has been argued by cultural critics that one of the main problems of modernity is waste management—how to come to terms with the waste and destruction that modern consumer culture produces.[39] It must somehow be expelled and turned into "otherness," so that the self and identity can be created. The first of the two, "The Garbage Collector," is a realistic story about the pathos of waste. Its sociology turns on the notion of the degradation of work by the threat of atomic war. Modernity, through the rational management of civil defense, turns a meaningful job into alienation. The second story, "The Pedestrian," involves a writer who wanders the modern urban wasteland at night looking for meaning in the fragments of the devastated landscape.

Bradbury's garbage collector is a type of common man who works on a garbage truck, seeing garbage as "bad" but also as something that can be tolerated, even enjoyed, as long as it is seen as a game. But when he realizes that he will be called upon to collect bodies in the event of war, this suddenly transforms his attitude toward his work, making it "strange." As much as the sociological, there are psychological depths to this story as well. What was previously a game in which he and his partner could interpret social status from the refuse they collected is now threatened by the notion that he will have to think about how to organize dead bodies on the truck. Thinking about this situation introduces the notion of transgression of boundaries (will the bodies be thrown together indiscriminately, women with men, animals with humans, and so on). Even more dehumanizing, he realizes that he might even get used to the idea of doing that. Although not an imaginative man, in the end he begins to see and think about the white maggots seething in the garbage. These images evoke the horrifying experience of abjection, which is the threat of the collapse of the extinction of meaning. The irony of the last sentence, spoken by the wife in welcoming her children home to dinner, has to be appreciated by the reader. Of course we realize what the family meal now means and why the garbage collector no longer wants to eat—it will produce more garbage.

The sociology of "The Pedestrian" turns also on the reversal of social norms, a favorite technique of satire. Bradbury envisages a time in the near future in which nearly everyone is so wrapped up in the experience of mass media that it is considered abnormal—indeed bordering on the criminal—for anyone to take a solitary walk at night. Mr. Leonard Mead is "arrested" on his walk, but, ironically, crime has declined to such an extent that only one patrol car remains, and that is run by robotic means. He is not taken to a jail, but to a psychiatric center for "regressive" tendencies. The story is satiric because Mead addresses the denizens of the "tomb-like" house with rhetorical questions about what they might be watching on television, questions that have broader implications for the society of spectacles as a whole. He asks them ironically where the cowboys are rushing off to, and whom the U.S. Cavalry is rescuing tonight. Graveyard, tomb, desert—these are Bradbury's chronotopic metaphors for what has happened to the real world in the television landscape (long before Baudrillard theorized about the postmodern).

Fantasy writers, not realists, were again among the first to describe important but unnoticed changes in our perception of the world. The distinction between the imaginary and the real, which still exists for Mead, has disappeared for most of the inhabitants of this future city. It's clear that in this future no one reads anymore or tries to construe the meaning of things. Rather, people inhabit simulations with ready-made meanings, a kind of programmed fantastic. Mead, a writer who hardly writes anymore, is out to find what meaning he can in what the city has rejected as abject, in the ways that the natural world has begun to reclaim the city—with flowers and grass growing out from under the unused, buckling cement sidewalks.

The inverted world that we see in "The Pedestrian" is recognizably that of "Long After Midnight" and "The Fireman," which are earlier versions of what eventually became *Fahrenheit 451*. Indeed, Clarisse, whom we first meet in "Long After Midnight," is another pedestrian, like Leonard Mead, who triggers a profound response in Montag, the fireman. In effect, Bradbury expanded the world of "The Pedestrian" into a satirical novel about the effects of mass culture. Clarisse's role is enormously important in all three versions of the *Fahrenheit* text, and even though she disappears early in the novel, Clarisse embodies what the modern world so achingly lacked for Bradbury: the experience of beauty and feeling, an otherness that is not to be colonized or expelled, denatured or killed (though that is what the modern world does to her), but that is to be honored and welcomed as the meeting of self and Other in a "beautiful we," the end of power, the experience of freedom in reverie.[40] As a writer in love with the world, who thought that the world needed us to see it in order to reveal its true beauty, Bradbury could never embrace the nihilistic sublime of characters such as Beatty (Leahy in the earlier version). Any artist who could create a second House of Usher that is beautiful and alluring, though fatal to those without imagination, has met abjection and bitterness but overcome them.

My aim in this chapter has been to situate certain of Bradbury's postwar writings in the context of the cultural politics of modernism. One of the ironies of Bradbury's literary fortune has been that, while he has become an acknowledged cultural icon of the twentieth century, his writings are still compared not to a tradition of satire, but to the commercial cuteness of

Norman Rockwell.[41] His unabashed nostalgia for popular culture is perhaps to blame for this impression. In my view Bradbury has always been a writer who has aspired to more than just celebrating a sentimental nostalgia for small-town life, though arguably this is a large part of his popular appeal today. For me Bradbury's writings have always provided a rich field of potentially "other" meanings that have made him a part of serious modern literature. I am not alone in this understanding. Recent discussions of the cultural politics of modernism that weigh the contributions of prominent science fiction authors such as H. G. Wells, Yevgeny Zamyatin, and Arthur C. Clarke often mention Bradbury as someone who has helped us understand modernity and "live on" in the post-holocaust world of today.[42] It may be that his awareness of what is passing—that October country with its autumnal imagery and smoldering fires—is far more acute than his sense of what is to come, but these stories still remain as sparks in the carnival bonfire that can renew the world. Bradbury himself summed up his feelings about this complex and contradictory period in American culture by returning to L. Frank Baum and his Oz in 1974 and by saying that his fears were now in abeyance, that the realists were losing way to a conception of man as a loving companion to the universe.[43] By such hopes he intended to continue living, in the spirit of Mr. Electrico.

NOTES

1. See the tribute to Bradbury published by *The Nostalgia Digest* (Autumn 2012): 1–2.
2. Bradbury often gave his most relaxed and revealing biographical musings to small magazines. One of the fullest accounts he ever gave of the Mr. Electrico experience and his involvement in popular culture and carnival was to Brad Linaweaver, *Wonder* No. 8 (1992): 2–17. I am relying primarily on the account Bradbury gave to Linaweaver. Mr. Electrico's performance consisted of sitting in an electric chair, allowing electricity to flow through his body, and then rising to touch people in the audience with a silver sword. I'm tempted to contrast Bradbury's experience with Lovecraft's experience of Nyarlathotep/Tesla discussed in the previous chapter.
3. For an account of this complex textual and thematic history, see Jonathan R. Eller and William F. Touponce, *Ray Bradbury: The Life of Fiction* (Kent, OH: Kent State University Press, 2004), 51–104.
4. Mikhail Bakhtin, *Rabelais and His World*, translated by Helene Iswolsky (Bloomington: Indiana University Press, 1984), 101–36.
5. Eller, *Ray Bradbury: The Life of Fiction*. Bradbury granted me an interview concerning the role of carnival in his writings, which I edited as an afterword to Eller and Touponce, *Ray Bradbury: The Life of Fiction*, 433–435. My involvement with Bradbury and carnival started in the late 1980s. At the time, Bradbury was kind enough to read and comment on my Bakhtinian reading of *Something Wicked This Way Comes*. In an encouraging letter, Bradbury called me a true reader and a friend (personal letter, 2 May 1988). Selected bibliographical references to this article and others can be found in *The Life of Fiction*, 560.
6. For a discussion of the aura of the chronotope, see Gary Saul Morson and Caryl Emerson, *Mikhail Bakhtin: Creation of a Prosaics* (Stanford: Stanford University Press, 1990), 374–75. The authors give as an example of chronotopic aura the castle in Gothic fiction, which is not just a building, but an image saturated with its own experience of time and space, and traces of previous generations.

7. Michael André Bernstein, *Bitter Carnival: Ressentiment and the Abject Hero* (Princeton: Princeton University Press, 1992).
8. Herschel B. Chipp, ed., *Theories of Modern Art* (Berkeley: University of California Press, 1968), 493.
9. Otto Friedrich, *City of Nets* (New York: Harper & Row, 1986), 96.
10. David L. Ulin, ed., *Writing Los Angeles: A Literary Anthology* (New York: Library of America, 2002).
11. Chipp, ed., *Theories of Modern Art*, 496–97.
12. Bradbury adored both artists and wrote stories about them: "The Watchful Poker Chip of Henri Matisse" (1954) and "In a Season of Calm Weather" (1957; later retitled "The Picasso Summer" for film and for story reprints since 1980). The first is a satire on the pretensions of the avant-garde, and the second is a poignant story of a man who discovers Picasso drawing an elaborate "bacchanal" on a sandy Mediterranean beach, which is later washed away by the tide.
13. Wendy Steiner, *Venus in Exile: The Rejection of Beauty in 20th-Century Art* (New York: Free Press, 2001), 115.
14. Ray Bradbury, "Day after Tomorrow: Why Science Fiction?" *Nation* (2 May 1953): 364. This sentence has been excised from later reprints of this article in Bradbury collections.
15. Kingsley Amis, *New Maps of Hell* (New York: Ballantine, 1960), 94.
16. Amis did, however, consider Robert Sheckley, together with Pohl and Kornbluth, to be the primary examples of this new form of satire aimed at exposing the various forms of persuasion (especially the language of advertising). "Neo-menippean" was the term self-consciously and self-mockingly used by Sheckley to describe his writings (though at a later date; see *Galaxy*, July 1975, 12). The term is not perhaps well known to most readers. Traditional menippean satire (the best-known example of which is Lewis Carroll's *Alice in Wonderland*) contains debates involving role reversals, a direct connection with the decrowning rituals of Saturnalia. What is more, a medley of other literary forms and speech genres may be appropriated by the debate. Usually, menippean satire is cheerfully intellectual and less aggressive than satire *per se*, although it holds up contemporary intellectual life to gentle ridicule (see discussion, below, of "Bright Phoenix"). For those unfamiliar with Bakhtinian terminology, another term for this literary mode is "anatomy" (Northrop Frye), the most famous example of which is Burton's *Anatomy of Melancholy*.
17. Matthew Hodgart, *Satire* (New York: McGraw-Hill, 1969), 115.
18. For an account of Bradbury's genre contacts, see my introduction to Ray Bradbury, *The Collected Stories of Ray Bradbury*, edited by William F. Touponce and Jonathan R. Eller (Kent, OH: Kent State University Press, 2010).
19. Katerina Clark and Michael Holquist, *Mikhail Bakhtin* (Cambridge, MA: Harvard University Press, 1984), 307.
20. Bernstein, *Bitter Carnival*, 23.
21. Amis, *New Maps of Hell*, 92.
22. The stories under discussion here are collected in Ray Bradbury, *A Pleasure to Burn: Fahrenheit 451 Stories* (New York: Harper, 2011).
23. Mikhail Bakhtin, *Problems of Dostoevsky's Poetics*, edited and translated by Caryl Emerson (Minneapolis: University of Minnesota Press, 1984), 133.
24. Bakhtin, *Problems of Dostoevsky's Poetics*, 132.
25. Gilles Deleuze and Felix Guattari, *Anti-Oedipus: Capitalism and Schizophrenia* (New York: Viking Press, 1977), 47.
26. Ray Bradbury, *Pillar of Fire and Other Plays for Today, Tomorrow and Beyond* (New York: Bantam, 1975). Bradbury also calls him a "sympathetic madman" (x).
27. Deleuze and Guattari, *Anti-Oedipus*, 329.
28. Bakhtin, *Problems of Dostoevsky's Poetics*, 111.
29. See my genre analysis in *Ray Bradbury: The Life of Fiction*, 199–201.
30. Bradbury revisited and dialectically reversed the idea of cultural "touchstones" in "To the Chicago Abyss," *Fantasy and Science Fiction* (May 1963). In this story, which is set in a post-apocalyptic world, an old man remembers all the scintillant junk of popular culture in the hopes that this mediocrity will stimulate civilization to rebuild on a higher level of excellence.

31. For an analysis of the culture industry (the term is Adorno's) in *Fahrenheit 451*, see William F. Touponce, *Ray Bradbury and the Poetics of Reverie* (Ann Arbor, MI: UMI Research Press, 1984), 85, and passim.

32. Mikhail Bakhtin, *The Dialogic Imagination*, edited by Michael Holquist (Austin: University of Texas Press, 1981), 199–200.

33. Eller and Touponce, *Ray Bradbury: The Life of Fiction*, 90–92.

34. Later, and for inclusion in *The Martian Chronicles*, Bradbury added passages linking the story to the landscape of Mars. The presence of this story in *The Martian Chronicles* was somewhat troublesome for Bradbury. He loved it as expressing his concerns about the cultural politics in the 1950s. Indeed, it mentions the fear of the word "politics" becoming identified with communism, and the cultural situation in which art and literature were being twisted into knots and thrown in all directions by societal pressures. But its bitter theme didn't fit *The Martian Chronicles* as a colonization chronicle. Nevertheless, in that framework the obvious point of the story is that ordinary Earth morality, which represses fantasy, must not be allowed to take over on Mars. As in "The Exiles," Bradbury's Mars was intended to be a chronotopic refuge for fantasy.

35. Bakhtin, *Problems of Dostoevsky's Poetics*, 179n22. Bakhtin notes that "he had a very keen ear for everything carnivalistic in contemporary life."

36. See discussion in Steiner, *Venus in Exile*, 1–131.

37. Bernstein, *Bitter Carnival*, 25.

38. Bradbury's second House of Usher, which makes an appearance in "The Mad Wizards of Mars," was changed to the Emerald City of *The Wizard of Oz* when published in *Fantasy and Science Fiction* as "The Exiles," perhaps because Bradbury felt he needed a decidedly American fantasy reference. The basic themes and structure of the narrative are pretty much the same in all versions, but "The Mad Wizards of Mars" has significant differences in the choice of authors Bradbury puts on Mars, especially Hawthorne, who was removed as a character from later versions. New material on H. P. Lovecraft was added to this *F&SF* version, which was then removed in the "final" version included in *The Illustrated Man*. Even that version has been further changed to remove references to psychoanalysis. Anthony Boucher undoubtedly had something to do with the removal of Hawthorne and the insertion of Lovecraft. As an abject hero, however, the reclusive Lovecraft does not work. As we have seen, he was more problematic than abject. Although concerned about "the crisis," he does nothing to help the other exiles (as the great indifferentist he's depicted as immersed in writing his voluminous correspondence and eating ice cream). Undoubtedly Bradbury later removed him from the version included in *The Illustrated Man* to make the tone more bitter and desperate. Also, part of the *F&SF* story is concerned with the internal politics of the exiles on Mars, with Baum being upset by Poe's takeover of the Emerald City.

39. Steiner, *Venus in Exile*, 82–84.

40. Steiner, *Venus in Exile*, 115. Steiner sees *Fahrenheit 451* as one of several books providing a provocation against the notion of sublimity, which she argues tried to exclude women from modern art. *Fahrenheit 451* was subsequently published in *Playboy* magazine, famous for its display of the female body.

41. James Park, *Icons* (New York: Collier, 1991), 51.

42. Peter Conrad, *Modern Times, Modern Places* (New York: Alfred A. Knopf, 1999), 720.

43. Ray Bradbury, "Because, Because, Because, Because of the Wonderful Things He Does," in Michael Patrick Hearn, ed., *The Wizard of Oz*, The Critical Heritage Series (New York: Schocken Books, 1983), 251.

Index

Adorno, Theodor W., viii, xi, xiii, xvi, 7–8, 36, 41, 50n10, 63, 97, 137n31
allegory, xiii, xv, xviii, 22, 25, 27, 29, 33, 43, 71, 75–76, 77, 79, 80, 81, 84, 87, 96–97, 99, 105n73
Amis, Kingsley, 112–113
anacrisis, 124
aura (atmosphere), x, xi, xii–xiv, xvi, xvii, xviii, xxn15, 3–4, 6, 17, 26, 50n11, 59, 62, 64–67, 69–70, 71, 72, 73, 74, 75–77, 79, 81, 82, 83–84, 85, 87, 89, 92, 93, 94, 95, 96, 98–101, 102n12, 104n52, 110, 128, 130, 135n6

Bachelard, Gaston, 65
Bakhtin, Mikhail, viii, 85, 86, 109–110, 113, 114, 124, 129, 130–131, 136n16
Baum, L. Frank, 111, 134, 137n38
beauty, xii, xiii, xvi, xvii, xviii, 1–8, 9, 10, 16, 17–18, 21, 23, 24–29, 30–31, 33, 34–35, 37, 39, 40, 41–42, 43–44, 45–46, 47, 49, 62, 64, 65–66, 67, 68–69, 72, 76, 77–78, 82–83, 87, 90, 98, 104n46, 111, 123, 128, 134
Benjamin, Walter, viii, ix, x, xi–xii, xiii–xv, xvi–xvii, xviii, xxn18, 11, 36–37, 60, 65–66, 69, 72, 77, 81, 84, 84–85, 88, 89, 99, 100, 101, 109, 115, 128
Bradbury, Ray, vii–viii, x, xiv, xvii, xviii, 109–115; "Bonfire", 114, 123; "Bright Phoenix", 124; "Carnival of Madness" ("Usher II"), 128–131; "Day after Tomorrow: Why Science Fiction?", 112; *Fahrenheit 451*, xviii, 114–115; "The Fireman", 134; "The Garbage Collector", 133; *The Illustrated Man*, 137n38; "The Library", 123; "Long After Midnight", 114, 134; "The Mad Wizards of Mars" ("The Exiles"), 132–133; *The Martian Chronicles*, 130, 137n34; "Of All Things—Never to Have Been Born Is Best", 127; "The Pedestrian", 110–111, 116, 133–134; "Pillar of Fire", 119–123; *A Pleasure to Burn*, 110; "The Reincarnate", 66, 117; "The Scythe", viii; "The Smile", 128; *Timeless Stories for Today and Tomorrow*, 116; *Where Ignorant Armies Clash by Night*, 125–127
Brecht, Bertolt, 111

capitalism, ix–xi, xiv, xviii, xxn27, 3, 5, 7, 10, 21, 23, 25, 27–28, 29, 33, 34, 41, 49, 55n98, 57, 60, 62, 68, 82, 102n13, 134
carnival, xviii, 109–110, 111, 113–115, 117, 121, 122, 124–125, 128, 129, 130, 131–132
chronotope, 110, 135n6
cosmicism, 62, 72

Deleuze, Gilles and Felix Guattari, 121–122
demonic, the, viii, xiii, xiv, xvii, xviii, xixn4, 34, 61, 64, 65, 71, 76, 78, 82, 84, 85–86, 87, 89, 92, 95, 96, 99, 102n19, 103n31, 106n99, 115
Derrida, Jacques, xvi, xixn10
Dewey, John, ix–x
"Dover Beach" (Matthew Arnold), 115, 126, 127
Duchamp, Marcel, 128
Dunsany, Lord (Edward John Moreton Drax Plunkett), vii, x, xi, xvii, xviii, 1–2, 4, 7, 9–10, 35–37; *The Blessing of Pan*, 11, 43–45; "Carcassonne", 31; "The Cave of Kai", 18; *The Charwoman's Shadow*, 41–43; *The Chronicles of Roderiguez*, 3, 38; *The Curse of the Wise Woman*, 11, 45–46; "The Eye in the Waste", 13; "The Fall of Babbulkund", 25; *The Gods of Pegāna*, 12–13; "The Idle City", 32; "Idle Days on the Yann", 32–35; "In the Land of Time", 18; "The Journey of the King", 18–23; *The King of Elfland's Daughter*, 39–41, 69; "The Kith of the Elf-Folk", 25–27; "The Lord of Cities", 28–29; "Of the Thing That Is Neither God Nor Beast", 14; "On an Old Battlefield", 36; "Poltarnees Beholder of Ocean", 29–31; "Prayer of the Men of Daleswood", 35; "The River", 16–17; "Romance on the Modern Stage", 4–5, 50n14; "The Sayings of Imbaum", 15; *The Story of Mona Sheehy*, 11, 47–49; "The Sword of Welleran", 24, 29; "A Tale of London", 32; *Time and the Gods*, 15, 17–18; "Usury", 23–24

Edison, Thomas Alva, 81
Erfahrung (continuous experience), x, xi, xii, xvi–xvii, xviii, 42, 53n56, 60, 65, 72, 86, 90, 96, 100, 102n16
Erlebnis (momentary experience), xi, xiii, xvii, 53n56, 102n11, 102n16
experience, modern, vii–xi; and experiment, 89, 90, 96

fabulation, 5, 49n1

Freud, Sigmund, xiii, xiv, 61, 77
Frye, Northrop, x, 1, 2, 4, 5, 10–12

Goldmann, Lucien, xxn27, 55n97, 57, 60, 68
gothic, the, viii, xiv, 57, 73, 85, 91, 130, 135n6
grotesque, the, x, xvii–xviii, 39, 53n67, 61, 62–63, 64, 65, 71, 72, 75, 77, 81–82, 83, 87, 89–90, 91, 92–93, 94, 99, 102n19–103n20, 106n94, 131

hauntology, 64, 67, 103n30
Hemingway, Ernest, 130–131
Hoffmann, E. T. A., xvii, 102n19
HUAC (House Committee on Un-American Activities), 110

ideologeme, 79, 82

Jameson, Fredric, xvi, 2, 5, 36, 50n12, 52n48, 80

Koestler, Arthur, 112
Krutch, Joseph Wood, viii–ix

Lewis, Sinclair, 129
Lovecraft, H. P., vii, viii, x, xi, xiii, xvii, xviii, 57–67; *At the Mountains of Madness*, 62, 64, 98; "The Beast in the Cave", 61; "Beyond the Wall of Sleep", 76–77; "The Call of Cthulhu", 69, 71; *The Case of Charles Dexter Ward*, 64, 91, 96; "Celephaïs", 68–69; "The Colour out of Space", 73, 95; "Dagon", 62, 75–76, 77; *The Dream-Quest of Unknown Kadath*, xiii, 64, 96–97; "The Dunwich Horror", 69; "Ex Oblivione", xixn4; "Facts Concerning the Late Arthur Jermyn and His Family", 62; "From Beyond", 5, 62–63, 71, 79–80; "The Haunter of the Dark", 65; "Herbert West—Reanimator", 68, 88–90; "The Festival", 66; "The Horror at Red Hook", xvi; "The Music of Erich Zann", 58, 87; "The Nameless City", 82–84; "Nyarlathotep", 61, 80–82; "The Outsider", 63, 85–86; "Pickman's Model", xiv, 72; "The Picture in the

House", 71; "The Rats in the Walls", 91–93; "The Shadow out of Time", 63, 100–101; "The Shadow over Innsmouth", 98–97; "The Street", 79; "Supernatural Horror in Literature", 59, 63, 73–74; "The Unnamable", 66, 93–95; "The Whisperer in Darkness", 72; "The White Ship", 71, 78
Lukács, Georg, viii, xixn4, 103n31

Machen, Arthur, vii, 44, 69, 94, 122
Manson, Charles, 115
Marxist literary criticism, xi, xiii, xiv, xv, xvi, xviii, xixn10, 2, 3, 4, 5, 7, 8, 23–24, 26–27, 28, 29, 36, 46, 66, 68, 79, 81, 97, 109, 110
Matisse, Henri, 111, 123
melancholy, ix, xiii, xv, xvi, xvii, xviii, 20, 47, 58, 61, 117, 123, 126, 127
modernity, narrative of, vii–x

Nietzsche, Friedrich, vii, ix, 13, 15, 20, 23, 44, 61, 89
nostalgia, xvi, xvii–xviii, 18, 61, 109–110, 134
noveless, 52n55

opalescence, 6, 41, 54n93, 98
orientalism, 5, 6, 12, 15, 17, 19, 20–21, 25, 26, 32, 37, 40, 78
Orwell, George, 112–113
outside, experience of, xiii, 17, 19, 23, 43, 61, 62–63, 66, 72, 74, 81, 85–86, 95, 98, 101, 119

picaresque, the, 92–93
Picasso, Pablo, 123, 136n12
Poe, Edgar Allan, 6, 36, 69, 72, 74, 76, 119, 122–123, 125, 128, 129–130, 131, 132, 137n38
political unconscious, the, xvi, 3–4, 13, 25, 28, 40, 41, 42, 43, 46, 49, 50n12, 65, 66, 102n13, 121
Pollock, Jackson, 111
Proust, Marcel, xii, xiii, 65, 101

Rabelais, François, 112, 114, 132
realism, vii, xiv, xvi, xvii, xviii, 1, 4–5, 11, 41, 49, 50n12, 77, 96, 97, 128–129, 130–133
reverie, 7, 14, 16–17, 27, 28, 39, 65, 67, 72, 74, 76, 77, 115, 116, 123, 127, 134, 137n31
romance, viii, x, xvi, 1–4, 5, 10–12, 15, 24, 25, 29–30, 32, 34, 36, 37, 38, 41, 43, 44–45, 47, 48, 49, 50n12, 59
Romero, George A., 118–119

satire, 35, 61, 111, 112–114, 117, 131, 133, 134, 136n16
Schopenhauer, Arthur, 87
Shakespeare, William, 123, 125, 132
shock, xi, xii, xiii, xiv, xvii, xviii, 61, 62, 63, 68, 69, 70, 72, 76, 78, 79, 81, 82, 85–86, 87, 88, 90, 93, 95, 96, 97–98, 99, 101, 119
Sime, S. H., 13, 14, 15, 16, 24, 29, 52n46
spectral, the, viii, x, xiii, xiv, xv, xvii, xixn10, 24, 58–59, 63, 66, 69, 74, 75, 79, 80, 81, 83–84, 85, 86, 89, 91, 92, 93, 94, 95–96, 98, 100, 101, 103n30, 122, 123
storyteller, the, vii–viii, xi, xii, xv, xvi–xvii, xviii, 2, 5, 11, 13, 14, 17, 26, 31, 33, 35, 43, 46, 49, 50n14, 64, 69, 73, 75, 86, 91, 95, 100, 101, 109, 115
sublime, the, 10, 13, 29, 30, 34, 87, 106n90, 134
supernatural, the, vii, viii, x, x–xi, xii, xiv, xvi, xvii, xviii, xixn10, 1, 11, 12, 29, 33, 36, 40, 43, 44, 45, 46–47, 48, 57, 58, 59, 60, 63, 64, 65, 66, 67, 68, 72–74, 79, 83, 84, 89–90, 91, 92, 93–95, 96, 98, 105n61, 109, 117, 121, 132
surrealism, xiv, 111
symbolism, xvi, 16, 21, 36, 77, 78, 90, 97, 102n12, 113, 117, 118, 123–125, 127

Tennyson, Alfred Lord, 2, 31, 42, 50n14
Tesla, Nicola, 81, 135n2
trace, the, xi, xii, xv–xvi, 66, 69, 71, 72, 75, 93, 94–96, 98, 99–100, 101, 104n39, 121, 135n6

Yeats, William Butler, 6, 9, 35, 49, 69

About the Author

William F. Touponce (Ph.D. in comparative literature, University of Massachusetts, 1981) is emeritus professor of English at Indiana University, Indianapolis. In 2004 he co-authored a comprehensive survey of Ray Bradbury's life and career: *Ray Bradbury: The Life of Fiction*. In 2007 he became the first director of the Center for Ray Bradbury Studies, a part of the Institute for American Thought. Until his retirement in 2012, he was general editor of *The Collected Stories of Ray Bradbury* and edited a journal devoted to Bradbury, *The New Ray Bradbury Review*, now in its third year of publication. He is the author of several critical studies on science fiction authors, including Frank Herbert and Isaac Asimov, as well as two other monographs on Ray Bradbury and numerous articles and reviews in the field of children's literature.